Programming with Turing
and Object Oriented Turing

Peter Grogono

Programming with Turing and Object Oriented Turing

Springer-Verlag

New York Berlin Heidelberg London Paris
Tokyo Hong Kong Barcelona Budapest

Peter Grogono
Department of Computer Science
Concordia University
Montreal, Quebec H3G 1M8
Canada

Cover Image ©1995 Michael Schimpf/Panoramic Images, Chicago, All Rights Reserved

Library of Congress Cataloging-in-Publication Data
Grogono, Peter.
    Programming with Turing and Object Oriented Turing
  / Peter Grogono
      p.   cm.
    Includes bibliographical references and index.
    ISBN 0-387-94517-2 (softcover : acid-free paper)
    1. Object-oriented programming (Computer science) 2. Turing
  (Computer program language) 3. Windows (Computer programs)
    I. Title.
QA76.64.G76 1995   95-10802
005.13'3 —dc20

Printed on acid-free paper.

Production managed by Laura Carlson; manufacturing supervised by Joe Quatela.
Edited by Sharon H. Nelson, Metonymy Productions.
Photocomposed from text prepared by Metonymy Productions using TeX and LaTeX.
Printed and bound by Hamilton Printing Co., Rensselaer, NY.
Printed in the United States of America.

9 8 7 6 5 4 3 2 1

ISBN 0-387-94517-2 Springer-Verlag New York Berlin Heidelberg

Preface

The programming language Turing is named for the British mathematician and computer scientist Alan Mathison Turing (1912–1954). Turing's contributions to computer science began in 1936, when he published a landmark paper on the limits of mechanical computation. The mathematical model introduced in the paper is now known as a "Turing machine" and forms the basis of the modern theory of computability. During World War II, Turing played an important role in the design of the Colossus, an electronic machine that deciphered coded messages. In 1951, he proposed a test, now called the Turing test, to answer the question: Can a machine think? Today, the most distinguished award given by the world's largest association for computing professionals, the Association for Computing Machinery, is called the Turing Award.

The programming language Turing was designed by Richard C. Holt and James R. Cordy at the University of Toronto as a first language for computer science courses. Turing is a practical language suited to general-purpose applications. Like the work of the person for whom it is named, the language Turing serves well in both the theoretical and practical domains. Most of the software that supports Turing, including the Turing compiler, is written in Turing. This book includes all the features of Turing and provides an introduction to the object oriented features of the more recent language, Object Oriented Turing (OOT).

Turing is particularly appropriate as a first language for learning and teaching. It incorporates many of the advantages while avoiding most of the disadvantages of earlier languages. The following four features make Turing particularly suitable as a first language and as a pedagogical tool.

- Turing is learned in easy stages. As a first step, we can write one-line programs in Turing. We can continue by writing programs of increasing complexity, adding one or two new features at a time. This distinguishes Turing from languages that require knowledge of advanced programming concepts before even simple programs can be written.

- Turing is defined by simple rules with few exceptions. With a little effort, it is easy to learn the entire language. This distinguishes Turing from languages that breed gurus and wizards who revel in arcane and obscure features.

- Turing is a standardized language. Most Turing programs written on a PC will run on a Macintosh or a UNIX workstation and give the same results. Only a few features of Turing, such as graphics, do not work in the same way on all systems. This distinguishes Turing from languages that require programs to be adapted for different systems.

- Turing has a formal definition and semantics. This distinguishes Turing from languages defined by a lengthy, complex, and potentially ambiguous report written in a natural language.

Effective programming requires capabilities in four separate but related areas. First, we achieve the capability to write programs in a particular language. This requires knowledge of the syntax, semantics, and style of the language. Second, we learn how to choose control and data structures that are appropriate for each problem and to demonstrate that they do in fact solve the problem correctly. Although the techniques vary from one language paradigm to another, this capability is largely independent of any particular language. Third, because most programming problems can be solved using techniques that are well understood and widely documented, we acquire a repertoire of standard algorithms and data structures. Fourth, because new problems arise, we learn to design new algorithms and data structures. *Programming with Turing* focuses on the capabilities of writing programs and of choosing appropriate control and data structures.

A book that teaches a programming language ideally satisfies two requirements. It provides a narrative that reveals successively more advanced features of the language and a reference source in which particular features of the language can be found quickly. Each section of *Programming with Turing* is constructed to make use of the material and examples presented in previous sections. Each chapter ends with a collection of exercises intended to develop confidence and familiarity with Turing and with general principles of programming. At the same time, *Programming with Turing* is organized to serve as a reference source: each section covers a specific topic; each chapter includes summaries; and appendices offer quick reference for particular features.

Many of the examples and exercises are about hobbies, physics, and other areas of application. They show some of the ways in which the ability to understand and use basic computational skills can enrich our lives. In addition, they offer a sample of programming tasks and of what programming is about.

I could not have written *Programming with Turing* without the Turing software and technical assistance provided by Ric Holt and Chris Stephenson at Holt Software Associates. I am grateful to Sharon H. Nelson at Metonymy Productions for detailed and thorough editing.

January 1995   P. G.
                                                                     Montreal

How to Install the Software

Appendix K, on page 375, explains how to install WinOOT from the disk included with this book. Appendix L, on page 376, explains how to run WinOOT. Before installing WinOOT, you should ensure that at least 2 megabytes of virtual memory are available to Windows

Contents

List of Figures

Programming with Turing
and Object Oriented Turing

Chapter 1

First Concepts

A program is a text. Writing a program is like writing an instruction manual. After we have written a program or a manual, other people can read it. The important difference between a manual and a program is that a computer can run a program but it cannot run a manual. Consequently, a program must convey information in a form that a human reader can understand and a computer can process. Because programmers spend more time writing and changing existing programs than writing new ones, it is important to write programs that are easily understood by people as well as efficiently processed by computers.

Developing the skill of reading programs is as important as developing the skill of writing them. For that reason, this book contains many examples of programs, both complete and partial. Here is a strategy that many people find helpful when learning to program. First, we read an example program carefully, understanding as much as we can. Second, we make some simple changes to the program and check that the changes have the expected effect. Finally, we write a program that has a similar structure but performs a different task.

In this chapter, we discuss simple Turing programs that consist of a few lines. The first section introduces most of the basic features of Turing by means of examples. These features enable us to write simple programs immediately. Later sections of this chapter provide a systematic account of each feature and may be used for reference.

1.1   Writing Simple Programs

The best way to learn a programming language is to use it. We start by writing short programs and, as we gain confidence, our programs grow longer and more complex. Programming languages differ in the extent to which they support this kind of learning and growth. Some languages are at their best when programs are short; a ten-line program is fine but a thousand-line program is unmanageable. Other languages do not allow short programs: we have to write dozens of lines to accomplish anything at all. In Turing, we may write programs of any size, from one line to thousands of lines.

We begin with a discussion of some very short programs. Each program performs a simple calculation and displays some results on the screen. The results provide quick confirmation that the programs are doing what we expect them to do.

1.1.1   The put Statement

Programs usually print or display the results of their computations. The programs in this section use Turing's put statement to display their results on the screen. The first program is very simple indeed. It consists of a single line:

    put 1995

When the program is run, it displays "1995" at the top left of the screen or output window.

This program consists of a single *statement*. The statement is called a "put statement" because it begins with the word "put". The put statement consists of the word put and one or more *expressions*. When Turing encounters a put statement, it computes and displays the expressions that follow put.

Expressions

In the statement put 1995, the number "1995" is a simple expression. We can build more complicated expressions using the arithmetic operators "+", "−", "×", and "÷". Since standard keyboards do not have the symbols "×" and "÷", Turing uses the symbols "*" and "/" instead.

Example 1.1   Displaying Results

Suppose that a swimming pool is 100 feet long and 50 feet wide. The program

    put 100 * 50

computes the surface area of the water: 5,000 square feet. Turing displays this number, and all other numbers, without commas:

    5000

Suppose that the swimming pool is 3 feet deep at one end, 12 feet deep at the other end, and the bottom is a uniform slope. Then the volume of water is obtained by multiplying the surface area by the average depth.

The program

    put $100 * 50 * (3 + 12)/2$

computes this value and displays the result:

    37500

Evaluating Expressions

Turing evaluates expressions using the conventional rules of algebra. Multiplications and divisions are performed before additions and subtractions. For instance, $10 - 2 * 3 = 10 - 6 = 4$. When we need to perform addition or subtraction first, we use parentheses. The parentheses in $100 * 50 * (3 + 12)/2$ ensure that Turing evaluates $3 + 12$ before dividing by 2.

Strings

An unadorned number does not convey much information. A program should display more than the results of calculations: it should also display verbal information to help its users understand the results.

The technical name for a phrase or, in general, any sequence of symbols in a program, is *string*. When we write a string in a Turing program, we must enclose it in quotes. When Turing displays a string, it does not display the quotes. For example, the program

    put "This string has no quotes."

displays

    This string has no quotes.

The keyword put may be followed by several numbers or strings, in which case Turing requires a comma between items. To aid readability, we insert a blank after each of these commas.

Example 1.2   Displaying Useful Information

Ponds, unlike swimming pools, are usually circular. Suppose that a pond has a radius of 20 meters. The program

```
put "The surface area is ", 3.14159 * 20 * 20, " square meters."
```

displays the result

```
The surface area is 1256.636 square meters.
```

Turing does not put blanks before or after numbers. If we want blanks around numbers, we must include them in the messages that precede and follow numbers. In Example 1.2, there is a blank after "is" and a blank before "square". If we had left out these blanks, as in the program

```
put "The surface area is", 3.14159 * 20 * 20, "square meters."
```

Turing would display

```
The surface area is1256.636square meters.
```

Sequences

If a program consists of several statements, Turing executes each statement in turn. A list of statements is called a *statement sequence*, or simply a *sequence*.

Example 1.3   A Statement Sequence

Assume that the pond in Example 1.2 has a maximum depth of 2 meters and that its bottom is part of a sphere. The following program calculates the area of the surface and the volume of the water in the pond.

```
put "The area of the pond is ", 3.14159 * 20 * 20, " square meters."
put "The volume of water in the pond is ",
    3.14159 * 2 * 2 * (3 * 20 − 2)/3, " cubic meters."
```

The second put statement is written on two lines. Splitting a line does not affect the meaning of a program in most cases, but we must not split a line in the middle of a string. For example, we must write the string "The area of the pond is " entirely on one line.

When this program is run, it displays

```
The area of the pond is 1256.636 square meters.
The volume of water in the pond is 242.949627 cubic meters.
```

Formulas

Formulas written in mathematical notation often contain implicit multiplications. For example, the program in Example 1.3 uses the fact that if r is the radius of the pond and d is its maximum depth, the volume of the water is $\pi d^2 (3r - d)/3$. In this formula, πd^2 is short for $\pi \times d \times d$. In Turing, we must write the multiplications explicitly, using the multiplying operator "$*$".

1.1.2   Constant Declarations

For a person reading a program, names are more informative than numbers. A *constant declaration* introduces a name into the program and associates a value with the name. The following declaration associates the value 3.14159 with the name *Pi*.

   const *Pi* := 3.14159

Once we have written this declaration, we can use the name *Pi* instead of the number 3.14159 elsewhere in the program.

Naming

Using a name has several advantages over using a numerical value. First, a person reading the program understands the purpose of the number. Although 3.14159 is a number that most people recognize, there are very few other numbers with this property. The number 640, for instance, conveys much less information than the name *AcresPerSquareMile*.

Second, it is easy to make a mistake in typing a string of digits. To type numbers accurately is more difficult than to type words accurately, and mistakes in numbers are less obvious than mistakes in words.

Finally, even if we fail to notice an error in a name, Turing may discover it. If we declare the constant *Pi* but write *Po* later in the program, Turing will complain that *Po* has not been declared. If we write 3.14519 instead of 3.14159, the error probably will not be detected until somebody notices that the answers are wrong.

The advantages of naming apply not only to well-known numbers such as *Pi*. We can give a name to any number that appears in a program. This is a step towards *self-documenting programs* — programs that need no explanation other than the declarations and statements they contain.

When the statements of a program do not provide sufficient explanation, we can add comments to the program. A *comment* is a phrase or sentence that explains an aspect of the program that is not obvious. The symbol % introduces short comments in Turing. Section 1.6 includes a detailed discussion of comments.

Example 1.4   Programming with Names

In Example 1.3, we had to explain that "20" was the radius of the pond and "2" was its depth. The following version of the program uses constant declarations to name these values and therefore does not require such explanations. This program also introduces the exponent operator, "**". The expression $Radius ** 2$ is Turing's notation for $Radius^2$, or "$Radius$ squared".

> % Compute the surface area and volume of a pond.
> const $Pi := 3.14159$
> const $Radius := 20$
> const $Depth := 2$
> put "The surface area is ", $Pi * Radius ** 2$, " square meters."
> put "The volume of water in the pond is ",
> $Pi * Depth ** 2 * (3 * Radius - Depth)/3$, " cubic meters."

The output of the program is unchanged from that of Example 1.3.

> The area of the pond is 1256.636 square meters.
> The volume of water in the pond is 242.949627 cubic meters.

Discussion

It is important to choose meaningful names for the constants declared in a program. In the program of Example 1.4, the names $Radius$ and $Depth$ clearly indicate the meanings of the constants. The program would work just as well if we used the names R and D instead of $Radius$ and $Depth$, but the purpose of the variables would not be apparent to a human reader.

A name rarely provides a complete explanation of the meaning of a number. There is nothing about the name $Radius$ that is particular to ponds; $Radius$ could just as easily refer to a balloon. We could use longer names, such as $PondRadius$ or $RadiusOfPond$, but this would not necessarily be an improvement. Long names are hard to read, and it is not easy to understand a program that contains many long names. It is better to explain with a comment that the program is about ponds and to use the names $Radius$ and $Depth$.

1.1.3   The **get** Statement

All the programs we have seen so far behave in a very simple way: they display some results and then stop. They would be more useful if they could ask us for some input data, do some calculations with the data, and then tell us the results.

The **get** statement enables a program to obtain information from the user via the keyboard. The simplest form of the **get** statement is

    get ☐

in which the box stands for the name of a variable.

Variables

Variables are like constants in that they have names and values. The difference between variables and constants is that the value of a variable changes while the program runs, whereas the value of a constant never changes. The effect of the **get** statement is to assign a value to a variable.

Example 1.5   Asking for Information

The program in this example first asks for the radius of a pond and then displays the surface area of the pond. It contains a declaration that introduces a variable named *Radius* and a **get** statement that obtains the value of *Radius*.

```
const Pi := 3.14159
var Radius : real
put "Please enter radius:   "
get Radius
put "The area of the pond is ", Pi * Radius ** 2, " square meters."
```

Here and elsewhere in this book, characters displayed by Turing programs, such as "`Please enter radius:`", are printed in typewriter style. Characters entered by the user are printed in italics.

After we run the program, the screen might look like this:

```
Please enter radius:
```
    50
```
The area of the pond is 7853.975 square meters.
```

The program reaches the first **put** statement and displays the message "`Please enter radius:   `". The effect of the next statement, **get** *Radius*, is that the program waits for the user to enter a number using the keyboard. In this example, the user enters "50". The program does not respond until the user presses the ENTER key. The user can correct mistakes using the BACKSPACE key, which erases the last character entered.

Variable Declarations

In Example 1.5, we declare the name *Radius* with the statement

        var *Radius* : real

The word var in this statement indicates that *Radius* will be a *variable* rather than a constant as it was in Example 1.4. The word real indicates that the value of *Radius* is a real number. Turing distinguishes *real numbers*, which have a fractional part, from *integers*, which do not. For example, 3 is an integer, but 3.14159 is a real number.

We can make a small but useful improvement to the program in Example 1.5. We add two dots to the end of the first put statement. It now reads

        put "Please enter radius: " ..

The effect of this change is that Turing will not start a new line after displaying the message. After we run the modified program, the screen will look like this:

        Please enter radius: *50*
        The area of the pond is 7853.98 square meters.

1.1.4   Errors

However careful we are in writing programs, some errors are bound to creep in. Modern programming languages and systems are designed to detect errors and report them to us. Turing detects and reports errors during two phases of processing.

During the first phase, the program is translated into a simpler form that is easier for the computer to process. This phase is called *compiling the program* and it is performed by the Turing *compiler*. The second phase, during which the program is run, occurs after the program has been successfully compiled. This phase is called *executing* or *running* the program.

Turing may detect errors during either phase. Errors detected during compilation are called *compile-time errors*. Errors detected during execution are called *run-time errors*.

In the following program, both statements result in compile-time errors. The first statement is illegal because Turing requires a colon before the equal sign in a declaration. The second is illegal because *N* is declared to be an integer but the value assigned to it is not an integer. In this book, we use the symbol "⊘" to mark constructions that are illegal or undesirable in Turing.

var $X = 3$ ⊘
const N : int := 9.5   ⊘

The following program also contains an error, but in this case Turing does not discover the error until the program is run. When we run the program, the second statement assigns the value zero to Q. The third statement attempts to divide P by Q, and it is at this point that Turing detects the error.

const P := 20
const Q := 0
put P div Q ⊘

All errors are serious, but compile-time errors are less serious than run-time errors. If a program has compile-time errors, we must correct the errors and recompile the program before we can run it. It is not possible to run a program that contains compile-time errors.

Run-time errors are more difficult to diagnose and correct than compile-time errors, for the obvious reason that they cannot be detected until we test the program by running it. Even testing a program does not necessarily reveal all of its run-time errors.

It is not for academic reasons that language designers and programmers attempt to provide programs that are self-documenting and free of errors. Programs perform critical tasks such as controlling pacemakers and monitoring air traffic. An undetected run-time error in a program may have serious or even tragic consequences.

1.2   Learning to Read Programs

The programs in Section 1.1 contain symbols of several different kinds. The symbols include words, such as get and *Radius*; numbers, such as *Pi*; operators, such as "+" and "*"; and punctuation marks, such as ",". Some words, such as get, have a fixed meaning in Turing. We introduce other words, such as *Radius*, as names for constants and variables. In this section, we look at keywords and identifiers and explain their roles in a program.

1.2.1   Keywords

The keywords we have seen so far are const, var, put, and get. In this book, the keywords in Turing programs are written in sans serif type. In the programs we see on the screen and in most printouts, keywords and variables are not distinguished typographically.

Keywords have a fixed meaning in a Turing program. Furthermore, we can use them only in the contexts for which they are designed. For example, the keyword const always introduces a constant declaration. We cannot use keywords as names or change their meaning in any way. A complete list of Turing's keywords appears in Appendix A on page 356.

1.2.2 Identifiers

Identifier is the technical term for a name that we choose ourselves when we are writing a program. So far, we have used identifiers for constants, such as *Pi*, and for variables, such as *Radius*. In this book, all identifiers are written in italics to distinguish them from keywords and strings. In actual programs, keywords, identifiers, and strings are all written in the same font.

Rules for Identifiers

Six rules govern the choice of identifiers in Turing.

- The first character of an identifier must be a letter.

- Any characters after the first must be letters, digits, or the underscore ("_").

- An identifier cannot have more than 50 characters.

- A Turing keyword cannot be used as an identifier.

- Two identifiers are distinct unless all their characters match.

- Upper and lower case letters do *not* match.

The following names satisfy the rules and are therefore legal Turing identifiers:

  X   K37   Pi   curvature_constant   R2D2   LastEstimate

The following names are not legal identifiers:

  5th   Pied Piper   fred@sunu.com   _Sweep   ⊘

The first starts with a digit, the second contains a blank, the third contains other illegal characters, and the last starts with an underscore. The following identifiers are distinct because upper and lower case letters do not match:

  Nova_Scotia   NOVA_SCOTIA   nova_scotia

Choosing Identifiers

Choosing appropriate names is an important component of good programming. Appropriate names help the reader to see what the program is intended to do. Though we may generalize about names, it is not always true to say that a short name such as X is bad or that a long name such as *Horizontal_ Component* is good. The appropriateness of a name depends on how the name is used in a program. For instance, the name X might be appropriate in a program of 5 lines but it would not serve well in a program of 5,000 lines. The short programs in this book do not always provide enough context to enable us to choose a meaningful name.

In general, very short names do not convey an obvious meaning and, like abbreviations, are best avoided. For instance, it does not take much longer to type *Radius* than *Rad*, and the meaning of *Radius* is self-evident. Conversely, very long names are tedious to write, hard to read, and invite errors. Names such as *Number* and *Value* are too vague to be useful. Names that contain ones and zeros may lead to confusion and errors. The best names explain themselves; names such as *Length*, *Width*, *Radius*, and *InterestRate* serve well as identifiers.

Here are some guidelines for choosing useful identifiers.

- Choose informative names.
- Avoid very short names.
- Avoid very long names.
- Avoid abbreviations.
- Avoid ones and zeros.

Whatever convention we adopt for writing names, it is important that we use it consistently. The convention used in this book is that the first letter of a name is upper case and the rest of the letters are lower case. When the identifier consists of several words, the first letter of each word is in upper case. Typical names are *Radius*, *FirstRecord*, and *MaxValue*.

1.3 Introduction to Standard Types

Every constant, variable, and expression in a Turing program has a *type*. The type determines the possible values of the entity and the operations we can apply to it. Turing provides four *standard types* and facilities for defining an unlimited number of *user-defined types*. The standard types are integer, real, string, and Boolean. The corresponding Turing keywords are int, real, string, and boolean.

The information provided in this introductory section is all you need to use standard types in simple programs. Chapter 3 provides a complete and detailed description of the standard types.

1.3.1   Integers and Reals

The types integer and real are both *numeric types.* Integers are "whole numbers" such as 1, 99, and −17. Reals are numbers that may have fractional parts, such as 1.5 and 99.99.

The computer can represent a fractional value precisely only if its denominator is a power of 2. Fractions such as $\frac{1}{2}$, $\frac{5}{8}$, and $\frac{975}{2048}$ have precise representations; fractions such as $\frac{1}{3}$ do not. It is not possible to represent irrational numbers, such as $\sqrt{2}$, or transcendental numbers, such as π, precisely.

Numeric Operators

Figure 1.1 shows some examples of the use of numeric operators. The third column shows the types of the operands and the fourth column shows the type of the result.

Statement	Output	Operand Types	Result Type
put $2 + 3$	5	integer	integer
put $2.5 + 3$	5.5	mixed	real
put $5.0 * 2.0$	10	real	real
put $11/3$	3.666667	integer	real
put $12/3$	4	integer	real
put 11 div 3	3	integer	integer
put 11.9 div 3	3	mixed	integer
put 11 mod 3	2	integer	integer
put 12.0 mod 3	0.0	mixed	real
put 12.0 mod 3.5	1.5	real	real

Figure 1.1   Evaluation of Numeric Operators

The numeric operators "+", "−", "*", "/", "div", and "mod" all require two operands, which may be integers or reals. The operator "−" can also be used with only one operand, as in the expression $-X$. The type of the result of "+", "−", "*", and "mod" depends on the types of the operands: if both operands are integers, the result is an integer; if either operand is real, the result is real.

The operators "/" and "div" both perform division. The result of X/Y is always real, and the result of X div Y is always an integer, with the remainder discarded. The result of X mod Y is the remainder when X is divided by Y.

1.3.2 Strings

A value of type string is a sequence of up to 255 characters. In Turing programs, we write strings between quotes. The quotes distinguish the string from the surrounding text in the program but are not part of the value of the string.

The shortest string has no characters at all. It is written "" and is called the *empty string*.

The character "\" (backslash) plays a special role in strings, acting as an *escape* character. The most common use of the backslash is in "\n", which Turing translates as a line break. The statement

```
    put "This string would fit\non one line."
```

displays

```
    This string would fit
    on one line.
```

Concatenation

We can use the operator "+" with string operands. The result is the two strings joined together or, in technical language, concatenated. The statement

```
    put "A professor is one who talks " +
     " in someone else's sleep.\n" +
     "[W. H. Auden]"
```

displays

```
    A professor is one who talks in someone else's sleep.
    [W. H. Auden]
```

In addition to concatenating strings, we can discover how many characters they contain and we can select individual characters. The function *length* counts the number of characters in a string. For example, the expression *length* ("Mango") evaluates to 5. The value of *length* ("") is 0.

Indexing

To select an individual character of a string S, we use an expression of the form $S(N)$ in which N is an integer between 1 and the length of the string. For example, "Mango" (1) is "M" and "Mango" (4) is "g". This operation is called *indexing* the string. If we index a character that is not in the string, Turing reports an error. For example, "Mango" (0) and "Mango" (6) both give errors.

1.3.3   Booleans

The type **boolean** has precisely two values: true and false. The keywords **true** and **false** denote these values in Turing programs. Expressions with Boolean values occur often in programs. They are called by a variety of names, including *predicates*, *Boolean expressions*, *conditional expressions*, or simply *conditions*.

Comparison Operators

Although **true** and **false** are valid conditions, Boolean values are usually obtained by comparison. For example, the expression $Num = 3$ has the value **true** if the current value of the integer variable Num is 3, and it has the value **false** otherwise. Similarly, $Num > 3$ is **true** if the current value of Num is greater than 3. The comparison operators are summarized in Figure 1.2.

The operands of a comparison operator must be of the same type, and the type may be **int**, **real**, or **string**. We can compare Boolean values, but only with the operators "=" and "≠".

Mathematical Symbol	Turing Expression	Meaning
$=$	$X = Y$	X is equal to Y
$\neq$	X not= Y	X is not equal to Y
$<$	$X < Y$	X is less than Y
$\leq$	$X <= Y$	X is less than or equal to Y
$>$	$X > Y$	X is greater than Y
$\geq$	$X >= Y$	X is greater than or equal to Y

Figure 1.2   Comparison Operators and Their Meanings

We cannot write Boolean expressions in a put statement. The function *BoolStr*, defined below, uses techniques described in Chapter 5 to convert a Boolean value to a string that we can display.

```
function BoolStr (Expr : boolean) : string
    if Expr then
        result "true"
    else
        result "false"
    end if
end BoolStr
```

As a simple example of the use of *BoolStr*, the program

> put *BoolStr* $(2 + 2 = 5)$

displays `false` because the value of the Boolean expression $2 + 2 = 5$ is false.

Comparing Strings

The values of Boolean expressions with numeric operands are fairly easy to predict on the basis of the meanings of the comparison operators. Boolean expressions with string operands, however, do not always give the expected results. If A and B are strings containing lower case letters only, then $A < B$ is true if the word A would come before the word B in the dictionary. For example,

> put *BoolStr* (`"apple"` $<$ `"banana"`)

displays `true`.

Comparison of strings containing only upper case letters works in the same way. For example,

> put *BoolStr* (`"MANGO"` $\leq$ `"CHERRY"`)

displays `false`. When we mix upper and lower case letters, the results are not necessarily the same as dictionary order.

Turing compares the numeric codes of characters rather than the characters themselves. Character codes are determined by the system on which Turing is running but usually will be ASCII codes. A table of ASCII codes appears in Appendix E on page 368. In ASCII, the letters "A" through "Z" have codes 65 through 90, and the letters "a" through "z" have codes 97 through 122. The ASCII code of lower case "r" is 114 and the ASCII code of upper case "S" is 83. Consequently, the statement

> put *BoolStr* (`"raspberry"` $<$ `"Strawberry"`)

displays `false`.

If the strings contain characters other than letters, the situation is even worse. The only way to determine the result of a string comparison is to use a table of character codes. Programs should not depend on the codes of particular characters unless such a dependency is unavoidable.

1.4   Declarations

A *declaration* introduces a new identifier into the program and associates some properties with it. For example, a constant declaration introduces an identifier with a type and a value as properties. In this section, we describe constant and variable declarations.

1.4.1   Constant Declarations

A constant declaration associates a name with a type and a constant value. The standard form of constant declaration is

    const ⬚ : ⬚ := ⬚

in which the first box stands for a name, the second box stands for a type, and the third box stands for a value.

The declaration

    const *MaxSteps* : int := 100

introduces a new constant with name *MaxSteps*, type int, and value 100. Turing can usually infer the type we intend from the value we provide. Consequently, we are allowed to omit ": int" from this declaration. Constant declarations with types omitted have the form

    const ⬚ := ⬚

in which the first box stands for a name and the second box stands for an expression. After the declarations

    const *MaxSteps* := 100
    const *MinorAxis* := 250.0
    const *Title* := "The Theory of Cuckoo Clocks"

the constant *MaxSteps* has type int, *MinorAxis* has type real, and *Title* has type string.

There are a few situations in which we must use the full form of constant declaration. The intent of the declarations

  const *MaxSteps* := 100
  const *Diameter* : real := *MaxSteps*

is to introduce the integer constant *MaxSteps* with value 100 and the real constant *Diameter* with value 100.0. If we had omitted ": real" in the second declaration, *Diameter* would have the same type as *MaxSteps*, namely int.

1.4.2 Variable Declarations

A variable declaration introduces the name of a variable into the program and specifies the type of the variable. The standard form of a variable declaration is

  var ⬚ : ⬚ := ⬚

in which the boxes stand for a list of names, a type, and an expression, respectively. Names in the list are separated by commas. Variable declarations have the same structure as constant declarations, except that we are allowed to introduce several variables in a single declaration. The effect of the declaration is to introduce each name into the program as a variable with the given type and value.

The declaration

  var *X*, *Y*, *Z* : real := *MaxCoor*/2

introduces three real variables with names *X*, *Y*, and *Z*.

As with constant declarations, we can omit the type of the variable if Turing can infer the type from the value. The form of the declaration is

  var ⬚ := ⬚

in which the first box stands for a list of one or more names and the second box stands for an expression. Turing infers the type of the variable from the form of the expression and gives each variable in the list the same type and value. For example, the declarations

  var *Message*, *Status* := " "
  var *TitleWidth* := *length* ("Ingredients")

introduce two string variables and an integer variable.

Alternatively, we may omit the value from a variable declaration. The form of the declaration is

var ⬜ : ⬜

in which the first box stands for a list of one or more names and the second box stands for a type. In the sequence

> var *Reply* : string
> get *Reply*

the variable *Reply* is declared as a string without an initial value. There is no need to provide an initial value because the statement following the declaration will read a value from the keyboard.

Initialization

Variables introduced by declarations without initial values are *uninitialized*. Turing reports an error if we attempt to use the value of an uninitialized variable. The following program reports such an error when the put statement is executed.

> var *MagicNumber* : int
> put *MagicNumber*   ⊘

To avoid such errors, it is best to provide initial values whenever possible. If there is no initial value, there should be a statement that provides a value, such as a get statement, close to the declaration.

1.5   Output and Input

The put and get statements are similar in structure. The put statement consists of the keyword put followed by expressions; the get statement consists of the keyword get followed by variable names. These expressions and names collectively are called *arguments*.

1.5.1   Output Statements

As we have seen, a put statement consists of the keyword put followed by one or more arguments. Arguments are separated by commas. Optionally, the last argument may be followed by the symbol " .. ". Turing executes a put statement by converting each argument to a string of characters and sending the characters to the screen. After displaying all of the arguments, Turing moves the cursor to the beginning of the next line *unless* there is a " .. " symbol.

In the examples below, a put statement is followed by a box containing the corresponding output.

If the argument is a string, Turing displays only the characters of the string.

    put "Hello"   `Hello`

If the argument is an integer, Turing displays its exact value.

    put 379   `379`

If the argument is a real number, Turing displays it with a decimal point but without trailing zeros.

    put 6.5000   `6.5`

If the fractional part is zero, Turing does not display the decimal point.

    put 99.00   `99`

Turing does not display more than six digits after the decimal point. The last digit may be rounded; in this example, Turing displays "7" rather than "6".

    put 0.123456789   `0.123457`

If a real number is very large, Turing displays it in floating-point notation.

    put 100000000.0   `1e8`

Similarly, if a real number is very small, Turing uses floating-point notation.

    put 0.00000002345   `2.345e-8`

Formatting Expressions

We use *formatting expressions* to provide fine control over the output. In the statement

    put "Hello" : 10

": 10" is a formatting expression. Its effect is to ensure that at least 10 characters are displayed. This particular kind of formatting expression is also called a *width specifier* because it specifies the width of the output. Turing puts five blanks *after* the string "Hello".

    put "Hello" : 10   `Hello⌴⌴⌴⌴⌴`

If the width specifier has a value smaller than the length of the string, Turing prints the entire string.

```
    put "Hello" : 3
```
⟦ Hello ⟧

We can use width specifiers with integers as well as with strings. Turing inserts blanks *before* the number.

```
    put 379 : 6
```
⟦ ␣␣␣379 ⟧

Width specifiers also work with real numbers.

```
    put 6.7 : 7
```
⟦ ␣␣␣␣6.7 ⟧

An argument with a real value may be followed by two or three formatting expressions. The value of any formatting expression must be a positive integer. The first expression is always a width specifier, as in the preceding examples. The second formatting expression specifies the number of digits to be displayed after the decimal point.

```
    put 6.7 : 4 : 4
```
⟦ 6.7000 ⟧

The third formatting expression specifies floating-point notation and the number of digits that Turing should provide in the exponent field.

```
    put −6.7 : 12 : 4 : 2
```
⟦ ␣␣-6.7000e00 ⟧

Turing normally inserts a line break character after writing the arguments of a put statement. If the put statement is followed by two dots, " .. ", the line break is suppressed. Note that there should not be a comma before the two dots.

The keyword skip, used as an argument in a put statement, has the effect of inserting a line break. It is equivalent to \n within a string. The following two put statements have the same effect. They display two lines on the screen and leave the cursor positioned at the end of the second line.

```
    put "Please reply with a number.\nPut your number here: " ..
    put "Please reply with a number.", skip, "Put your number here:  "  ..
```

1.5.2   Input Statements

A get statement consists of the keyword get followed by one or more variable names. The variable names are separated by commas. Each variable must have been declared as an integer, real, or string. We consider each case in turn.

Reading Integers and Reals

The following program reads an integer and displays it.

```
var N : int
get N
put N
```

When this program is run, it stops at the **get** statement and waits for input from the keyboard. At this point, we should enter an integer value consisting of an optional sign, "+" or "−", followed by one or more digits. We then press the ENTER key to indicate that the input is complete. We can enter blanks either before or after the number.

We can input the number one thousand in any of the following ways:

1000   +1000   ⊔⊔⊔+1000⊔⊔⊔

Real values are entered in a similar way. The following program reads a real number and displays it.

```
var X : real
get X
put X
```

The real numbers we can enter consist of a sign, an integer part, a fractional part, and an exponent part. For example, we might enter −2.735e−8. This number has sign "−", integer part "2", fraction part ".735", and exponent part "e−8". The only part that Turing requires is the integer part; the other parts are optional. For example, we could enter 2, which Turing would read as the real number 2.0.

Here are some of the ways in which we can enter the number one million as a real number:

1000000   ⊔⊔+1000000   1000000.00⊔⊔
1e6   +1.0e+06   ⊔⊔100e4

Because Turing does not accept blanks or commas in numbers, we cannot enter one million in either of the following ways:

1⊔000⊔000   ⊔⊔1,000,000   ⊘

Reading Strings

To see how Turing treats strings, suppose that we declare a string variable S and then use a **get** statement to read a value into it. What happens depends on the form of the **get** statement and the characters entered by the user, as shown in Figure 1.3. The first two lines show the effect of the statement **get** S. Turing reads

Statement	Characters Entered	Value of S
get S	drums	drums
get S	drums are noisy	drums
get S	"drums are noisy"	drums are noisy
get S	""	(empty string)
get S : 4	drums	drum
get S : *	drums are noisy	drums are noisy

Figure 1.3   Using the get Statement to Read Strings

only as far as the first blank. Consequently, if the user enters several words, as on the second line, S will contain only the first word.

The third line shows that the user can force Turing to read blanks by enclosing the input string in quotes. The fourth line is a special case of the same rule; the user sets S to the empty string by entering "".

Formatting Expressions

The programmer can control the number of characters read by including formatting expressions in the get statement. On the fifth line, ": 4" after S specifies that Turing will read at most four characters. On the sixth line, ": *" after S specifies that Turing will read characters, including blanks, until the user presses ENTER.

Turing allows us to read several values with one get statement. The values do not have to be all the same type. If we run the program

```
var N : int
var S : string
var X : real
get N, S, X
```

and, when it pauses for input, we enter

```
3
"is bigger than"
2.9
```

the variables N, S, and X receive the values 3, "is bigger than", and 2.9, respectively. Note that each entry must be on a separate line.

1.5.3   Interactive Programs

A program that requires several lines of input without prompts is likely to confuse its users. Consequently, it is usually best to write **put** and **get** statements in pairs; each **put** statement prompts for one item and the corresponding **get** statement reads that item. We conclude this section with a program that uses **put** and **get** statements in this way.

Example 1.6   An Interactive Program

The following program asks the user for some information and then issues a personalized greeting.

```
var GivenName, FamilyName : string
var BirthYear : int
put "Enter your given names:   " ..
get GivenName : *
put "Enter your family name:   " ..
get FamilyName : *
put "Enter the year in which you were born:   " ..
get BirthYear
put "Your name is ", GivenName, " ", FamilyName,
   skip, "and you are ", 1995 − BirthYear, " years old."
```

Each **get** statement in this program is preceded by a **put** statement. The **put** statement tells the user what the program is expecting. We often use alternating **put** and **get** statements in this way to achieve the effect of a dialogue between the user and the computer.

The **get** statements that read names use ": *" to ensure that the program reads everything the user enters. The **put** statements display blanks to separate the parts of a name correctly. An interaction with this program might appear on the screen like this.

```
Enter your given names: Augusta Ada
Enter your family name: Byron
Enter the year in which you were born:   1816
Your name is Augusta Ada Byron
and you are 179 years old.
```

This program does not attempt to check its input. If the user responded to the third request with the string *None of your business*, the program would fail and Turing would issue an error message.

1.6   Comments

A *comment* in a program is a piece of text intended for people rather than for a computer to read. Comments do not affect the computation performed by a program and, in fact, Turing discards comments when it executes a program.

Turing provides two forms of comment. The short form is a message that begins with the character "%" and continues to the end of the line. Any text on the left of the "%" is part of the program. Text on the right of the "%" is the comment. The comment may contain any characters, including "%".

A short comment is often all we need to explain the role of a constant or a variable in a program.

> const *EMsteel* := 2e11   %   N/m**2 (Elastic modulus of steel)
> var *MinMax* : real   %   Smallest of the results obtained in Phase 2

The second form of comment is used less often. A comment starts with "/*" and ends with "*/". The text of the comment can extend over several lines. We can use the second form of comment to introduce a group of declarations and statements.

> /* The next group of statements establishes the dimensions
>   of the box. The program asks the user for the length
>   and width. It calculates the depth according to Statute 83(a)
>   Subsection 2.2(iii). The area and volume are also computed
>   for use in Stage 4.
> */
> var *Length, Width, Depth, Area, Volume* : real
> put "Enter Length of box (feet):   " ..
> get *Length*
> put "Enter Width of box (feet):   " ..
> get *Width*
> *Area* := *Length* * *Width*
> *Depth* := *max*(*Area*/10, 1)
> *Volume* := *Length* * *Width* * *Depth*

Comments should provide information that a reader cannot obtain from the program. The comment in the following statement is useless because it says nothing we do not know already.

> $N := N + 1$ % Increment N

The comment would be more useful if it described what was being incremented.

    $N := N + 1$ % Increment the number of bottles

This comment is necessary only because N is a poor choice of identifier. If we had used *BottleCount* rather than N, the comment would be unnecessary.

The comment in the following program is useful because it supplies information not provided by the code.

    % Use Newton's Second Law to obtain the acceleration.
    Accel := *Tension/BobMass*

Most of the programs in this book do *not* contain comments. Every program is accompanied by explanatory text that serves as an unusually detailed comment in a non-standard format.

1.7 Summary

Numbers in parentheses refer to sections where material appears.

▶   Turing evaluates expressions using the rules of conventional algebra (1.1.1).

▶   Errors detected at compile-time are of more use to the programmer than errors detected at run-time (1.1.4).

▶   Appropriate identifiers make programs easy to read and understand (1.2.2).

▶   Turing has four standard types: int, real, string, and boolean (1.3).

▶   A declaration introduces a new constant or variable (1.4).

▶   A constant declaration defines the name, type, and value of a new constant (1.4.1).

▶   A variable declaration defines the name, type, and value of a new variable (1.4.2).

▶   The put statement displays values on the screen (1.5.1). Each argument of a put statement must be the keyword skip, or an expression with a value of type int, real, or string. An argument may be followed by formatting expressions separated by colons.

▶   The get statement reads data from the keyboard (1.5.2). Each argument of a get statement must be a variable with type int, real, or string. A string variable may be followed by a colon and a number or by "*". When responding to a get statement, the user can correct mistakes using the BACKSPACE key.

▶   Comments do not affect the action of the program but are helpful to people reading it (1.6). The character "%" introduces a comment that extends to the end of the current line. The symbol "/*" introduces a comment that extends as far as the symbol "*/".

1.8 Exercises

1.1   Use Turing to compute the following values.

(a) $3(17 + 46)$

(b) $\dfrac{48 + 32}{48 - 32}$

(c) $13^2 - 12^2$

(d) $\dfrac{\frac{2}{3} + \frac{3}{4}}{\frac{4}{5} + \frac{5}{6}}$

(e) $\dfrac{4}{3} \times 3.14159 \times 2^3$

(f) $\dfrac{1.9 \times 10^{30}}{\frac{4}{3}\pi(6.96 \times 10^8)^3}$

1.2   Write down the value that Turing will display when each of the following put statements is executed. Then execute the statements and compare the results with your predictions.

(a) put $100 - 50 - 30$

(b) put $100 - (50 - 30)$

(c) put $(3/2)/(3 \text{ div } 2)$

(d) put 20 div 2 div 2

(e) put 20 div 4 mod 2

(f) put 3 ** 3 ** 3

(g) put 3 ** 2 * 2

(h) put $793.7/17.4 - 793.7$ div $17.4 - 793.7/17.4$ mod 1

1.3   What does the following program display? Write a better program that does the same thing.

```
const ll0011 := 2
const l1001l := 3
const l10Ol1 := 4
put (ll0011 + l1001l) * (l1001l + l10Ol1)
```

1.4   A rectangular swimming pool is 66 feet long and 22 feet wide. It is 3 feet deep at the shallow end, 8 feet deep at the deep end, and the bottom slopes uniformly. Water weighs 62.5 pounds per cubic foot, and there are 2,240 pounds in a ton. Write a program that computes the surface area of the pool, the volume of water in it, and the weight of the water in tons.

1.5   Use Turing to find approximate answers to the following questions. State any assumptions you make.

(a) How many meals have you eaten in your life?

(b) How many heartbeats have you experienced?

(c) How long would you need to paddle a canoe around the world?

(d) One alcoholic drink is estimated to kill about 100,000 brain cells. If a man with 10^{12} brain cells has three drinks a day, how long will it be before he has no brain cells left?

1.6   Many computations involve *units*, such as feet, meters, seconds, and tons. It is important in programming to use compatible units and to perform appropriate conversions. Here are some problems that require conversion.

(a) If your rent is $350 per month, how much are you paying in cents per minute?

(b) Assuming that the earth completes a circular orbit with a radius of 93 million miles in 365.25 days, how fast is it moving in miles per hour? (Exercise 1.11 requires another calculation of the same value in different units.)

(c) Assuming that the moon completes a circular orbit with a radius of 240,000 miles in 28 days, what is its orbital speed in miles per hour?

(d) Microscopes that rely on quantum effects are sensitive to vibration. They must not be allowed to move at speeds of more than 10^{-8} meters per second. The continents drift at a speed of about 15 feet per century. Which speed is faster? Assume that 1 meter = 3.28 feet.

1.7   If F is a temperature measured in degrees Fahrenheit and C is the same temperature measured in degrees Celsius, then $C = 5(F - 32)/9$. Write programs that convert between the two temperature systems.

1.8   The wavelength λ and the frequency f of light or radio waves are related by $\lambda f = c$, where $c = 3 \times 10^8$ meters per second is the velocity of light. Write programs that convert between frequency and wavelength.

1.9   In countries that use imperial units, the gas consumption of a car is measured in miles per gallon. In countries that use the metric system, it is measured in liters per hundred kilometers. Write programs that convert from one system to the other. Assume that 1 mile = 1.61 kilometers and 1 imperial gallon = 4.546 liters. In U.S. liquid measure, 1 gallon = 3.785 liters.

1.10 The ability to calculate approximate answers mentally is very useful to programmers. For each of the following items, estimate the answer and then use Turing to obtain an accurate answer. For example, you might estimate the answer to the first question as follows: $768 \times 1280 \times 25 \approx 10^3 \times 10^3 \times 25 = 25$ million bits. The exact value is 23,592,960 bits, which is about 6% smaller than the estimate.

(a) A high resolution monitor displays 768 lines with 1,280 pixels on a line. Obtaining a wide range of colors requires 24 bits per pixel. How many bits are required to store an image? If the image is refreshed 60 times per second, what is the transfer rate in bytes per second? (1 byte = 8 bits.)

(b) A laser printer prints 1,000 dots per linear inch. It can print to within 1/4 inch of the borders of $8\frac{1}{2} \times 11$ inch paper. How many bits are required to print a page? What is the corresponding number of bytes?

(c) The active surface of a hard disk has a minimum radius of 2.5 inches and a maximum radius of 5 inches. There are eight surfaces, and the storage capacity of the disk is 105 megabytes. How many bits are stored on each square inch of a surface of the disk? You can interpret "mega" either as 10^6 or as $2^{20} = 1,048,576$.

(d) A hose delivering 4.5 gallons per minute is used to water a garden 35 feet long and 25 feet wide. How long must the sprinkler be left on to achieve the effect of a quarter of an inch of rain? (1 cubic foot = 10 gallons.)

(e) A compact disk contains many "samples" of sound. A sample corresponds to 22.7 microseconds of sound and requires 16 bits of storage for a single channel. A stereo disk has two channels and lasts for about one hour. How many bits are stored on it?

Assuming that the minimum radius of the recording surface is 0.9 inches and the maximum radius is 2.1 inches, how many bits are there in 1 square inch of the surface? (1 microsecond $= 10^{-6}$ seconds.)

(f) The playing surface of a long-playing record has a minimum radius of 3 inches and a maximum radius of 11.5 inches. The record rotates at $33\frac{1}{3}$ revolutions per minute, and the playing time is 30 minutes.

1. What is the total length of the groove?

2. What is the wavelength of concert A in the outermost groove?

3. What is the wavelength of concert A in the innermost groove?

The frequency of concert A is 440 cycles per second.

1.11 The following figure gives information about the sun, the moon, and the earth. Use it to answer the questions below. The answers will not be particularly accurate. This is not Turing's fault; the calculations make simplifying assumptions. For example, we assume that orbits are circular with the larger mass fixed at the center of the circle. In reality, orbits are ellipses and both bodies move.

Body	Mass (kg)	Radius (m)	Distance to Sun (m)	Distance to Earth (m)
Sun	1.90×10^{30}	6.96×10^8		
Earth	5.98×10^{24}	6.38×10^6	1.496×10^{11}	
Moon	7.40×10^{22}	1.74×10^6	1.496×10^{11}	3.844×10^8

(a) The volume of a sphere of radius r is $\frac{4}{3}\pi r^3$. Calculate the volume of the sun, the earth, and the moon in cubic meters.

(b) The density of any solid object is its mass divided by its volume. Calculate the density of the sun, the earth, and the moon in kilograms per cubic meter.

(c) The gravitational force between two bodies of masses M_1 and M_2, separated by a distance d, is GM_1M_2/d^2. Calculate the gravitational forces between the sun and the earth, the sun and the moon, and the earth and the moon. Do you notice anything surprising about these forces?

The results will be in Newtons, the metric unit of force. The value of G, Newton's universal constant of gravitation, is about 6.673×10^{-11} Newtons $\cdot$ meter^2 $\cdot$ kg^{-2}.

(d) The orbital velocity of a small body moving around a much larger body is $\sqrt{GM/d}$, in which G is the gravitational constant, M is the mass of the larger body, and d is the distance between the bodies. Calculate the orbital velocity of the earth around the sun and the moon around the earth. Use $sqrt(X)$ to compute $\sqrt{X}$ in Turing.

(e) The *period* of an orbit is the time required to complete one revolution. For an orbit of radius d and orbital velocity v, the period is $2\pi d/v$. Calculate the period of the earth's orbit around the sun and the moon's orbit around the earth.

(f) One day, gravity breaks down, and a group of engineers decides to attach the moon to the earth with a steel cable so that it won't fly away. Assuming that steel can support a tension of 5×10^8 Newtons per square meter, what is the minimum thickness of the cable?

Chapter 2

Assignment and Control

Programs may exhibit complex behavior even though they are built from simple components. The complexity arises from the interdependence of computations and data in the program. Obviously, the computations determine the results produced. Less obviously, but equally important, the result produced by each computation may affect a future computation. Managing the interdependence of computations and data is one of the major tasks of programming. Assignments and control structures are essential tools that help us to perform this task. *Assignments* give new values to variables. *Control structures* use results to control the order in which computations are performed.

The control structures that Turing provides are *sequence*: do one thing after another; *decision*: select one of several alternatives; and *repetition*: do one thing several times. These three control structures are fundamental to computer science. They occur in many different contexts, including programming, formal language theory, and data structures. With these control structures, we can write programs of unlimited size and complexity.

As we have seen in Chapter 1, readability is an essential component of program design. There are several ways in which we can ensure that programs remain readable as they grow larger. One is to minimize the amount of text between the declaration of a name and its uses. Another is to use indentation and spacing to give the program a pleasant appearance on the page. The last two sections of this chapter discuss these aspects of programming.

2.1   The Assignment Statement

An *assignment statement* gives a new value to a variable. The assignment statement enables the program to compute values and store them. The statement

$N := 7$

is an assignment statement. The symbol ":=" is called the *assignment operator*.
The effect of the statement is to change the value of the variable N to 7. The
previous value of N, whatever it was, is lost.

We can read the statement "$N := 7$" in several ways:

"The variable N is assigned the value 7."
"Assign 7 to N."
"N becomes 7."
"N gets 7."

The last of these, "N gets 7", is both the shortest version and the one preferred by
most experienced programmers.

Sometimes "$N := 7$" is read as "N equals 7". This is incorrect. It confuses
"=", the equality predicate, with ":=", the assignment operator. "$N = 7$" is an
expression that may be true or false; it is not a statement.

Assignment and Declaration

The assignment operator ":=" is familiar from the constant and variable declarations introduced in Chapter 1. We now have three ways in which to use it:

const $A := 7$
var $B := 8$
$C := 9$

The first of these does two things: it declares a constant with name A and value 7.
The second also does two things: it declares a variable with name B and value 8.
The third simply assigns the new value 9 to the variable C.

Names that appear in declarations, such as A and B, *must not* have been declared
previously. Names that are used without declaration, such as C, *must* have been
declared previously. In the assignment $C := 9$, we know that C must be a variable
because we can assign new values to variables but not to constants. If the program
has compiled successfully, there must be a declaration of C earlier in the text of
the program.

If we declare a variable without an initial value, Turing considers the variable to
be undefined. If we use an undefined variable in an expression or a put statement,

Turing reports a run-time error. We give a value to an undefined variable by using either a **get** statement, as described in Chapter 1, or an assignment statement.

Example 2.1   Using the Assignment Statement

We begin a program with the following declarations:

    const $A := 0$
    var B : int

The following three statements are illegal in the context of these declarations.

    $A := 3$ ⊘   Illegal assignment to a constant.
    put B ⊘   Illegal use of an undefined variable.
    put C ⊘   Illegal use of an undeclared variable.

The following two statements are legal in the context of these declarations.

    put A %   Legal use of a defined constant.
    $B := 5$ %   Legal assignment to a declared variable.

After we have assigned the value 5 to B, the statement put B becomes legal because B has been initialized.

Abbreviating Assignments

The same variable name may appear on both sides of an assignment statement. For example, the effect of the statement

    $N := N + 1$

is to increase the value of N by 1. If the value of N was 4, Turing first would evaluate $N + 1$, obtaining 5, and then would give N the new value, 5.

Statements of this form occur frequently in programming, and it is annoying to have to write the variable name twice. We don't mind writing N twice, but consider

    $OctopusCount := OctopusCount + 1$

Turing allows us to write this statement in the following shorter form:

    $OctopusCount += 1$

The short form is quicker to write, easier to read, and less prone to error. Turing also provides corresponding abbreviations for the operators "$-$" and "$*$", as shown in Figure 2.1.

Statement	Abbreviation
$V := V + E$	$V += E$
$V := V - E$	$V -= E$
$V := V * E$	$V *= E$

Figure 2.1   Abbreviated Assignments

2.2   Sequences

The sequence is the simplest of the three control structures introduced in this chapter. If we write statements one after another, Turing will execute them in the order in which we have written them. The statements constitute a *sequence*.

The order of a sequence of statements usually affects the meaning of the program. Statements depend on computations performed by previous statements. Normally, we cannot change the order of statements in a sequence without changing the meaning of the sequence. For example, after executing the assignments

$M := 10$
$N := 10 * M + 1$

we have $M = 10$ and $N = 101$. We cannot reverse the order of the statements because the second statement uses the value of M computed by the first statement.

Occasionally, the order of the statements does not affect the meaning of the program. For example, the following three statements can be written in any order provided that the variables they use have been declared previously in the program.

$X := 9 * X / 5$
$Y := 100.0$
get Z

2.3   Decisions

Many quite simple machines have a limited capacity for making decisions. For example, toasters, ovens, refrigerators, and many other appliances can "decide" to turn their motors on or off according to a measured temperature. Decisions of this kind are fundamental to programming.

In a sequence of statements, control passes from one statement to the next independently of the values of the variables. We obtain the additional flexibility required for making decisions by allowing the values of variables to affect the flow of control. *Decision statements* enable programs to select different actions depending on the values of variables. The if and **case** statements provide two different ways of doing this.

2.3.1   The if Statement

The if statement, in its simplest form, addresses a situation in which the program must choose between two alternatives. The program uses a Boolean expression, which must be either true or false, to choose the appropriate alternative.

Example 2.2   Using the if Statement

In a park, it is necessary to water the grass on Monday if less than half an inch of rain has fallen during the previous week. The following program would help the park-keeper to decide whether to water.

```
put "How much rain fell last week?   " ..
var RainFall : real
get RainFall
if RainFall < 0.5 then
   put "You should water the grass."
else
   put "It is not necessary to water the grass."
end if
```

When Turing reaches the if statement on the fourth line, it first evaluates the condition $RainFall < 0.5$. If the result is true, which it will be if less than half an inch of rain has fallen, Turing executes the statements following then. Otherwise, the result is false, and Turing executes the statements following else. In either case, *exactly one* of the sequences is executed.

Here are two examples of the program in use. In the first example, the condition is true, and Turing executes the then branch. In the second example, the condition is false, and Turing executes the else branch.

```
How much rain fell last week? .49
You should water the grass.


How much rain fell last week? .75
It is not necessary to water the grass.
```

Compound Conditions

It often happens that the appropriate action depends on more than one condition. We can handle these situations by writing an if statement as part of the sequence of statements following then or else. The resulting statement is called a *compound* if statement.

Example 2.3   A Compound if Statement

The town does not allow the grass in the park to be watered after it has issued a drought warning. We modify the program of Example 2.2 accordingly. If less than half an inch of rain has fallen, the program must ask if there has been a drought warning. The sequence following the first then contains declarations, a put and a get statement, and another if statement.

```
put "How much rain fell last week?   " ..
var RainFall : real
get RainFall
if RainFall < 0.5 then
   var Reply : string
   put "Was there a drought warning (y/n)?   " ..
   get Reply
   if Reply = "y" then
      put "There is a drought:  do not water the grass."
   else
      put "You should water the grass."
   end if
else
   put "It is not necessary to water the grass."
end if
```

The following dialogues illustrate the three possible responses of this program. In each case, the program executes one of the last three put statements.

```
How much rain fell last week? .4
Was there a drought warning (y/n)? y
There is a drought:  do not water the grass.

How much rain fell last week? .4
Was there a drought warning (y/n)? n
You should water the grass.

How much rain fell last week? .5
It is not necessary to water the grass.
```

In the final dialogue, exactly half an inch of rain is reported, and the program recommends not watering. The condition *RainFall* < 0.5 is true only if the rainfall was *less than* half an inch. It is false if there was *exactly* half an inch.

Local Declarations

We declared the variable *Reply* in Example 2.3 "inside" the first if statement. A declaration inside a statement is called a *local declaration*. We can use a local variable such as *Reply* only between its declaration and the final else of the program. Section 2.5 gives complete rules for names declared locally.

Input Validation

The following dialogue shows that there is a problem in the program of Example 2.3.

```
How much rain fell last week? .4
Was there a drought warning (y/n)? u
You should water the grass.
```

The response to the question **Was there a drought warning (y/n)?** sets the variable *Reply* to "u". The user probably intended to press "y" but pressed "u" by mistake. The program, however, compares "u" and "y" and finds that they are unequal. Consequently, it behaves as if the response was "n", which might confuse the user.

We can improve the program by rewriting the if statement so that it checks that the user's reply is either "y" or "n". If it is neither of these, the program should ask for a valid reply. We can achieve this by rewriting the inner if statement in the following way.

```
if Reply = "y" then
   put "There is a drought:  do not water the grass."
else
   if Reply = "n" then
     put "You should water the grass."
   else
     put "Please use 'y' or 'n' to answer."
   end if
end if
```

The repetition of end if is an awkward feature of the preceding statement. Since compound if statements in which else is immediately followed by if occur quite frequently in programming, Turing provides a more compact way of writing them. We change else if to the single keyword elsif and remove the end if. Here is the revised if statement:

```
if Reply = "y" then
   put "There is a drought:   do not water the grass."
elsif Reply = "n" then
   put "You should water the grass."
else
   put "Please use 'y' or 'n' to answer."
end if
```

Using the elsif construction, we can write if statements that are easy to read and that provide as many alternatives as are required by the problem we are solving. The next example illustrates the use of several alternatives.

Example 2.4   Cascaded if Statements

Figure 2.2 shows the tax rates in a mythical country, Turingia. Since there is no simple relationship between a Turingian citizen's income and the tax payable, a program that calculates tax must treat each income category as a distinct case.

Income ($)	Tax Rate (%)	Note
0 – 4,999	0	
5,000 – 9,999	7	
10,000 – 14,999	8	
15,000 – 24,999	10	
25,000 –		(1)

Note (1) For incomes of $25,000 and over, tax is 20% of the first $25,000 and 40% of income in excess of $25,000.

Figure 2.2   Tax Rates in Turingia

For a given income, the following program performs exactly one tax calculation and assigns the result to the variable *Tax*.

```
var Income, Tax : real
put "Enter your income after expenses ($):   " ..
get Income
if Income < 5000 then
   Tax := 0
```

```
      elsif Income < 10000 then
         Tax := 0.07 * Income
      elsif Income < 15000 then
         Tax := 0.08 * Income
      elsif Income < 25000 then
         Tax := 0.1 * Income
      else
         Tax := 0.2 * 25000 + 0.4 * (Income − 25000)
      end if
      put "Net␣income:␣␣␣", Income : 9 : 2
      put "Income␣tax:␣␣␣", Tax : 9 : 2
      put "Balance:␣␣␣␣␣␣", Income − Tax : 9 : 2
```

Here is an example of the program in action.

```
      Enter your income after expenses ($): 37000
      Net income:      37000.00
      Income tax:       9800.00
      Balance:         27200.00
```

Style

The statement

$$Tax := 0.2 * 25000 + 0.4 * (Income − 25000)$$

is a literal translation of Note (1) in Figure 2.2. Instead, we could have written the statement

$$Tax := 0.4 * Income − 5000$$

The expressions in these two assignments are mathematically equivalent. The second expression is merely a simplified version of the first. Whether a programmer should carry out simplifications like this is a subtle question. The advantage of the unsimplified version is that a person checking the program can easily see the relationship between the program and the instructions on the tax form. This may be more important than the very small amount of execution time saved by simplifying the expression.

2.3.2 The case Statement

The case statement performs a similar function to the if statement, but we use the case statement when the appropriate action depends on an integer value rather than on a Boolean value.

Example 2.5   A Simple case Statement

The following program asks the user to enter the current month as an integer between 1 and 12. It responds with a brief description of the expected weather for that month in Turingia, using a case statement to select the description.

```
var Month : int
put "Enter the month (1-12):   " ..
get Month
case Month of
    label 1, 2 : put "Bitterly cold"
    label 3 : put "Very cold and snowing"
    label 4 : put "Cold and wet"
    label 5 : put "Warm and wet"
    label 6 : put "Hot"
    label 7 : put "Hot and humid"
    label 8 : put "Humid"
    label 9, 10 : put "Cool"
    label 11, 12 : put "Cold and snowing"
    label : put "Invalid month"
end case
```

Case Expressions

In the phrase case *Month* of, the variable *Month* is used as a *case expression*. Turing evaluates the case expression, matches it to one of the labels that follow, and performs the corresponding action. If the user wanted to know what weather to expect in May, the following dialogue would occur.

```
Enter the month (1-12): 5
Warm and wet
```

In the dialogue above, the value of *Month* is 5, and the corresponding action is

```
    put "Warm and wet"
```

Case Labels

The weather is bitterly cold in both January and February. These months are combined in a single case with two label values, 1 and 2, leading to the same action. Similarly, there is a single action for September and October (labels 9 and 10), and for November and December (labels 11 and 12). There can be as many label values as necessary for each action. The labels do not have to appear in order. The following case statement, like the one in the program above, uses a given month to choose an action.

```
var Month : int
put "Enter the month (1-12):   " ..
get Month
case Month of
   label 1, 2, 3, 4, 9, 10, 11, 12 :
      put "The month has an 'r' in it."
   label 5, 6, 7, 8 :
      put "The month does not have an 'r' in it."
   label :
      put "Invalid month"
end case
```

Default Actions

The following dialogue shows what happens if the user does not comply with the instructions given by either the program above or the weather prediction program of Example 2.5.

```
Enter the month (1-12): 13
Invalid month
```

The number 13 does not match any of the numbers following label in the case statement. Turing performs the action corresponding to the final label, which does not have a number, and displays "Invalid month". This is called the *default action* of the statement.

Turing does not require a case statement to have a default action. If there is no default action and the case expression does not match a label, Turing reports an error. If there is a default action, it must be the last action of the case statement.

Menu Selection

The case statement provides a convenient way of writing programs that offer a choice to the user. Suppose that a program displays the following menu.

```
You can:
a) Add a new name.
d) Delete a name.
f) Find a name.
q) Quit.
Enter your choice:
```

The user presses a key, and the program responds by performing the appropriate action. It seems natural to use the case statement for this application, but there is a problem: case labels must be integers; they may not be letters.

The predefined function *ord* solves this problem by converting a character value to an integer. If C is a character string with exactly one character, then *ord* (C) is the numeric code for the character in C. Example 2.6 uses *ord* to provide the integer required for a case label.

Example 2.6   Using *ord* in a case Statement

The following program displays a menu that offers each of the four choices mentioned above and allows the user to choose an action. The string variable *Choice* records the user's reply. The case statement uses the numeric value of the reply to select the correct action. The program accepts both upper and lower case letters in replies. Each box stands for the code of an action.

```
put "You can:"
put " a) Add a new name."
put " d) Delete a name."
put " f) Find a name."
put " q) Quit."
put "Enter your choice:   " ..
var Choice : string
get Choice
case ord (Choice) of
   label ord ("a"), ord ("A") : % Add a new name.
       ┌────────┐
       └────────┘
   label ord ("d"), ord ("D") : % Delete a name.
       ┌────────┐
       └────────┘
   label ord ("f"), ord ("F") : % Find a name.
       ┌────────┐
       └────────┘
   label ord ("q"), ord ("Q") : % Quit.
       exit
   label :
       put "Please enter one of a, d, f, or q.\n"
end case
```

The program works correctly but is insecure. If the user enters more than one character, the program fails with an error message because *ord* accepts only a single character. We will see how to remove this insecurity by using the string functions described in Section 3.4.

2.4   Repetition

Repetition, in various forms, is close to the heart of programming. Most of the tasks that computers perform consist of quite simple operations carried out over and over again. Almost all programs contain statements that are executed more than once.

Although the statements do not change, the data on which they operate do change. In some cases, the computations are essentially independent of one another. For example, a grading program might process each record in a student file to obtain the grade for the student. In other cases, each computation depends on previous computations. A program that computes square roots, for example, does so by finding better and better approximations to the correct value of the root. Each approximation depends on the previous one.

Turing provides two statements to control repetition: the loop statement and the for statement. The loop statement, as its name suggests, provides a simple and general way of constructing loops. A *loop* is a control structure that contains a sequence of statements that are executed several times. The for statement is a specialized kind of loop statement.

2.4.1   The loop Statement

A loop statement consists of the keyword loop, a sequence of statements that will be executed repeatedly, and the phrase end loop. Executing a sequence of statements repeatedly is called *iterating* the sequence. The statements that are iterated form the *body* of the loop. When the statements in the body stop executing, we say that the loop has *terminated*. At least one of the statements must be an exit statement that terminates the loop.

Example 2.7   A Simple Loop

The following program reads positive numbers from the keyboard and adds them together. When the user enters a negative number, the program displays the total and stops.

```
var Total := 0.0
loop
    var Current : real
    put ":  " ..
    get Current
    exit when Current < 0.0
```

```
    Total += Current
end loop
put "Total = ", Total
```

In the following dialogue, the user has entered three positive numbers followed by a negative number, -1, which terminates the loop.

```
: 2.5
: 3
: 4.5
: -1
Total = 10
```

Loop Execution

The variable *Total*, which accumulates the sum of positive numbers entered by the user, is declared with initial value 0.0 before the **loop** statement. The body of the loop consists of one declaration and four statements between **loop** and **end loop**. We use the variable *Current* within the body of the loop to store the number most recently obtained from the user by the **get** statement. During each iteration of the loop body, Turing reads a new value for *Current* and, if it is positive, adds it to *Total*.

Eventually, the user enters a negative number. Turing evaluates the condition *Current* < 0.0, obtaining the result **true**. The **exit** statement then terminates the loop. The negative value of *Current* is *not* added to *Total* because Turing exits from the loop immediately, without executing the statement *Total* $+=$ *Current*. The last statement of the program, immediately following the **loop** statement, displays the final value of *Total*.

Example 2.8   Using an Unconditional **exit** Statement

We can use the **exit** statement without a **when** clause, in which case its effect is to terminate the loop unconditionally. The following program determines whether the number provided by the user is a power of two.

```
put "Enter number:   " ..
var Original, Copy, Power := 0
get Original
Copy := Original
loop
    if Copy = 1 then
        put Original, " = 2**", Power
        exit
```

```
  elsif Copy mod 2 ≠ 0 then
    put Original, " is not a power of 2."
    exit
  else
    Copy := Copy div 2
    Power += 1
  end if
end loop
```

Here are two examples of the program in action.

```
Enter number: 32
32 = 2**5
```

```
Enter number: 24
24 is not a power of 2
```

The value of the number that the user enters is stored in the variable *Original*. The program must store this value because it is used in the displayed messages. But we also need a variable that will be halved during each iteration of the loop. The second variable is called *Copy* in the program. It has the same initial value as *Original*, but its value changes as the program runs.

The value of *Copy* mod 2 is the remainder when *Copy* is divided by 2. Thus the expression *Copy* mod 2 ≠ 0 is **true** if *Copy* is an odd number.

Each time the program starts a new cycle of the loop, there are three cases to consider, depending on the value of *Copy*. First, if the number is equal to 1, it is a power of 2 because $2^0 = 1$. Second, if the number is odd and greater than 1, it cannot be a power of 2. For these cases, no further looping is necessary and the exit statement terminates the loop. Finally, if the number is even, we divide it by 2 and execute the loop again.

If the value of *Original* is 32, as in the first example above, *Copy* receives the values 32, 16, 8, 4, 2, and 1. Since the final value is 1, the original value must be a power of 2. In the second example, *Copy* receives the values 24, 12, 6, and 3. Since 3 is an odd number greater than 1, the original value is not a power of 2.

If we start the program in Example 2.8 and enter 0, the loop will not terminate. The variable *Copy* receives the value 0. Since the conditions *Copy* = 1 and *Copy* mod 2 ≠ 0 are both false, Turing executes the **else** clause of the **if** statement. The assignment *Copy* := *Copy* div 2 does not change the value of *Copy* because 0 divided by 2 is 0, and so the **if** and **elsif** conditions are still false. Both termination conditions remain false, and the loop will execute until the user interrupts the program.

There is no general way of deciding whether a loop will terminate, but there is a necessary condition that we should always check: the statements in the body of the loop must change the value of at least one of the variables in the termination condition. This condition is not satisfied by the program in Example 2.8. When *Copy* is zero, the exit conditions are not satisfied and the assignment

$$Copy := Copy \text{ div } 2$$

does not change the value of *Copy*. Consequently, the loop continues until the user interrupts the program.

Nested Loops

The statements in the body of a loop may be loop statements. A statement that contains two or more loops, one inside the other, is called a *nested* loop statement.

Example 2.9   Nested Loops

The following program is an extended version of the program in Example 2.8. It consists of two loops, one nested inside the other. The outer loop reads numbers from the keyboard. Positive numbers are tested to see whether they are powers of two. Negative numbers are reported as errors. Zero terminates the program.

```
loop
    var Original, Copy : int
    put "Enter number (0 terminates):  " ..
    get Original
    if Original = 0 then
        exit
    elsif Original < 0 then
        put "Please enter a positive number."
    else
        Copy := Original
        var Power := 0
        loop
            if Copy = 1 then
                put Original, " = 2**", Power
                exit
            elsif Copy mod 2 ≠ 0 then
                put Original, " is not a power of 2."
                exit
            else
                Copy := Copy div 2
                Power += 1
```

```
      end if
    end loop
  end if
end loop
```

Here is an example of this program in action.

```
Enter number (0 terminates): 32
32 = 2**5
Enter number (0 terminates): -3
Please enter a positive number.
Enter number (0 terminates): 0
```

2.4.2   The for Statement

The for statement is a specialized version of the loop statement. We use the for statement when we need to execute a sequence of statements for a fixed range of values. A typical application of the for statement is to display a table of values.

Example 2.10   Using the for Statement to Display a Table

We usually know how many rows and columns a table will have before we display it. Consequently, we use for statements to display tables. Here is a program that displays the volume of water contained in circular ponds with radii from 5 to 25 meters. We use the same formula as before: $V = \pi d^2 (3r - d)/3$.

```
const Depth := 1.0
const Pi := 3.14159
put "Radius␣␣␣Volume"
for Row : 1 .. 5
  var Radius := 5.0 * Row
  put Radius : 5 : 1, " ",
      Pi * Depth ** 2 * (3 * Radius − Depth)/3 : 8 : 1
end for
```

The effect of the program is to execute the statements between for and end for five times, giving Row the values $1, 2, \ldots, 5$ in turn. The first occurrence of Row in the for statement is a declaration. For this reason, we do not need to declare Row elsewhere in the program. The formatting expressions ": 5 : 1" and ": 8 : 1" ensure that the rows of the table will be correctly aligned.

Here is the output generated by this program.

```
Radius    Volume
   5.0    14.7
  10.0    30.4
  15.0    46.1
  20.0    61.8
  25.0    77.5
```

Nested Loops

If the table has more than two or three columns, it may be possible to calculate the values of the column entries using a for statement. We can nest for statements just as we nested loop statements in Example 2.9.

Example 2.11   Nested for Statements

The following program displays a table of the volumes of various ponds. Like the program in Example 2.10, this program varies the radius of the pond from 5 to 25 meters. This program also varies the depth of the pond from 1 to 5 meters. Both values are determined by for statements, with one statement nested inside the other.

```
const Pi := 3.14159
put "Depth" ..
for Column : 1 .. 5
    const Depth : real := Column
    put Depth : 10 : 2 ..
end for
put skip, "Radius"
for Row : 1 .. 5
    const Radius := 5.0 * Row
    put Radius : 5 : 0 ..
    for Column : 1 .. 5
        const Depth : real := Column
        const Volume := Pi * Depth ** 2 * (3 * Radius − Depth)/3
        put Volume : 10 : 2 ..
    end for
    put ""
end for
```

The constants *Row* and *Column* index the rows and columns of the table. The constant *Depth* has the same value as *Row*, but it is a real constant. The keyword real is necessary in the declaration of *Depth* because otherwise Turing would infer its type as int, the type of *Column*.

Here are the results displayed by the program.

Depth	1.00	2.00	3.00	4.00	5.00
Radius					
5.	14.66	54.45	113.10	184.31	261.80
10.	30.37	117.29	254.47	435.63	654.50
15.	46.08	180.12	395.84	686.96	1047.20
20.	61.78	242.95	537.21	938.29	1439.90
25.	77.49	305.78	678.58	1189.62	1832.59

Style

We could have written the program of Example 2.11 using fewer statements. For example, we could write the formulas directly in the put statements instead of giving them names in constant declarations. The declarations of *Radius*, *Depth*, and *Volume* clarify the purpose of the program. Without them, we would have to explain the purpose of the formulas. Here as elsewhere, we are more concerned to make programs understandable than to make them short.

The Controlled Variable

In a for statement, the variable that follows the keyword for is called the *controlled variable*. In the following for statement, the controlled variable is *Counter*.

for *Counter* : 1 .. 10

☐☐☐☐

end for

The phrase 1 .. 10 determines both the values assumed by the controlled variable and the number of iterations performed by the for statement. The box stands for statements that will be executed ten times, with *Counter* assuming the values $1, 2, \ldots, 10$. We can refer to the value of the controlled variable only between for and end for. Turing increments the controlled variable implicitly and does not allow the program to change its value.

If the controlled variable is not mentioned in the body of the loop, we do not need to declare it.

Example 2.12 Omitting the Controlled Variable

The for statement in the program below executes forty times, doubling the value of *Pos* and halving the value of *Neg* during each iteration, without referring to the controlled variable, *Count*.

```
var Pos, Neg := 1.0
for Count : 1 .. 30
    put Pos : 15, Neg : 15
    Pos *= 2
    Neg := Neg/2
end for
```

Since the controlled variable *Count* is not used in the body of the loop, we do not need to declare it. We could replace the third line of the program by

```
for : 1 .. 30
```

without changing the behavior of the program. When the program runs, it displays a table that starts as shown below.

1	1
2	0.5
4	0.25
8	0.125
16	0.0625
32	0.03125
64	0.015625
128	0.007813
256	0.003906
512	0.001953
1024	9.765625e-4
...	...

Loop Bounds

The key step in designing a for statement is the choice of the initial and final values of the controlled variable. In the for statement

```
for Count : M .. N
    ┌─────────┐
    └─────────┘
end for
```

the M is the *lower bound* of the loop and the value of N is the *upper bound* of the statement. The number of iterations is $N - M + 1$ if $M \leq N$ and zero if $M > N$. The fact that the for statement does nothing if the lower bound is greater than the upper bound is important because it helps us to construct loops that work correctly in limiting cases. For example, we can process the characters of a string S using a loop of the form

```
for P : 1 .. length (S)
    ┌──────────┐
    └──────────┘
end for
```

If S is the empty string, the **for** statement does nothing, which is usually what we want.

Example 2.13 Processing Strings with a **for** Statement

The code below takes a string *OldString* and produces a new string *NewString* that is the same as *OldString* but with blanks removed. If *OldString* is the empty string, the **for** statement does nothing, and *NewString* remains empty. The expression *OldString* (P) denotes the Pth character of the string *OldString*.

```
NewString := ""
for P : 1 .. length (OldString)
    if OldString (P) ≠ " " then
        NewString += OldString (P)
    end if
end for
```

Counting Backwards

Occasionally, we want the value of the controlled variable to decrease rather than increase during execution of the loop. Turing provides the keyword **decreasing** for this purpose. The program below uses a **for** loop with a decreasing counter to display numbers in reverse order.

```
put "Counting backwards:   " ..
for decreasing Count : 10 .. 0
    put Count, " " ..
end for
```

When this program runs, it displays the following output:

```
Counting backwards:   10 9 8 7 6 5 4 3 2 1 0
```

A decreasing loop does nothing if the first bound is smaller than the second bound. For example, the following statement does not display anything.

```
for decreasing Count : 1 .. 5
    put Count
end for
```

Comparing for and loop Statements

Every for statement in a Turing program can be rewritten as a loop statement. The for statement in the following code computes the sum of the integers
$First, \ldots, Last$.

```
var Sum := 0
for N : First .. Last
    Sum += N
end for
put Sum
```

The code below uses a loop statement to achieve the same effect.

```
var Sum := 0
var N := First
loop
    exit when N > Last
    Sum += N
    N += 1
end loop
put Sum
```

These two statements show that the for statement is not strictly necessary in
Turing: every for statement could be rewritten as a loop statement. However,
the for statement is extremely useful in practice. By encapsulating the lower and
upper limits, the termination condition, and the incrementing step, it provides a
more readable and concise program than a loop statement.

2.4.3   Designing Loops

A large proportion of programming errors is due to faulty loop design. This is not
surprising because a loop has three components — initialization, iteration, and
termination — that must work together in a precise way. It is not difficult to
design good loops if we keep in mind the three components: how to start the loop,
how to carry on, and when to stop.

To start the loop, we must set all of the relevant variables to suitable values. Sums
and counters should be zero, strings should be empty, and conditions should
be false. These are general recommendations: other values will sometimes be
required for particular circumstances.

Having chosen the initial values, we think about the effect of each iteration. The
loop should have a *goal*, and each iteration should *make progress* towards the goal.

If we are computing a sum, we should add something to it; if we are counting, we should increment the counter, and so on. The last and most important factor is when to stop. There is an obvious criterion — when we have achieved the goal — but we must be careful to ensure that the loop can actually reach the goal.

Example 2.14   A Counting Loop

We construct a loop that counts the number of times the letter "e" occurs in a given string, S. If P is a positive integer between 1 and the length of the string S, then the expression $S(P)$ gives the Pth character of the string. The loop scans the string from left to right, examining each character. We use P as an index to locate the character, and a counter, C, to count the "e"s. Initially, we need $P = 1$, indexing the first character of the string, and $C = 0$, indicating that we have not yet seen any "e"s.

To make progress, we examine the current character, $S(P)$, and increment the counter if it is an "e". We also advance the index, P. The code is

```
if S (P) = "e" then
    C += 1
end if
P += 1
```

The loop should stop at the end of the string. When we inspect the last character of the string, we have $P = length(S)$. This suggests the following loop.

```
var P := 1
var C := 0
loop
    if S (P) = "e" then
        C += 1
    end if
    exit when P = length (S)
    P += 1
end loop
```

There is a serious problem with this loop. If the string is empty, the program fails at the expression $S(P) =$ "e" because $S(P)$ attempts to index the first character of an empty string. Since the string is empty, $length(S)$ is zero and the initial value of the index, $P = 1$, is already too large. We see that the condition for terminating the loop should have been $P > length(S)$ and we should test it *before* we examine the string. The following loop incorporates this improvement.

```
var P := 1
var C := 0
loop
   exit when P > length (S)
   if S (P) = "e" then
      C += 1
   end if
   P += 1
end loop
```

We have already seen that the statements in the body of a loop may never be executed. The program above illustrates this. If the string S is empty, *nothing happens* except the exit test. Most well-written loops have the property that, under certain conditions, they do nothing. After you have written a loop, you should always check that, if there is nothing to do, the loop actually has no effect.

It is easier to design for statements than loop statements. This is because the for statement is designed to do the important things — initialize, make progress, and stop — automatically. We use for statements whenever they are appropriate. The following for statement provides a better solution to the problem of Example 2.14 than the solution shown there.

```
C := 0
for P : 1 .. length (S)
   if S (P) = "e" then
      C += 1
   end if
end for
```

Exiting from a Loop

There are, however, many situations in which we cannot use for loops because we do not know the range of values for iteration. In these situations, we must use an exit statement within a loop statement. The termination conditions under which the exit statement is executed determine the effect of the loop.

We should not use exit statements indiscriminately because a loop statement with several exit statements is hard to understand. The best kind of loop has one exit statement at the beginning of the loop. A useful feature of this kind of loop is that it has no effect if the termination condition is true when the loop starts.

The following loop statement subtracts π from the positive real variable X until the result lies between 0 and π. If X is initially less than π, its value does not change because the exit statement comes before the assignment statement.

```
const Pi := 3.14159
loop
   exit when X < Pi
   X -= Pi
end loop
```

The second best kind of loop has one exit statement that is the last statement of the loop. The loop statement below finds the number of digits, D, needed to display the positive integer N. Even if N is initially zero, we must display at least one digit. By placing the exit statement at the end of the loop, we ensure that D is at least 1.

```
var D := 0
loop
   N := N div 10
   D += 1
   exit when N = 0
end loop
```

Sometimes it is best to put the exit statement in the middle of the loop. A common example is a loop that reads a number, checks the value of the number, and then processes it.

There are a few situations in which it is better to use more than one exit statement in a loop. Multiple exit statements usually indicate different reasons for terminating the loop. For example, in Example 2.8, we used the loop

```
loop
   if Copy = 1 then
      put Original, " = 2**", Power
      exit
   elsif Copy mod 2 ≠ 0 then
      put Original, " is not a power of 2."
      exit
   else
      Copy := Copy div 2
      Power += 1
   end if
end loop
```

The two exit statements in this loop correspond to two situations: either $Copy = 1$ or $Copy$ is odd and greater than 1. It is possible to write this loop with only one exit statement:

```
loop
  if Copy mod 2 ≠ 0 then
    if Copy = 1 then
      put Original, "= 2**", Power
    else
      put Original, " is not a power of 2"
    end if
    exit
  else
    Copy := Copy div 2
    Power += 1
  end if
end loop
```

The disadvantage of the second version is that the two nested if statements are harder to read than the original single if statement.

2.5   Scopes and Local Declarations

A declaration introduces a new name into a program. If we can use the new name between its place of declaration and the end of the program, we say that the name is *global*.

The *scope* of a name is the region of the program in which we can use the name. If the name is global, its scope starts at its declaration and continues to the end of the program. The statements "X is global" and "X has global scope" mean the same thing. We say that a name is *visible* inside its scope.

The scope of every name in a Turing program begins at its declaration. Some scopes, however, do not include the whole of the rest of the program. These scopes are called *local scopes*. The declaration of a variable with a local scope is called a *local declaration*.

Each of the statements introduced in this chapter except the assignment statement — that is, the if, case, loop, and for statements — contains nested sequences of declarations and statements. Each nested sequence introduces a new scope. The scope of a declaration within a sequence starts at the declaration and ends at the end of the sequence in which it appears.

The scope of each declaration in a simple program is illustrated in Figure 2.3. Each box indicates the scope of a variable; the name of the variable appears in the top right corner of the box and is not part of the program. For example,

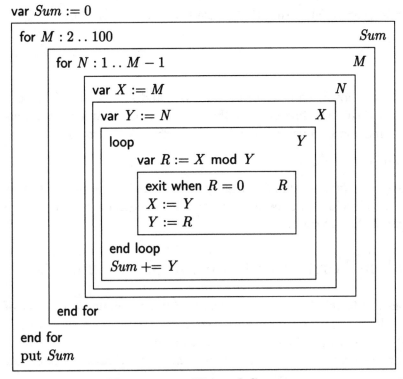

Figure 2.3   Nested Scopes

the largest box shows the scope of Sum, which includes all the code after the declaration of Sum.

Declaration Before Use

The basic scope rule of Turing is called the "declaration before use" rule. The declaration of a name must appear earlier in the program than the first use of the name. For example, Turing accepts the program

```
var N : int := 99
put N
```

but it does not accept

```
put N              ⊘
var N : int := 99
```

because the second version uses N in the put statement before it declares N in the variable declaration.

Turing has a control structure that is used only to limit a scope. In the statement

> begin
> ⬜️
> end

the box stands for a sequence of declarations and statements. The scope of any declaration within the box ends at the keyword **end**. It is not often necessary to use **begin** and **end** because the other control structures provide local scopes.

Discussion

The scope of a variable should usually be as small as possible. If a variable is used only inside a loop, we should declare it at the beginning of the loop, not at the beginning of the program.

2.6   The Form and Content of Statements

The programs in this book are all formatted in accordance with a set of conventions. By following conventions, we give programs a consistent appearance that makes them pleasant to look at and easy to read. Formatting conventions convey more than pleasing appearance, however. The conventions we adopt should reflect the structure of the program.

This section shows the relationship between form and content. For each statement that has been introduced in this chapter, we define a general form and show how the statement should be written in a program.

The general form of the assignment statement is

> ⬜️ := ⬜️

The left box stands for the name of a variable and the right box stands for an expression. The variable and the expression must be the same type (int, real, string, or boolean) except that if the variable is declared to be real, the expression may have either an integer or a real value. The effect of the assignment statement is to make the value of the expression the new value of the variable.

In an if statement, the statement sequences are indented. The first if, each **else** or elsif, and the final **end if** are aligned on the left.

> if ⬜️ then
> ⬜️
> elsif ⬜️ then
> ⬜️
> . . . .

else
☐
end if

In all cases, Turing executes exactly one of the statement sequences. It evaluates the conditions in turn. If one of the conditions is **true**, Turing executes the corresponding statement sequence and then goes to the statement following **end if**. If none of the conditions is **true**, Turing executes the statement sequence following **else**.

The **else** part of the if statement may be omitted. A statement of the form

if ☐ then
☐
end if

has no effect if its condition evaluates to **false**.

In a **case** statement, each label should be indented with respect to the **case** keyword. The statements following a label should be further indented unless they are short enough to fit on the same line as the label.

case ☐ of
    label ☐ :
      ☐
    . . . .
    label :
      ☐
end case

In a **loop** statement, the declarations and statements in the body of the loop should be indented with respect to the **loop** keyword. The **loop** statement has the general form

loop
☐
end loop

in which the box stands for a sequence of declarations and statements. The sequence will usually contain one or more **exit** statements of the form

exit when ☐

in which the box stands for a Boolean expression.

Turing executes the statements between **loop** and **end loop** over and over again. Looping stops as soon as Turing encounters an **exit** statement with a true condition.

The general form of a **for** statement is

for ☐ : ☐
☐
end for

The first box stands for a variable name. The variable is called the *controlled variable* of the **for** statement. The second box stands for a *range specification*. The third box stands for a sequence of declarations and statements called the *body* of the **for** statement.

The most common form of range specification is $M \mathrel{..} N$, in which M and N are integer expressions. The expressions M and N are the lower and upper *bounds* of the iteration, respectively. Turing executes the body with the controlled variable having values $M, M+1, \ldots, N$. The number of iterations performed is $N-M+1$. The **for** statement is legal even if $M > N$. In this case, the predicted number of iterations is negative, and Turing does not execute the body at all.

Conventions

In this book, we use some additional conventions to improve the readability of programs.

Keywords appear in bold type:

const   **int**   **put**

Identifiers appear in italics:

FamilyName   *Radius*

Character strings and results appear in typewriter type:

`"Alan Mathison Turing"`

Operators are written in conventional mathematical form rather than in Turing form. Appendix B on page 357 shows the correspondence between the symbols used in this book and the symbols shown on the screen or in a listing of the program produced by a printer.

2.7   Summary

Numbers in parentheses refer to sections where material appears.

▶   The assignment statement changes the value of a variable (2.1).

▶   The if statement chooses between two or more courses of action depending on the value of a Boolean expression (2.3.1).

▶   The case statement chooses between two or more courses of action based on the value of an integer expression (2.3.2). Each action in a case statement is introduced by a label. If there is a default action, it has an empty label and appears at the end of the case statement.

▶   The loop statement has a body that is executed zero or more times (2.4.1).

▶   Execution of an exit statement terminates the loop (2.4.1).

▶   The for statement has a body that is executed zero or more times (2.4.2).

▶   Loop design requires care (2.4.3).

▶   Each identifier in a program has a scope (2.5).

▶   Most Turing statements contain local scopes in which identifiers can be declared (2.5).

▶   The keywords then, loop, for, and begin introduce new scopes, as do labels in a case statement (2.5).

▶   There is a preferred layout for each kind of statement (2.6).

2.8   Exercises

2.1   Use loop statements to compute the following values:

(a) $1 + 2 + 3 + \cdots + 100$

(b) $1 + 1/2 + 1/3 + \cdots + 1/100$

(c) $1 - 1/2 + 1/3 - \cdots + 99/100 - 1/100$

(d) $1/2 + 2/3 + 3/4 + \cdots + 99/100$

(e) $\dfrac{100 - 0}{1} + \dfrac{99 - 1}{2} + \dfrac{98 - 2}{3} + \cdots + \dfrac{51 - 49}{50}$

(f) $2 \times \dfrac{2}{1} \times \dfrac{2}{3} \times \dfrac{4}{3} \times \dfrac{4}{5} \times \dfrac{6}{5} \times \dfrac{6}{7} \times \cdots \times \dfrac{2n}{2n - 1} \times \dfrac{2n}{2n + 1}$ for a suitable value of n.

For large values of n, the result should be close to π.

2.2   Write down the results you would expect each of the following programs to display. Then run the programs and see if your predictions were correct.

(a) ```
var M := 0
var N := 10
loop
    exit when M ≥ N
    M += 1
    N -= 1
end loop
put M : 3, N : 3
```

(b) ```
var S := 0
for P : 1 .. 6
    S += P
end for
put S
```

(c) ```
var N : int
get N
loop
    exit when N = 0
    put N mod 10 ..
    N := N div 10
end loop
```
```

(d) var $K := 7$
    loop
        put $K : 3$ ..
        if $K = 1$ then
            exit
        elsif K mod $2 = 0$ then
            $K := K$ div 2
        else
            $K := 3 * K + 1$
        end if
    end loop

(e) var $N := 1$
    loop
        put $N : 3$ ..
        case N of
            label 1 :
                $N += 2$
            label 2, 4 :
                $N := N$ div 2
            label 3 :
                $N += 1$
        end case
    end loop

2.3   Often we can find a precise criterion for loop termination. The loop in the following program will terminate if the user enters a number less than or equal to 10.

    var N : int
    get N
    loop
        put $N ** 2$
        exit when $N \geq 10$
        $N += 1$
    end loop

For each of the following statements, find a termination criterion. Assume that M and N have been declared as integer variables.

(a) loop
      exit when $M = N$
      M += 1
      N -= 1
   end loop

(b) loop
      exit when $M < N$
      M -= N
   end loop

(c) loop
      exit when $N > 100$
      M += N
   end loop

(d) loop
      M += N
      exit when $M > 100$
   end loop

(e) loop
      exit when $N = 0$
      N := N div 10
      put N mod 10 ..
   end loop

2.4   The gear ratio of a bicycle is sometimes measured by the distance the bicycle travels when the pedals make one complete rotation. This distance is given by X in the formula $X = \pi DF/R$, in which D is the diameter of the rear wheel, F is the number of teeth on the front sprocket, and R is the number of teeth on the rear sprocket. A typical 12–speed bicycle has two front sprockets, with 42 and 52 teeth, and six rear sprockets, with 13, 15, 17, 20, 24, and 28 teeth. Write a program that displays a table giving the distance travelled for each combination of sprockets. Assume that the diameter of the rear wheel is 27 inches.

2.5   Write a program that reads a list of numbers and displays the largest and smallest numbers in the list. Choose a suitable marker to end the list, for example a negative number.

2.6   Write a program that reads an integer and determines whether it is prime. A prime number has no factors other than itself and 1. Thus 2, 3, 5, 7, 11, and so on are prime.

2.7 Write a program that expresses a sum of money in coins. In Canada or the United States, the user might enter 63 (cents), in which case the program would display

```
2 quarters 1 dimes 0 nickels 3 cents
```

2.8 Write a program that reads a sentence and displays the first letter of each word of the sentence. For example, if the user entered "**And seek for truth in the groves of Academe.**", the program would display

```
A s f t i t g o A
```

2.9 Write a program that converts digits to words. For example, if the user enters *1993*, the program would display **one nine nine three**.

2.10 Write a program that reads a date in the form of two integers, month and day, and displays the number of days since January 1 of that year. For example, the input *2 6*, corresponding to February 6, should produce the response **37**. Assume that the year is not a leap year. The program should report an error if the date is invalid.

2.11 Modify Exercise 2.10 so that it reads the year as well as the month and day. The revised program should check whether the year is a leap year and, if so, adjust the number of days accordingly if the date is later than March 1. A year has a leap day, February 29, if its last two digits are divisible by 4. For example, 1992 and 1996 are leap years. If the last two digits are "00", however, the year has a leap day if the first two digits are *not* divisible by 4. Thus 1900 was a leap year but 2000 will not be.

2.12 Write a program that reads a list of items and displays their cost and tax. Each item consists of a quantity, which is an integer; a unit cost, which is a real number; and a code, which is a letter. The code must be one of: O, indicating that there is no tax; N, indicating that there is a normal tax of 4%; or L, indicating that there is a luxury tax of 9%. To illustrate the calculation, suppose that there is an item "5 4.00 N". This indicates that there are five units at $4 each, with normal tax. The amount payable is $20.80. The program should read all the items in the list and then display the amount payable and the portion of it that is tax.

2.13 Write a program that reads a value x and displays the value of e^x. Use the series
$$1 + x + \frac{x^2}{2!} + \frac{x^3}{3!} + \cdots + \frac{x^n}{n!}.$$
Choose a value for n that gives accurate results for $1 \le x \le 10$.

2.14 Write a program that reads a positive real number and displays its square root. Suppose the number read is x and the square root is q. As a first approximation, set q to 1. Newton's rule says that if $q' = (x/q+q)/2$, then q' is a better approximation to $\sqrt{x}$ than q. Use a loop with an assignment statement to obtain a series of approximations to $\sqrt{x}$. Terminate the loop when
$$\left| 1 - \frac{x}{q^2} \right| < 10^{-6}.$$

For a real number R, the Turing expression $abs\,(R)$ gives the absolute value, $|R|$, of R.

Chapter 3

Standard Types and Expressions

The concept of *type* is pervasive in computer science. It is not a particularly mysterious concept. In fact, we use types every day in normal conversation. Types enable us to refer to families of objects that have properties in common with one another.

The word "fruit" is an example of a type. Like any type, it has instances: apples, oranges, mangoes, and pomegranates are all instances of the type fruit or, more simply, are fruits. If we know that something is a fruit, we have certain expectations of it: it probably grew on a tree, has a skin, has seeds or pits, and may be good to eat. Types help us to think and speak concisely. It is quicker to say "I like eating fruit" than to say "I like eating apples, oranges, mangoes, pomegranates . . .".

Types in programming languages such as Turing play a similar role to types in natural languages. The type of a variable tells us what we can do with the variable. If we know that a variable is an integer, for instance, we know that we can display it, increment it, or divide it by seven, although we may not know its actual value.

The *standard types* of a language are types that are built into the language and cannot be changed in any way by programmers. The standard types of Turing are int, real, boolean, and string. They are fully described in this chapter. Turing also provides methods that we can use to define new types. These are discussed later in the book.

3.1   The Role of Types in Programs

Types in programming languages serve a number of useful purposes.

Types help us to read and understand programs. A declaration such as

> var *BeanCounter* : int

informs us that *BeanCounter* will have integer values. While this might seem to be a rather small amount of information, it is better than none at all. In complex programs that use many types in addition to the standard types, the explicit association of a type with every variable is an important part of the documentation.

Types enable the compiler to detect errors in the program. Suppose that N is an integer and S is a string. If we attempt to calculate $N + S$, the computation will fail because strings cannot be added to integers. In a typed language such as Turing, this error would never occur because we have to declare the types of N and S. The compiler would detect and report the error in the expression $N + S$ before we run the program.

Types can improve the efficiency of programs. With type information, the compiler can translate an expression such as $A + B$ to a single "add" instruction. Without type information, the program would have to examine the types of A and B at run-time, add them if they had the same type, and report an error otherwise.

Operators and Operands

Chapter 1 introduced the four standard types of Turing: integers, reals, Booleans, and strings. Before proceeding to the detailed descriptions of the standard types, we review the relevant concepts.

Expressions consist of operators and operands. An operand may be a variable, a constant, or a literal. In the program

> const $M := 5$
> var $N := M + 3$

"+" is an operator, 5 and 3 are literals, M is a constant, and N is a variable.

The structure of a literal depends on its type. For example, 5 is an integer literal but 5.0 is a real literal. Constants and variables are identifiers, and their structure does not depend on their type.

Turing operators are either *unary prefix* or *binary infix*. A unary prefix operator has one operand and is written before its operand. In the expression -46, the symbol "$-$" is a unary prefix operator. A binary infix operator has two operands and is written between them. In the expression $357 - 23$, the symbol "$-$" is a binary infix operator. As these examples show, the operator "$-$" can be either unary prefix or binary infix, depending on its context. The same is true of "$+$": both $19 + 523$ and $+390$ are legal expressions.

Convention

The sentence "E evaluates to V", in which E is a Turing expression and V is the corresponding value, occurs frequently in this chapter. We will use the symbol "$\longrightarrow$" to stand for "evaluates to". For instance, the string "$2 + 2 \longrightarrow 4$" is read "when Turing evaluates the expression $2 + 2$, it obtains the value 4".

3.2 The Types int and real

Turing has two standard numeric types: the type of integers, denoted by the keyword int, and the type of real numbers, denoted by the keyword real. Since integers and reals have much in common, we describe them together in this section.

3.2.1 Values of int and real

The values of the type int are whole numbers like 0, 17, 38, 534, and -43. Turing uses 32 bits to represent integers and, consequently, their values range from $-M$ to $+M$, where $M = 2^{31} - 1 = 2,147,483,647$. The values of the type real are numbers with fractional parts, like 0.7 and -16.95.

In the usual style of writing numbers, the decimal point has a fixed position between the integer part and the fractional part. This style does not work well for very large or very small numbers because many digits are needed. Scientists and engineers prefer to express numbers in a standard form, such as $d.ddd$, in which each d denotes a digit, and to multiply the number by a power of ten. For example, the mass of the earth is written "5.977×10^{24} kg" rather than as "$5,977,000,000,000,000,000,000,000$ kg". Numbers written in this way are called *floating-point* numbers because the position of the decimal point is determined by the value of the exponent rather than by the way in which we write the number.

Most computers use a floating-point representation, but the "point" is a binary point rather than a decimal point. In other words, the exponent is a power of 2 rather than a power of 10. Usually, we do not worry about the representation that the computer uses because Turing provides real numbers that are adequate for most calculations. On the PC, for example, real numbers have about 15 decimal digits of precision and may have values as small as 10^{-323} and as large as 10^{308}.

3.2.2 Integer Literals

Integer literals consist of decimal digits. Although we are accustomed to using commas to indicate thousands and millions, Turing does not allow commas in numbers. The following are valid integer literals:

    0   7   94   100000000

The number 26,537 is not a valid integer literal because it contains a comma.

We can write negative numbers, such as -999. Strictly, however, this is an expression consisting of the unary operator "-" and the integer literal "999". The distinction between literals and expressions is rarely significant in actual programs because wherever Turing allows a literal, it also allows a constant expression.

3.2.3 Real Literals

Real literals have an integer part, a fractional part, and an exponent part. In the literal

    12.345E-6

the integer part is "12", the fractional part is ".345", and the exponent part is "E-6". The value of the corresponding number is 12.345×10^{-6}, or 0.000012345. Turing does not require all of the parts of a real literal to be present, provided that there is no ambiguity.

The following literals all denote the **real** value $1,000,000$:

    1000000.0   1e6   10.0e+5   .1E007

The following literals do *not* denote the **real** value $1,000,000$:

    1000000   e6   .e6   1000000E   ⊘

Turing considers the first to be an integer because it has no fraction or exponent. The second is an identifier because it begins with "e". The third and fourth are illegal: ".e6" begins with "." and "1000000E" ends with "E". Four rules govern the real literals.

- The literal must contain at least one of ".", "e", or "E".
- If there is a decimal point, there must be at least one digit before it or after it.
- If there is an "e", it must be followed by one or more digits.
- There may be a sign ("+" or "−") between "e" and the digits.

3.2.4 Numeric Expressions

Numeric expressions consist of operands and the operators "+" (add), "−" (subtract), "*" (multiply), "/" (divide and round), "div" (divide and truncate), "mod" (modulus or remainder), and "**" (exponent). All of the operators may be used as *binary infix operators* written between their two operands. The operators "+" and "−" may also be used as *unary prefix operators* written before their single operand.

Precedence

In an expression with more than one operator, operator precedence determines the order of evaluation. For example, Turing evaluates $X+Y*Z$ by multiplying Y by Z and then adding the result to X. When operators have the same precedence, Turing evaluates from left to right. In the evaluation of $X+Y+Z$, Turing adds Y to X and then adds Z to the result. We can override the precedence rules by using parentheses. For example, Turing evaluates $(X + Y) * Z$ by first adding Y to X, then multiplying the result by Z.

Figure 3.1 Operator Precedence

Figure 3.1 summarizes the precedence rules for all Turing operators, including some that are not discussed in this section. The operators are arranged in rows according to their precedence. The operator "**" has the highest precedence, and "⇒" has the lowest precedence. The operators "+" and "−" appear twice because they may be used with either one or two operands. Expressions such as $N * -1$ are legal in Turing because the unary "−" has higher precedence than "*". Turing evaluates this expression as $N * (-1)$.

Result Type

The type of the result of an operator depends on the types of its operands. In most cases, the result is integer if both operands are integers and real otherwise. The division operators are different: "/" always yields a real result, and "div" always yields an integer result. Figure 3.2 shows some examples.

Expression	Value	Operand Types		Result Type
2 + 2	4	int	int	int
2 * 2.1	4.2	int	real	real
15/2	7.5	int	int	real
15.9 div 2	7	real	int	int
15 mod 4	3	int	int	int
15 mod 4.5	1.5	int	real	real
2.5 ** 2	6.25	real	int	real

Figure 3.2   Expressions and Their Types

Computers cannot perform mixed type arithmetic. Adding an integer to a real, for example, produces nonsense. Turing therefore performs conversions before it evaluates operators. If we write $2 + 3.5$, Turing will convert the integer 2 to the real 2.0 before performing the addition. The result in this case is the real number 5.5. The same principle applies to more complicated expressions, sometimes with surprising effects. In Example 7.3, later in the book, we use the expression $440 * 2 ** ((Key - 9)/12)$ to calculate the frequency of a note Key semitones above middle C. Although Key, 9, and 12 are integers, the presence of "/" in $(Key - 9)/12$ makes this subexpression real. Consequently, the value of the entire expression is real although all of its operands are integers.

3.2.5   Properties of Operators

Turing is designed so that we rarely have to worry about the details of how expressions are evaluated. We write the expressions using standard algebraic syntax and Turing obtains the value we expect. On rare occasions, we need to know the meaning of a complicated expression and it becomes important to know the precise rules. This section describes those rules.

Overflow and Underflow

Suppose the theoretical value of an integer expression is N. If the absolute value of N is too large, that is $|N| \geq 2^{31}$, Turing will not be able to evaluate the expression and will report an error when we run the program. This kind of error is called *integer overflow*. Similarly, if a real expression has a value that is too large to compute, the result is *real overflow*. Furthermore, if an expression has a value that is not zero but is too small to be represented, the result is *real underflow*.

Turing cannot evaluate any of the following:

$$2 ** 40 \quad 10.0 ** 1000 \quad 10.0 ** -1000$$

Evaluation of the first causes integer overflow; the second causes real overflow; and the third causes real underflow. Overflow cannot be ignored because ignoring it would lead to incorrect results. The result of a calculation that underflows can be set to zero without introducing a serious error. Consequently, Turing handles overflow by stopping the program and reporting an error message but handles underflow by setting the result to zero and continuing execution.

Division and Modulus

Turing defines the integer division operator, div, by the following equation:

$$A \text{ div } B = \lfloor A \div B \rfloor$$

If $B = 0$, Turing reports an error. Otherwise, "$\div$" denotes exact, mathematical division, and $\lfloor \ldots \rfloor$ denotes the "floor" function, which truncates towards zero. For example $11 \text{ div } 3 \longrightarrow 3$ because $\lfloor 11 \div 3 \rfloor = 3$ and $-11 \text{ div } 3 \longrightarrow -3$ because $\lfloor -11 \div 3 \rfloor = -3$.

If we use div with real operands, we run the risk of integer overflow. Turing can evaluate the real value $2.0 ** 40$, but it cannot evaluate the integer value $2.0 ** 40 \text{ div } 5$ because the result (approximately 2.2×10^{11}) cannot be expressed as an integer.

Turing defines the remainder operator, mod, by the following equation:

$$A \text{ mod } B = A - B * (A \text{ div } B)$$

Using the definition of div, this is equivalent to

$$A \text{ mod } B = A - B \times \lfloor A \div B \rfloor$$

For example:

$$
\begin{aligned}
11 \text{ mod } 3 \quad &= \quad 11 - 3 \times \lfloor 11 \div 3 \rfloor \\
&= \quad 11 - 3 \times 3 \\
&= \quad 2
\end{aligned}
$$

Although the operator mod is usually used with integer operands, the definition allows us to use mod with real as well as with integer operands. The value of the Turing expression $20.0 \bmod 2\pi$ is the remainder when 20.0 is divided by 2π, computed as follows:

$$
\begin{aligned}
20.0 \bmod 2\pi &\approx 20.0 \bmod 6.283185 \\
&= 20.0 - 6.283185 \times \lfloor 20.0 \div 6.283185 \rfloor \\
&= 20.0 - 6.283185 \times 3 \\
&= 1.150444
\end{aligned}
$$

Definitions of div and mod differ from one programming language to another. In some languages, mod is defined so that if K is positive, the value of $N \bmod K$ is one of the numbers $0, 1, \ldots, K - 1$, whatever the value of N. In Turing, this is *not* so, because if N is negative and K is positive, then $N \bmod K$ is negative. For example, $-5 \bmod 3 = -2$.

Exponentiation

The exponential operator, "$**$", raises a number to a power. The exponent may be an integer, as in $2 ** 3 \longrightarrow 8$, or a real number, as in $9.0 ** 0.5 \longrightarrow 3.0$. The exponential operator is more complicated than the others because the type of the result is not necessarily the same as the type of the operands. For example, the expression $2 ** -2$ is illegal because the result, 0.25, would be real, not int. The expression $-1 ** 0.5$ is also illegal because the result, $\sqrt{-1}$, would be complex, which is not a Turing type. Figure 3.3 summarizes the rules for exponentiation.

Expression	Operand Types		Result	Restrictions
$M ** N$	int	int	int	$N \geq 0$
$X ** M$	real	int	real	
$M ** Y$	int	real	real	$M \geq 0$
$X ** Y$	real	real	real	$X \geq 0$

Figure 3.3   Properties of the Exponent Operator

Comparison

The comparison operators "$=$", "$\neq$", "$<$", "$\leq$", "$>$", and "$\geq$" are used to compare int and real values. They yield Boolean values; for example $2 \leq 99 \longrightarrow$ true and $1.0 \neq 1.0 \longrightarrow$ false.

It is best not to use the operators "=" and "≠" with real operands. Two real values X and Y may be theoretically equal, but unless they have been computed in exactly the same way, it is unlikely that $X = Y$ will be true. This is because calculations with real quantities are not exact. The value of $X = Y$ will be false even if X and Y differ only in one bit. The best way to check that X and Y are close is to compare their ratio to 1. The test should be

$$\left| 1 - \frac{X}{Y} \right| < \epsilon$$

where ϵ is a small number. In Turing, this test might become

    abs $(1 - X/Y) > \texttt{1e-6}$

If this expression is true, X and Y differ by less than one part in a million. The advantage of the test is that it works for variables of any size. A test of the form

    $|X - Y| < 10^{-6}$

is of no use if X and Y are very small (consider $X \approx 10^{-20}$) or very large (consider $X \approx 10^{20}$).

3.2.6 Predefined Numeric Functions

A *function* in a programming language takes a number, does some calculations, and gives back another number. For example, *sqrt* is a function: it accepts a number X and returns the square root of X, or $\sqrt{X}$. This function and a number of others are *predefined functions* in Turing. "Predefined" means that the language provides them; we can compute $\sqrt{X}$ without knowing how to compute a square root. The predefined numeric functions of Turing are summarized in Figure 3.4. A complete list of predefined functions and procedures appears in Appendix D on page 358.

There are two versions of *abs*, *max*, and *min*. For each of these functions, the type of the argument may be integer or real, and the result type is the same as the argument type. The other functions accept integer or real arguments, but the results are always real. For example,

    max $(-4, 99) \longrightarrow 99$

because both operands are integers, but

    max $(3.0, 99) \longrightarrow 99.0$

because the first operand, 3.0, forces Turing to consider *both* operands as real.

There are two versions of each of the trigonometric functions. The functions *sin* and *cos* assume that their arguments are in radians. The function *arctan* returns

Function	Result	Domain	Description
abs (M)	int		Absolute value
abs (X)	real		Absolute value
arctan (X)	real		Inverse tangent (radians)
arctand (X)	real		Inverse tangent (degrees)
cos (X)	real		Cosine (radians)
cosd (X)	real		Cosine (degrees)
exp (X)	real		Exponent (e^X)
ln (X)	real	$X > 0$	Natural logarithm $(\log_e X)$
max (M, N)	int		Maximom of M and N
max (X, Y)	real		Maximom of X and Y
min (M, N)	int		Minimom of M and N
min (X, Y)	real		Minimom of X and Y
sign (X)	int		Sign of X $(-1, 0,$ or $1)$
sin (X)	real		Sine (radians)
sind (X)	real		Sine (degrees)
sqrt (X)	real	$X \geq 0$	Square root $(\sqrt{X})$

Figure 3.4   Predefined Numeric Functions

its result in radians. The functions *sind*, *cosd*, and *arctand* are similar, but they use degrees instead of radians. Conversion between radians and degrees is simple: 2π radians = 360 degrees, and 1 radian is approximately 57.2958 degrees.

The value of *exp* (x) is e^x, and the value of *ln* (x) is the logarithm of x with base e, the "natural" logarithm. In both cases, $e \approx 2.7182818$. We can obtain logarithms to another base b by using the formula

$$\log_a N = \frac{\log_b N}{\log_b a} \ .$$

For example, to find $\log_{10} 1000$ in Turing, we use

$$ln\,(1000)/ln\,(10) \longrightarrow 3$$

3.3   The Type boolean

Boolean values are either true or false. The comparison operators "=", "≠", "<", "≤", ">", and "≥" yield Boolean values. For example, $2 = 3$ yields false. We can also introduce Boolean variables into our programs. For example, the value of *Finished* might be false until a certain calculation has been completed and true thereafter.

Since **boolean** is a keyword, we always give it a lower case "b" in programs. This is consistent with the other types of Turing: int, real, and string. When the word "Boolean" is not being used as a keyword, however, it has an upper case "B" because it is derived from a proper name. George Boole (1815–1864) was the inventor of modern mathematical logic. Boolean expressions are also called conditions or predicates.

3.3.1   Values of Boolean

The values of the type **boolean** are true and false, represented in Turing by the keywords **true** and **false**. These keywords do not appear frequently in programs. For example, we do not need to write **true** in statements such as

   if *PrinterDown* = **true** then ....

because the following statement does the same thing:

   if *PrinterDown* then ....

Similarly, a conditional statement that assigns values to a Boolean variable, such as

```
var BigNum : int
var ReallyBig : boolean
....
if BigNum > 10000000 then
   ReallyBig := true
else
   ReallyBig := false
end if
```

can often be written in a simpler way:

   ReallyBig := *BigNum* > 10000000

3.3.2   Boolean Expressions

There are four Boolean operators: "not" is a unary prefix operator; "and", "or", and "$\Rightarrow$" are binary infix operators. The operator $\Rightarrow$ is usually read "implies". In Turing programs, it is written with two characters, as "=>".

The Boolean operators have meanings that are close to their informal meanings in English. Figure 3.5 shows their precise meanings. The first two columns of the table give the four possible assignments of truth values to P and Q. Subsequent columns give the corresponding truth value of an expression. For example, in the third row, P is false, Q is true, and the fourth column says that P and Q is false.

P	Q	not P	P and Q	P or Q	$P \Rightarrow Q$
true	true	false	true	true	true
true	false	false	false	true	false
false	true	true	false	true	true
false	false	true	false	false	true

Figure 3.5   Truth Table for Boolean Operators

It is easier to remember the essential properties of the Boolean operators than it is to memorize the entire truth table.

- "not P" is false if P is true and true if P is false.

- "P and Q" is true if P and Q are both true, and false otherwise.

- "P or Q" is false if P and Q are both false, and true otherwise.

- "$P \Rightarrow Q$" is false if P is true and Q is false, and true otherwise.

Evaluating Boolean Expressions

How should the expression "P and Q" be evaluated? One possibility would be to evaluate P, then evaluate Q, and finally use the truth table to find the value of P and Q. This may not be the best approach, however. Consider the expression

$$Y \neq 0 \text{ and } (X-1)/Y > 3$$

Suppose that $Y = 0$. The first operand of the expression $Y \neq 0$ is false. The second operand, $(X-1)/Y > 3$, leads to failure because of the division by zero. The truth table shows that if P is false then "P and Q" is false whether Q is true or false.

An alternative strategy for evaluating "P and Q" would be first to evaluate P and then, if P is false, return the result false immediately. In other words, Q is evaluated only if P is true. Turing evaluates "P and Q" in this way, which means that we can write expressions such as "$Y \neq 0$ and $(X-1)/Y > 3$" knowing that they will not fail.

Turing also uses a shortcut in the evaluation of "P or Q". If P is true, Turing assumes that "P or Q" is true without evaluating Q. Similarly, if P is false, Turing assumes that "$P \Rightarrow Q$" is true without evaluating Q. As the following example shows, shortcut evaluation can simplify programs.

Example 3.1   Using Shortcut Evaluation

A hot-air balloon has volume V and mass m. The density of the atmosphere around the balloon is ρ, and the density of the hot air inside the balloon is ρ'. The balloon will leave the ground if $V \geq m/(\rho - \rho')$. The following program determines whether the balloon will leave the ground.

```
var DenseDiff := ColdDensity − HotDensity
if DenseDiff ≠ 0 and Volume ≥ Mass/DenseDiff then
   put "The balloon leaves the ground."
end if
```

If we omit the test $DenseDiff \neq 0$, the program will fail if the densities are equal. If Turing did not use shortcut evaluation, we would have to write two if statements:

```
var DenseDiff := ColdDensity − HotDensity
if DenseDiff ≠ 0 then
   if Volume ≥ Mass/DenseDiff then
      put "The balloon leaves the ground."
   end if
end if
```

The practical advantages of shortcut evaluation are to some extent offset by its theoretical disadvantages. If $Y = 0$, the expression "$Y \neq 0$ and $(X-1)/Y > 3$" has no mathematical meaning, but Turing evaluates it anyway. Furthermore, shortcut evaluation destroys the important property of commutativity for **and** and **or**. In logic, both of these connectives are commutative, enabling us to reason with the identities

$$P \text{ and } Q \equiv Q \text{ and } P$$
$$P \text{ or } Q \equiv Q \text{ or } P$$

Since these identities are not true for Turing operators, we must be particularly careful when we use logic to reason about Turing programs.

3.3.3   Assertions and Invariants

An *assertion* is a statement in a Turing program that says something about the values of variables at that point in the program. There are several kinds of assertion. The simplest kind of assertion consists of the keyword **assert** followed by a Boolean expression:

> **assert** $N \neq 0$
> **assert** $length\,(S) > 0$ **and** $index\,(S, ".") = 0$

When Turing reaches an assertion, it evaluates the Boolean expression. If the result is **true**, the program continues. If the result is **false**, the program stops and displays an error message of the form

> `Line 514:  Assert condition is false`

Assertions usually have no effect on the program except to slow it down slightly. It is therefore worthwhile to consider why anyone would want to use them.

When we are writing a program, we have certain beliefs about the values of the variables we use. For example, when we write an expression such as X/Y, we believe that Y will not be zero when Turing evaluates the expression. Assertions provide a way of including our beliefs in the code. When we write "**assert** $Y \neq 0$", we are saying that if our theory of how this program works is correct, Y will not be zero at this point.

There are two advantages to expressing our beliefs in this way. First, assertions record steps in the creation of a program that might otherwise be lost or forgotten. They are a form of documentation that may be useful either to the author of the program or to someone else who wants to modify it.

Second, when an assertion yields **false**, there must be an error in the program. The assertion enables us to pinpoint the error quickly. Without the assertion, the error would still be present, but we might have much more difficulty finding it.

Using Assertions

The following outline suggests a way of using an assertion. The dots stand for a section of the program that may be large; the first two statements might be separated by several pages in a listing of the program.

$Y :=$ *a complicated expression*

. . . .

assert $Y \neq 0$

$Z := X / Y$

The assertion is not useful in this program. Omitting it would make little difference because, if $Y = 0$, the program will fail at the division anyway. Suppose instead that the assertion was near the assignment to Y.

$Y :=$ *a complicated expression*

assert $Y \neq 0$

. . . .

$Z := X / Y$

In this version of the program, failure of the assertion draws attention to the actual problem, the assignment to Y.

The failure of an assertion should indicate that something has gone wrong in a way that we did not anticipate when we wrote the program. Assertions should not be used to provide a quick and easy way of detecting mistakes made by the person using the program. The two programs in the following example illustrate these different uses.

Example 3.2   Using Assertions

The following program asks the user to enter a number N. If the number does not lie between 0 and 25, the assertion is false and the program fails.

```
var N : int
put "Enter number of voters:   " ..
get N
assert 0 ≤ N and N ≤ 25
```

This is not an appropriate way to use an assertion. The assertion might cause the program to fail because the user did not understand the instructions or made a mistake. The program should be written in the following way to allow the user to have another chance.

```
var N : int
loop
   put "Enter number of voters:   " ..
   get N
   exit when 0 ≤ N and N ≤ 25
   put "Please enter a number between 0 and 25."
end loop
assert 0 ≤ N and N ≤ 25
```

The assertion now expresses the programmer's belief that when the loop terminates, N will have an acceptable value. The example is somewhat artificial because the assertion appears only three lines after the exit statement that says the same thing. In the context of a larger program than this one, an assertion of this kind would serve as both a check of the logical correctness of the program and a helpful piece of documentation.

Invariants

A *loop invariant* is a Boolean expression that should be true at the beginning of every execution of the body of the loop. In Turing, we can document loop invariants by placing an invariant statement at the front of the body of a for or loop statement. The invariant statement consists of the keyword invariant followed by a Boolean expression. Turing evaluates the condition and reports an error if it is false.

Example 3.3   Using a Loop Invariant

Given positive integers *Dividend* and *Divisor*, the following loop computes the quotient, *Quot*, and the remainder, *Rem*, when *Dividend* is divided by *Divisor*.

```
var Dividend, Divisor, Quot, Rem : int
put "Enter dividend and divisor:   " ..
get Dividend, Divisor
assert Dividend ≥ 0 and Divisor > 0
Quot := 0
Rem := Dividend
loop
   invariant Dividend = Quot * Divisor + Rem
   exit when Rem < Divisor
   Quot += 1
   Rem -= Divisor
end loop
assert Dividend = Quot * Divisor + Rem and 0 ≤ Rem and Rem < Divisor
put "Quotient:   ", Quot, " Remainder:   ", Rem
```

The loop invariant $Dividend = Quot * Divisor + Rem$ is true after initialization of the variables, at the beginning of each iteration, and after the loop has terminated. Turing evaluates this expression at the beginning of each iteration and would report an error if it ever became false.

Style

Assertions take time to evaluate. Consequently, programs with assertions run slightly slower than programs without assertions. The effect is small, usually no more than a few percent. The small loss in performance is compensated for by a large saving in the time required to develop a program. Assertions speed up development by helping us to locate errors precisely and rapidly.

It is not easy to write good assertions, but a few guidelines may be helpful.

- Assertions should be designed to catch errors, or to help the reader, or both.

- Assertions should not say things that are obvious or necessarily true.

- Assertions should not be complex or inefficient.

It is tempting to use assertions during development and then to remove them when the program is finished. This has been compared to wearing your life jacket during land practice and leaving it behind when you go to sea. The analogy is amusing but not really accurate. The important point is that most programs are never finished; they continue to evolve, and assertions contribute to their successful evolution.

3.3.4   Designing Boolean Expressions

Boolean expressions play a number of important roles in programs. For example, they determine the results of choices made by the program, control the termination of loops, and assert useful facts about the state of the computation. In each of these roles, the correctness of the Boolean expression is crucial to the correctness of the program. Consequently, it is important that we write Boolean expressions that are easy to read and understand.

Negation

Negation can make Boolean expressions hard to understand. For instance, frequent use of not before a Boolean variable is an indication that the variable name is unsuitable. Suppose that a program contains many occurrences of the expression "not *Finished*". If we change the name *Finished* to a name with the opposite meaning, such as *Active*, we can change every occurrence of "not *Finished*" to the simpler form "*Active*".

It is easy to misunderstand a decision statement with a negative condition, such as

```
if not P
  then A
  else B
end if
```

The following statement has the same effect and may be easier to read.

```
if P
  then B
  else A
end if
```

If we have to use negation in a compound expression, it is important to use deMorgan's laws correctly. Here they are expressed in Turing notation:

$$\text{not } (P \text{ and } Q) \ = \ \text{not } P \text{ or not } Q$$
$$\text{not } (P \text{ or } Q) \ = \ \text{not } P \text{ and not } Q$$

Using deMorgan's laws and the properties of comparison operators, we can write compound Boolean expressions in many different ways. There are no general rules because the best way of writing an expression depends on its role in the program. We can express the condition "female and not over 18", for instance, in at least four different ways:

```
Female and not Age > 18
not Male and not Age > 18
not(Male or Age > 18)
Female and Age ≤ 18
```

Of these, the last is probably the most readable. The best choice, however, would depend on the application.

3.4   The Type string

The first electronic computer ever made, ENIAC, computed with numbers only. By the time construction had been completed, computing pioneers had realized that computers would have to process characters as well as numbers. Today, computers process both numbers and text efficiently. In fact, many people use personal computers almost entirely for word processing. We can write programs that process text in Turing. Underlying all text operations is the type string.

3.4.1   String Declarations

There are two ways in which we can declare strings. The following declarations illustrate both.

> var *Short* : string (10)
> var *Long* : string

The first declaration says that *Short* is a string that will contain at most 10 characters. Actual values of *Short* may contain fewer than 10 characters but not more. Thus the assignments

> *Short* := ""
> *Short* := "Not long."

are legal, but the assignment

> *Short* := "Not short enough."   ⊘

is not legal.

The maximom length of a string is 255 characters. Turing will not accept a declaration such as

> var *SuperString* : string (1000)   ⊘

If the declaration does not specify a maximom length, Turing provides the *default length* of 255 characters. The string *Long*, declared above, has a maximom length of 255 characters.

For short programs, it is usually easiest to ignore the length argument and to use the default length. In a program that uses large numbers of strings, however, we should specify maximom lengths to avoid wasting large amounts of memory.

3.4.2   Values of String

Values of the type string are sequences of up to 255 characters chosen from the character set of the computer on which Turing is running. It is difficult to give a general description of the characters we can use in strings because they depend on both the kind of computer we use and the country in which we live. The general rule is that the characters allowed are at least the "graphic" characters of the character set of the system we are using. In ASCII, the most widely used character set, the graphic characters have codes from 32 through 125. A table of the ASCII graphic characters appears in Appendix E on page 368.

The character "\" (backslash) plays a special role in strings. It indicates that the next character in the string is to be translated into a different character. For

String	Translation
\\	\ (backslash)
\"	" (quotation symbol)
\b	Backspace
\d	Delete
\e	Escape (ASCII ESC)
\f	Form feed
\n	End of line
\r	Return
\t	Tab

Figure 3.6   Using "\" in Strings

example, the effect of the backslash in the string "\t" is to translate "t" into the tab character. The letter following "\" may be either upper or lower case; the strings "\t" and "\T" are both equivalent to one tab character. The uses of the backslash in strings are shown in Figure 3.6.

3.4.3   String Expressions

String expressions are simpler than numeric expressions because there are only two operations: concatenation and selection. "Concatenation" means "joining together". The concatenation of "whirl" and "pool" is "whirlpool". If X and Y are strings in a Turing program, the expression $X + Y$ yields their concatenation. The string resulting from concatenation must not contain more than 255 characters. Some people say "catenation" rather than "concatenation"; the two words have the same meaning.

The following three examples of string concatenation demonstrate that Turing does not insert a blank, or any other character, between the concatenated strings. In the third example, note that the string " ", which contains one blank, is not the same as the empty string, "", which contains no characters at all.

```
"con" + "cate" + "nation" ⟶ "concatenation"
"joining" + "together" ⟶ "joiningtogether"
"joining" + " " + "together" ⟶ "joining together"
```

We can use the operator " +=" with strings. As with numbers, the statement
$S += T$ is an abbreviation for $S := S + T$. The statement

$$Chars += "]"$$

adds the character "]" to the end of the string variable *Chars*.

String Indexing

The characters of a string are numbered, or *indexed*, from left to right. The
first character has index 1. If S is a string with N characters, then the numbers
$1, 2, \ldots, N$ are *legal indexes* for S. If M and N are legal indexes for S, and
$M \leq N + 1$, then the expression $S(M \ldots N)$ is the string consisting of the Mth
through Nth characters of S.

Suppose that the variable *Fruit* contains the string **"pomegranate"**. Then

$Fruit(1 \ldots 3) \longrightarrow$ **"pom"**
$Fruit(5 \ldots 8) \longrightarrow$ **"gran"**
$Fruit(4 \ldots 4) \longrightarrow$ **"e"**
$Fruit(9 \ldots 8) \longrightarrow$ **""**
$Fruit(1 \ldots 12)$ is an illegal expression

The third expression, $Fruit(4 \ldots 4)$, selects a single character, **"e"**. We can write it
in the shorter form $Fruit(4)$. In general, $S(M)$ gives the Mth character of the
string S, provided that M is a legal index. In the fourth expression, the first index
is greater than the second, and the result is the *empty string* — the unique string
that contains no characters. In general, $S(M \ldots M - 1)$ gives the empty string.
The first index, M, must be a legal index for S, but the second index, $M - 1$, need
not be. Thus $S(1 \ldots 0)$ is a legal way of writing the empty string. The expression
$S(2 \ldots 0)$ is *not* a legal way of writing the empty string, however, because of the
rule that requires $M \leq N + 1$.

The character "$*$", used as a string index, selects the last character of the string. If
N is an integer constant or expression, then $* - N$ is a legal string index if N is less
than the number of characters in the string.

Suppose that the variable *Fruit* contains the string **"Avocado"**. Then

$Fruit(* - 1 \ldots *) \longrightarrow$ **"do"**
$Fruit(5 \ldots *) \longrightarrow$ **"ado"**
$Fruit(2 \ldots * - 1) \longrightarrow$ **"vocad"**
$Fruit(* - 7)$ is an illegal expression

Comparing Strings

We can use the comparison operators "=", "≠", "<", "≤", ">", and "≥" with string operands. If the operands consist entirely of lower case letters, string A is "less than" string B if A would come before B in a dictionary. For example,

> "aardvark" ≤ "zebra" $\longrightarrow$ true
> "macrophage" > "macrophyte" $\longrightarrow$ false

If the letters have mixed cases or the operands contain characters other than letters, the rules are more complicated. Since Turing compares the ASCII codes of the characters, we have to know what the codes are in order to predict the result of a comparison. For example, the ASCII codes of the upper case letters are *smaller* than the codes of the lower case letters. Consequently, "Zebra" is "less than" "aardvark". The ASCII codes of all the characters that Turing uses appear in Appendix E on page 368.

3.4.4   Predefined String Functions

Turing provides four predefined string functions to improve the ease and efficiency with which we can process strings. Their names are *length*, *upper*, *repeat*, and *index*. There are also a number of functions that convert strings to other types; these are described in Section 3.5.

The Functions *length* and *upper*

The function *length* accepts a string and returns the number of characters in the string. The function *upper* returns the maximom length of the string, as given in its declaration. If we declare

> var *Name* : string(20) := "Pham"

then

> *length* (*Name*) $\longrightarrow$ 4
> *upper* (*Name*) $\longrightarrow$ 20

Example 3.4   Accessing Strings

A *palindrome* is a word that reads the same backwards and forwards. The words "dad", "mom", and "madam" are all palindromes. The following program reads a word and uses string indexing to determine whether it is a palindrome.

```
var Word : string
put "Enter word:   " ..
get Word
var Left := 1
var Right := length (Word)
loop
  if Left ≥ Right then
    put Word, " is a palindrome."
    exit
  elsif Word (Left) ≠ Word (Right) then
    put Word, " is not a palindrome."
    exit
  else
    Left += 1
    Right -= 1
  end if
end loop
```

The program first compares the first and last letters of the string. If they are not equal, the string cannot be a palindrome. If they are equal, the indexes *Left* and *Right* are each moved towards the middle of the string. The loop terminates when *Left* ≥ *Right*, which becomes true after both indexes have reached the middle of the string.

The program works correctly whether the number of letters in the string is even or odd. If the length is even, then *Left* = *Right*+1 during the last iteration. If the length is odd, then *Left* = *Right* during the last iteration. Since a letter cannot be different from itself, the string must be a palindrome. Finally, the program says that the empty string is a palindrome. This seems reasonable because the empty string has the same value whichever way we read it.

The Function *repeat*

The function *repeat* accepts two arguments, a string S and a positive integer N, and returns a string consisting of N copies of S joined together:

$$repeat\,(\text{"yum "}, 3) \longrightarrow \text{"yum yum yum "}$$

The function *repeat* is often used to build strings of blanks. Suppose that *Word* is a string and we want to place it into a field of *Width* characters. Assume that *length (Word)* ≤ *Width* and we execute the following assignments:

$$Left := Word + repeat\,(\text{" "}, Width - Length\,(Word))$$
$$Right := repeat\,(\text{" "}, Width - Length\,(Word)) + Word$$

The strings *Left* and *Right* will both have *Width* characters. *Left* will contain *Word* at its left end and *Right* will contain *Word* at its right end.

For example, if *Word* = `"apple"` and *Width* = 10, these assignments will yield the results

$$Left \longrightarrow \texttt{"apple\textvisiblespace\textvisiblespace\textvisiblespace\textvisiblespace\textvisiblespace"}$$
$$Right \longrightarrow \texttt{"\textvisiblespace\textvisiblespace\textvisiblespace\textvisiblespace\textvisiblespace apple"}$$

Pattern Matching

The function *index* accepts two string arguments, S and P, and returns the first position at which P occurs in S. If P does not occur in S, *index* returns 0. The string P is called a "pattern" and *index* performs *pattern matching*.

Suppose that we have assigned the value `"Pomegranates are delicious"` to the string variable *Description*. Then

$$index\,(Description, \texttt{"ate"}) \longrightarrow 9$$
$$index\,(Description, \texttt{"avocado"}) \longrightarrow 0$$
$$index\,(Description, \texttt{""}) \longrightarrow 1$$

We can use the function *index* to check that a particular character belongs to a set of characters. For example, to check that the Ith character of *Word* is a lower case letter, we could write

$$\text{if } index\,(\texttt{"abcdefghijklmnopqrstuvwxyz"}, Word\,(I)) \neq 0 \text{ then } \ldots.$$

If $Word\,(I)$ is a lower case letter, *index* returns a number between 1 and 26. If $Word\,(I)$ is not a lower case letter, *index* returns 0.

Example 3.5   Using a Pattern to Select Characters

Conventional use of the word "palindrome" is more general than Example 3.4 suggests. A string is considered to be a palindrome if its letters read the same backwards and forwards, regardless of any other symbols. The following program removes all characters other than letters from a given string.

```
var OldString, NewString := ""
put "Enter a string:   " ..
get OldString
for Pos : 1 .. length (OldString)
   if index ("abcdefghijklmnopqrstuvwxyz", OldString (Pos)) ≠ 0 then
      NewString += OldString (Pos)
   end if
end for
put NewString
```

3.5   Type Conversion

Turing provides a set of predefined functions that we use to convert values of one type into equivalent values in another type. Sometimes these functions are used implicitly, without our having to write them. For example, to evaluate $2.5 + 3$, Turing uses the predefined function *intreal* to convert the integer value 3 to the real value 3.0 before it completes the addition. When we write

> put 3

and Turing displays 3, there is a less obvious conversion; Turing has converted the integer value 3 to the character string "3". Similarly, a **get** statement requires an implicit conversion from the string that the user enters to the integer or real variable in the program. Although the implicit conversions are useful, there are rare occasions when we need to convert between types explicitly. The conversion functions described in this section perform this task.

3.5.1   Converting int to real

The function *intreal* accepts an integer argument and returns a real result. It rarely appears in programs because Turing introduces implicit conversions from integer to real wherever they are necessary. Since there is a real value that corresponds to every integer that Turing can represent, *intreal* can never cause overflow or underflow. Here are some examples of conversions:

> $intreal\,(16547) \longrightarrow 16547.0$
> $intreal\,(-5) \longrightarrow -5.0$

3.5.2   Converting int to string

The function *intstr* accepts either one or two integer arguments and returns a string result. The first argument is the integer to be converted. The second argument is the required length (number of characters) of the result. The second argument is optional. If there is only one argument, the string has minimom length:

> $intstr\,(55) \longrightarrow$ "55"

If we provide a width argument that is greater than necessary, Turing inserts leading blanks:

$$intstr\,(1993, 8) \longrightarrow \text{"}\text{␣␣␣␣}1993\text{"}$$

If we provide a width argument that is not big enough, Turing will use as much space as necessary:

$$intstr\,(1993, 2) \longrightarrow \text{"}1993\text{"}$$

The function *chr* converts an integer to a string with one character. The type of the result is string (1). If Turing is running on the PC, the integer must have a value in the range $1, 2, \ldots, 255$, excluding 128.

3.5.3   Converting real to int

There are three predefined functions that require a real argument and return an integer result. Each of them may cause integer overflow if the absolute value of the argument is greater than 2^{31}.

The function *ceil* returns the "ceiling" of its real argument. The *ceiling* of a real number X is the smallest integer N that is not less than X. Thus, if $ceil\,(X) = N$, then $N - 1 < X \leq N$.

The function *floor* returns the "floor" of its real argument. The *floor* of a real number X is the largest integer N that is not greater than X. Thus, if $floor\,(X) = N$, then $N \leq X < N + 1$.

The function *round* returns the integer closest to its real argument. Thus, if $round\,(X) = N$, then $N \leq X + 0.5 < N + 1$.

Example 3.6   Converting Real Numbers to Integers

The following program demonstrates the effects of the three functions for small real values. The assert statements check that we have made the correct assumptions about the functions.

```
var X := −1.4
loop
  var I := ceil (X)
  assert I − 1 < X and X ≤ I
  var J := floor (X)
  assert J ≤ X and X < J + 1
  var K := round (X)
  assert K ≤ X + 0.5 and X + 0.5 < K + 1
  put X : 8 : 1, I : 8, J : 8, K : 8
```

$X \mathrel{+}= 0.2$
exit when $X > 1.4$
end loop

When this program is executed, it displays these results:

-1.4	-1	-2	-1
-1.2	-1	-2	-1
-1.0	-1	-1	-1
-0.8	0	-1	-1
-0.6	0	-1	-1
-0.4	0	-1	0
-0.2	0	-1	0
0.0	0	-1	0
0.2	1	0	0
0.4	1	0	0
0.6	1	0	1
0.8	1	0	1
1.0	1	1	1
1.2	2	1	1
1.4	2	1	1

3.5.4   Converting real to string

There are several ways of converting a real value to a string. Accordingly, Turing provides several functions so that we can obtain precisely the format we need.

The simplest of the functions that converts a real number to a string is *realstr*. The expression *realstr* (R, W) converts the real value R to a string containing at least W characters. The following steps describe the effect of the conversion but not the precise way in which it is actually performed.

First, the real number R is converted to a string with six digits after the decimal point. Second, trailing zeros after the decimal point are removed. If all of the digits are zero, the decimal point is also removed. Finally, if the string has fewer than W characters, blanks are inserted at the left until there are exactly W characters.

The function *frealstr* accepts the same two arguments as *realstr* and a third argument giving the number of digits after the decimal point. The expression *frealstr* (R, W, F) converts the real number R using the same three steps as above, but the value of F replaces the number "6" in the first step.

Statement	Conversion
put I	$intstr\,(I)$
put $I : W$	$intstr\,(I, W)$
put R	$realstr\,(R, 1)$
put $R : W$	$realstr\,(R, W)$
put $R : W : F$	$frealstr\,(R, W, F)$
put $R : W : F : E$	$erealstr\,(R, W, F, E)$

Figure 3.7   Conversion Functions and put Statements

The function *erealstr* converts a real value to a floating-point representation. The expression *erealstr* (R, W, F, E) gives a string version of the real number R that has at least W characters, up to F digits after the decimal point, and E digits in the exponent.

The put statement makes implicit use of the conversion functions described here. For example, the statement "put 3" converts the integer 3 to the string "3" and then displays this string. Figure 3.7 shows how put statements use conversion functions.

3.5.5   Converting string to int

The function *strint* accepts a string and returns the value of the corresponding integer. The string should contain leading blanks, a sign, and digits. The leading blanks and the sign are optional, but there must be at least one digit. The strings that *strint* accepts correspond closely to the strings a user can enter in response to a get statement with an int argument. The following examples illustrate the effect of *strint*:

$strint\,(\texttt{"999"}) \longrightarrow 999$
$strint\,(\texttt{"⌴⌴⌴⌴1993"}) \longrightarrow 1993$
$strint\,(\texttt{"⌴⌴⌴-43120"}) \longrightarrow -43120$

The predefined function *ord* requires a string of one character as an argument. That is, *ord* (S) is legal if *length* $(S) = 1$; the value of *upper* (S) does not matter. The result returned by *ord* (S) is the ASCII code of the character contained in S. The following examples illustrate some of the possibilities:

$ord\,("\sqcup") \longrightarrow 32$

$ord\,("A") \longrightarrow 65$

$ord\,("a") \longrightarrow 97$

$ord\,("")$ is an illegal expression

$ord\,("AB")$ is an illegal expression

3.5.6 Converting string to real

The function *strreal* accepts a string and returns the value of the corresponding real number. The strings that *strreal* accepts correspond closely to the strings a user can enter in response to a **get** statement with a **real** argument. The following examples illustrate the effect of *strreal*:

$strreal\,("999") \longrightarrow 999.0$

$strreal\,("\sqcup\sqcup\sqcup\sqcup1.993e3") \longrightarrow 1993.0$

$strreal\,("\sqcup\sqcup\sqcup-43.12000") \longrightarrow -43.12$

$strreal\,("1e6") \longrightarrow 1000000.0$

3.6 Summary

Numbers in parentheses refer to sections where material appears.

▶ Turing has four standard types: int, real, boolean, and string (3.1).

▶ Literals denote values of standard types (3.1).

▶ Integers and real numbers have a finite set of values (3.2.1).

▶ Turing represents integers as 32-bit, signed quantities (3.2.1). Consequently, the range of integers is $-M \, .. \, + M$, where $M = 2^{31} - 1 = 2,147,483,647$.

▶ Real numbers are stored in floating-point format and have a precision of at least 15 decimal digits and a typical range $10^{-323} \leq |R| \leq 10^{309}$ (3.2.3).

▶ The numeric operators are "+", "−", "*", "/", "div", "mod", and "**" (3.2.4).

▶ The operators "+" and "−" may be used as either unary or binary operators (3.2.4).

▶ Operands of binary operators may be both integers, both reals, or mixed (3.2.4).

▶ The order of evaluation is determined by precedence rules (3.2.4). Precedence may be overridden by parentheses.

▶ If mod has a negative argument, the result is negative (3.2.5).

▶ Each trigonometric function has two forms, one for degrees and one for radians (3.2.6).

▶ The value of a Boolean expression is either true or false (3.3).

▶ Boolean expressions may not be fully evaluated; if the first operand of "and", "or", or "⇒" determines the value of the expression, Turing does not evaluate the second argument (3.3.2).

▶ Assertions and invariants are Boolean expressions (3.3.3). Turing evaluates the argument of each assert or invariant statement and reports an error if the result is false.

▶ Strings may contain from 0 to 255 characters (3.4).

▶ String comparisons are based on character codes (3.4).

▶ The character "\" acts as an escape character in strings; it must be followed by another character (3.4.2).

▶ The operator "+" concatenates strings (3.4.3).

▶ Programs often require values to be converted from one type to another (3.5).

3.7   Exercises

3.1   Give the value of each of the following expressions.

   (a) $99 - -1$
   (b) $4 * 2.3$
   (c) $-2 ** 3$
   (d) $-5.0 ** -1$
   (e) $10.0 ** -5$
   (f) $1 ** (-0.5)$
   (g) $3 + 7$ div $2 + 3$
   (h) $3 + 7$ div $(2 + 3)$

3.2   State whether each of the following literals is legal. If it is, state its type.

   (a) 14756
   (b) -17
   (c) 16.
   (d) 1e17.5
   (e) -2e-3
   (f) 01.125
   (g) "The␣string's␣the␣thing!
   (h) "59"
   (i) \n\n\n
   (j) "\\\"\\\"

3.3   Assuming that K, L, M, and N have been declared as integers, X, Y, and Z have been declared as real numbers, and S and T have been declared as strings, explain how the following expressions will be evaluated by Turing and what the results will be. Assume that overflow does not occur.

   (a) $K + L ** 2/N > X$ and L div $M/Y > 0$
   (b) $(M + N) ** K$
   (c) (M/N) div K
   (d) $M/(N$ div $K)$

(e) $Z / Y / Z$

(f) $L + length (S + T)$

(g) $length (S (* - M \; .. \; *)) - M$

(h) $length (repeat (S, K))$ div $length (S)$

(i) $length (intstr (M, L))$

(j) $ceil (X) - floor (X)$

3.4   Write a program that reads a string, removes characters other than letters from the string, converts the letters to lower case, and decides whether the final string is a palindrome. Use as much code as possible from Examples 3.4 and 3.5.

3.5   Print a table showing the values of the six trigonometric functions for the angles $0°, 10°, 20°, \ldots, 360°$. The functions *sin* and *cos* are predefined Turing functions. The other four functions are defined as

$$\tan \theta = \sin \theta / \cos \theta$$
$$\sec \theta = 1 / \cos \theta$$
$$\csc \theta = 1 / \sin \theta$$
$$\cot \theta = \cos \theta / \sin \theta$$

For some angles, the functions have infinite values. For these angles, the program should write the string `"inf"` instead of a number.

3.6   Write a program that displays the table shown as Figure 3.5. Use the function *boolstr*, defined in Section 1.3, to display the values **true** and **false**.

3.7   Simple computations can give insight into many hobbies and activities. This exercise shows how simple programs give insight into the principles of photography.

(a) The *aperture* of a lens, F, is f/D, where f is the focal length of the lens and D is the diameter of the opening through which light passes. The aperture is controlled by a ring on the lens. The conventional aperture settings are $1, 1.4, \ldots, 32$. The general formula is $F = 2^{i/2}$ for $i = 0, 1, \ldots, 10$. Print a table of the 11 common aperture settings.

(b) When a lens is focused to a particular distance, objects at other distances are out of focus. For practical purposes, we assume that a point-sized object is in focus if its image on the film has a diameter less than a small quantity, c. For 35 mm cameras, c is usually taken to be 3×10^{-5} meters.

If a lens, set to aperture F, is focused to a distance $h = f^2/cF$, all objects from f^2/cF to infinity will be in focus. We call h the *hyperfocal distance* for aperture F. Assuming $f = 0.05$ meters, write a program that computes h for each aperture setting.

(c) If the lens is focused to a distance v, objects at a distance d will be in focus if

$$\frac{1}{1 + vcF/f^2} \leq \frac{d}{v} \leq \frac{1}{1 - vcF/f^2} .$$

Write a program that asks the user for a focal length, f, and a distance, v, and computes the maximom and minimom values of d for each aperture setting.

3.8   The frequencies of the notes of a piano are $440 \times 2^{n/12}$, in which the smallest value of n is -48, corresponding to the lowest A, and the largest value is 39, corresponding to the highest C. Print a table showing these frequencies.

3.9   The tuning of a musical instrument is a compromise between pure harmonies and the ease of modulation between keys.

(a) The standard pitch for tuning is concert A, which has a frequency of $f_0 = 440$ Hertz. An E that is a perfect fifth above concert A has a frequency $f_1 = (3/2)f_0$. The E actually played on a modern instrument has a frequency $f_2 = 2^{7/12}f_0$. Compute f_1, f_2, and the ratio between them.

(b) The interval I between two tones f_1 and f_2 is usually measured in semitones according to the formula $I = 12 \ln (f_1/f_2)/ \ln 2$. Compute the interval between f_1 and f_2 in part (a).

Chapter 4

Defining New Types

A successful programming language must satisfy a number of requirements. First, it must enable us to use the computer efficiently. Second, it must provide a notation that enables us to describe clear and concise solutions to a wide variety of problems. Third, it must provide features that enable us to extend and adapt the basic notation to apply it to complex problems.

The types of a language contribute to all three of these requirements. The standard types of Turing, described in Chapter 3, correspond closely to the primitive instructions of the processor that executes the programs. Consequently, standard types provide efficiency. Moreover, since the vast majority of calculations use these types, we can solve many problems without needing other types.

Turing also provides facilities for defining new types. New types are sometimes called "user-defined" types. They enable us to extend the language to meet the needs of specific problems. Once we can define new types, we can begin a programming task by choosing types that are appropriate for the particular problem.

This chapter introduces subranges, enumerations, and arrays. Subranges and enumerations help us to detect errors early in program development. Arrays provide a simple but important way of structuring data. All three kinds of type definition bring the language of programming closer to the language of problem solving.

4.1   Subranges

Variable declarations are an important part of a program because they provide useful information both to the compiler and to readers. A declaration such as "*N* : int" does not convey much, but we have already seen how to improve it by choosing a name that is more expressive than *N*. We can make a further improvement by using a type that conveys more information than int.

The standard type int provides a wide range of integer values. For most purposes, we do not actually need all these values.

Consider these variable declarations:

        var *Marks* : int   % Marks for an assignment
        var *Row, Column* : int   % Position on the screen
        var *Trees* : int   % Number of trees in a garden
        var *Years* : int   % Acceptable dates

We would expect values of *Marks* to be between 0 and 100. If *Row* and *Column* define the position of the cursor on the screen or in a window, we would expect the value of *Row* to be between 1 and 25 and the value of *Column* to be between 1 and 80. For *Trees*, values between 0 and 20 would include all but the largest gardens. In each declaration, we can see obvious limits for the range of values of each variable. We can specify limits on integer values by declaring variables as *subranges* rather than as integers.

Example 4.1   Integer Subranges

The declarations above, rewritten as subranges, look like this:

        var *Marks* : 0 .. 100   % Marks for an assignment
        var *Row* : 1 .. 25   % Vertical position on the screen
        var *Column* : 1 .. 80   % Horizontal position on the screen
        var *Trees* : 0 .. 20   % Number of trees in a garden
        var *Years* : 1980 .. 2000 % Acceptable dates

The first of these declarations says that *Marks* is an integer variable with its values restricted to the subrange 0, 1, 2, . . . , 100. We can use *Marks* in the same way that we use variables of type int. We can use it, for example, in expressions with numeric operators and operands, in **get** statements, and in **put** statements. But if we request an operation that gives *Marks* a value outside its limits, Turing will stop the program and report an error.

For example, the statement

   $Marks := 103$

will stop the program with an error message. If the value of *Marks* becomes 100, the following statement will also stop the program:

   $Marks \mathrel{+}= 1$

The expression $0 .. 100$ is called a *type specifier*. In general, an expression of the form *Lower* .. *Upper* specifies a valid subrange type if *Lower* and *Upper* are integer values that can be computed at compile-time and $Lower \leq Upper$. The subranges in the following code are illegal.

   var *BadRange* : $100 .. 0$ ⊘
   var *Lower*, *Upper* : int
   Lower := 0
   get *Upper*
   var *FlexRange* : *Lower* .. *Upper*   ⊘

The subrange in the declaration of *BadRange* is illegal because the lower bound is greater than the upper bound. The subrange in the declaration of *FlexRange* is illegal because the value of *Upper* cannot be determined until the program is executed.

We can give names to subrange types in a *type declaration*. For example, the declarations

   type *RowType* : $1 .. 25$
   type *ColumnType* : $1 .. 80$

introduce two new subrange types that we can use in variable declarations:

   var *Row* : *RowType*
   var *Column* : *ColumnType*

The declarations of *Row* and *Column* have exactly the same effect as the corresponding declarations in Example 4.1.

There is an obvious similarity between a subrange type and the bounds of the controlled variable in a **for** statement and, in fact, we can use the name of a subrange type in a **for** statement.

Example 4.2   Using Named Subranges

Assuming that the type *ColumnType* has been declared as above, the statement

```
for Col : ColumnType
    put "*" ..
end for
```

has the same effect as the statement

```
for Col : 1 .. 80
    put "*" ..
end for
```

There are two differences between **for** statement limits and subrange type names. First, the lower limit of a **for** statement does not have to be less than the upper limit. The statement

```
for : 1 .. 0
    put "This sentence is not displayed."
end for
```

is legal, although it does nothing, but 1 .. 0 is not a legal subrange type. Second, Turing does not allow a subrange type to be used after the keyword **decreasing**. Thus, in any **for decreasing** loop, the limits must be expressions.

Discussion

If we removed all of the subrange declarations from a working program and replaced them by **int** declarations, the behavior of the program would be the same as it was before the changes. This raises the question of why we would use subranges at all.

There are important arguments for using subranges in programs whenever it is possible to do so.

First, subranges provide useful information for a person reading the program. Knowing the permitted range of values of a variable helps us to determine what it represents and how it will be used.

Second, subranges help us to detect errors quickly. An incorrect calculation that gives a variable a value outside its range will be discovered as soon as the incorrect value is assigned. If we use integers rather than subranges, the incorrect calculation may be hard to detect. In many cases, incorrect calculations cause mysterious errors in other parts of the program and lead to frenzied "debugging" sessions.

Third, subranges work well with arrays, which are described in Section 4.3 later in this chapter.

4.2   Enumerations

It is not always appropriate to express a range of values by using numbers, especially if the number of distinct values is small. For example, we could use the numbers 0 and 1 to represent Boolean values, but it is much easier to remember the meanings of **true** and **false**. A gardener writing a program would prefer to use names such as *HybridTea*, *Floribunda*, and *Climber* rather than the numbers 1, 2, and 3.

An *enumeration type* or, more simply, an *enumeration*, has a small number of values, each represented by a different name. The keyword **enum** introduces the list of names.

Example 4.3   Declaring Enumerations

Here are some declarations of enumeration types and variables:

> **type** *RoseType* : **enum** (*HybridTea*, *Floribunda*, *Miniature*,
>   *Climber*, *Rambler*, *Shrub*)
> **var** *Rose* : *RoseType*

> **type** *SpiceType* : **enum** (*Cardamon*, *Cinnamon*, *Coriander*,
>   *Cumin*, *Fennel*, *Fenugreek*, *Nutmeg*, *Turmeric*)
> **var** *OldSpice*, *NewSpice* : *SpiceType*

When we use a value of an enumeration, we must prefix it with the name of its type. The two names are separated by a dot ("."), for example:

> *Rose* := *RoseType*.*Floribunda*
> *OldSpice* := *SpiceType*.*Fenugreek*

As we see from the following example, we can use the same value name in more than one enumeration because the type names prevent ambiguity.

Example 4.4   Avoiding Ambiguity

After we have declared the enumerations

> **type** *Spectrum* : **enum** (*Red*, *Orange*, *Yellow*, *Green*, *Blue*, *Indigo*, *Violet*)
> **type** *TrafficLights* : **enum** (*Red*, *Yellow*, *Green*)

we can use *Spectrum*.*Green* and *TrafficLights*.*Green* without risk of confusion.

Functions for Enumerations

Several predefined functions and operators accept values of enumerations as operands. In addition, we can use values of enumerations in **for** and **case** statements and as operands of comparison operators.

The function names *succ* and *pred* are abbreviations for "successor" and "predecessor". The predefined function *succ* accepts an enumeration value and returns the next value of the enumeration, using the ordering given in the declaration. The last value has no successor, and Turing reports an error if we try to obtain it. Similarly, the predefined function *pred* accepts an enumeration value and returns the previous value of the enumeration. The first value has no predecessor, and Turing reports an error if we try to obtain it. The declarations of Example 4.3 yield the following results:

$$succ\,(Rose\,Type\,.\,Floribunda) \longrightarrow Rose\,Type.Miniature$$
$$succ\,(Rose\,Type\,.\,Shrub) \qquad \oslash$$
$$pred\,(Rose\,Type\,.\,Rambler) \longrightarrow Rose\,Type.\,Climber$$
$$pred\,(Rose\,Type\,.\,Hybrid\,Tea) \qquad \oslash$$

Turing represents values of enumerations as small integers starting at 0. The predefined function *ord* returns the integer value corresponding to the position of the given enumeration value in the declaration. Using the type declarations of Example 4.4 above:

$$ord\,(Spectrum\,.\,Red) \longrightarrow 0$$
$$ord\,(Spectrum\,.\,Green) \longrightarrow 3$$
$$ord\,(Traffic\,Lights\,.\,Green) \longrightarrow 2$$

We can use the comparison operators with values of an enumerated type. Since *Climber* precedes *Shrub* in the declaration of *RoseType*,

$$Rose\,Type\,.\,Climber < Rose\,Type\,.\,Shrub \longrightarrow \text{true}$$

We can use a **for** statement to perform an action for each value of an enumeration type. The box in the following statement stands for an action to be performed for each value of *RoseType*.

> **for** *Rose* : *RoseType*
>   ☐
> **end for**

Enumeration values can be used as labels in a **case** statement, as we see from Example 4.5.

Example 4.5   Enumerations as Cases

The program in this example uses a **case** statement to display a brief description of each kind of rose. There is no need for a default label because the value of *Rose* must be one of the labels provided.

```
case Rose of
  label Rosetype.HybridTea :
    put "The most popular roses are Hybrid Teas."
  label Rosetype.Floribunda :
    put "Floribunda give colorful, long-lasting displays."
  label Rosetype.Miniature :
    put "Miniature roses are usually less than 15 inches high."
  label Rosetype.Climber :
    put "Climbing roses are not easy to maintain."
  label Rosetype.Rambler :
    put "Ramblers are generally hardy."
  label Rosetype.Shrub :
    put "Anything else is probably a shrub."
end case
```

We can declare a subrange of an enumeration. Using the declaration of *Spectrum* from Example 4.4, we can declare the subrange of values from the blue end of the spectrum:

```
type Spectrum : enum (Red, Yellow, Orange, Green, Blue, Indigo, Violet)
type WaterColors : Spectrum.Green .. Spectrum.Violet
var Ocean : WaterColors
```

The values of the variable *Ocean* are determined by its base type, *Spectrum*. They are: *Spectrum.Green*, *Spectrum.Blue*, *Spectrum.Indigo*, and *Spectrum.Violet*.

Turing uses small integers to encode the values of enumerated types. The integers returned by the function *ord* are, in fact, just these encoded values. Although values of an enumerated type are represented as numbers, we cannot use them as numbers in the program. We cannot, for example, add, multiply, or display the values of an enumeration.

While this might seem to be a restriction, there is a good reason for it. At the level of abstraction of the program, it is irrelevant that each value of an enumeration is encoded as a number. It does not make sense to multiply a *Climber* by a *Shrub*, or to subtract *Green* from *Fennel*. By restricting the operations we can perform with enumerations, Turing prevents us from attempting meaningless calculations.

4.3   Arrays

An array is a collection from which we can select components by indexing. It is a simple example of a *data structure*. Arrays use the same principle as mailing addresses. The houses on a street have numbers. If we want to send a letter to a person on the street, we give the name of the street and the number of the house. Similarly, if we want to find a component of an array, we need the name of the array and the number of the component.

If we think of a variable as a box containing a single value, we can think of an array as a row of numbered boxes, each containing a value. Figure 4.1 shows a diagrammatic representation of a real variable, *Average*, with value 7.8, and an integer array, *Scores*, containing five values: 7, 9, 6, 10, and 7.

We declare the variables *Average* and *Scores* like this:

> var *Average* : real
> var *Scores* : array 1 .. 5 of int

The second declaration says that *Scores* is an array with components numbered 1 through 5 and that each component is an integer. The declaration contains the new keywords array and of.

Each component of an array has the same properties as a variable of the corresponding type. For example, each component of *Scores* is an integer variable that we can use in an expression or in a get, put, or assignment statement. We refer to the components of the array by *indexing*, or *subscripting*, them. The components of *Scores* are *Scores* (1), *Scores* (2), ..., *Scores* (5). Referring to a nonexistent component of an array is an error. For example, *Scores* (0) and *Scores* (6) are illegal expressions.

The number 2 in the expression *Scores* (2) is an *index* or *subscript*. A subscript is not necessarily an integer literal: any integer expression will do if its value is within the required range. The selector *Scores* $(2 * M - 3)$ is valid provided that the value of $2*M-3$ is an integer between 1 and 5. An expression whose value is a component of an array, such as *Scores* (2), is called a *selector*.

The for statement provides a natural way of processing the components of an array.

Average | 7.8 | Scores | 7 | 9 | 6 | 10 | 7 |

Figure 4.1   A Real Variable, *Average*, **and an Array,** *Scores*

Example 4.6   Processing an Array with for Statements

The following program asks the user for the value of each component of *Scores*, then prints the difference between each score and the average of all the scores. We use a subrange type, *Range*, as the index type of the array *Scores*.

```
type Range : 1 .. 5
var Scores : array Range of int
var Average := 0.0
for S : Range
   put "Enter score ", S, ":   " ..
   get Scores (S)
   Average += Scores (S)
end for
Average := Average/5
put skip, "Average score:   ", Average : 7 : 2
put "Relative scores:   " ..
for S : Range
   put Scores (S) − Average : 7 : 2 ..
end for
put ""
```

Here is a sample run of this program:

```
Enter score 1: 78
Enter score 2: 82
Enter score 3: 67
Enter score 4: 91
Enter score 5: 74

Average score:     78.40
Relative scores:    -0.40   3.60 -11.40  12.60  -4.40
```

Names for Array Types

As with enumerations and subranges, we can declare a name for the type of an array and use the type name in variable declarations. Continuing with the scoring example, we could write the following declarations. The variables *MyScore* and *YourScore* are both arrays containing integer components numbered 1 through 5.

```
type Range : 1 .. 5
type Marks : 0 .. 100
type ScoreType : array Range of Marks
var MyScore, YourScore : ScoreType
```

The general form of an array type is

array ☐ of ☐

in which both boxes stand for type names or type expressions. The first type is called the *index type* of the array. The index type must be the name of an enumeration or subrange type, or an expression of the form $M .. N$ in which M must be a constant but N may be a variable. Example 4.7 includes an array declaration in which the upper bound of the index type is a variable. The second type is called the *base type* of the array. The base type may be any type.

Example 4.7   Setting Array Bounds at Run-time

The following program reads numbers entered by the user and stores them in an array.

```
var Size : int
put "Enter number of components:  " ..
get Size
var Quant : array 1 .. Size of real
for N : 1 .. Size
   put "Enter quantity:   " ..
   get Quant (N)
end for
```

The first number that the user enters is stored in *Size*. Since the index type of the array *Quant* is 1 .. *Size*, this number determines the size of the array.

Functions

The predefined functions *lower* and *upper* take an array name as argument and return the lower and upper bounds of the array. The program

```
var Hist : array 0 .. 100 of int
put lower (Hist), " ", upper (Hist)
```

displays

```
 0 100
```

Example 4.8   Storing Words in an Array

The following program reads words and stores them in an array. The user must enter each word on a separate line. The program displays the words in the array after the user has pressed ENTER without entering a word or when the array becomes full.

First, we declare the number of words the array can hold, the maximum length of a word, and the array itself.

```
const MaxWords := 20
const MaxWordLen := 10
var Words : array 1 .. MaxWords of string(MaxWordLen)
```

The program consists of two loops. The first loop reads the words from the keyboard. If a word contains more than $MaxWordLen$ letters, it is truncated to $MaxWordLen$ letters before it is stored in the array.

```
var NumWords := 0
loop
  if NumWords = MaxWords then
    exit
  else
    put "Enter a word:   " ..
    var Word : string
    get Word
    exit when Word = ""
    NumWords += 1
    if length (Word) ≤ MaxWordLen then
      Words (NumWords) := Word
    else
      Words (NumWords) := Word (1 .. MaxWordLen)
    end if
  end if
end loop
```

The second loop displays the contents of the array. Since we know the number of words that have been stored, we use a for loop.

```
for Word : 1 .. NumWords
  put Words (Word)
end for
```

Style

The effect of the statement

```
if length (Word) ≤ MaxWordLen then
  Words (NumWords) := Word
else
  Words (NumWords) := Word (1 .. MaxWordLen)
end if
```

can be achieved more concisely by using the predefined function *min*. The following assignment statement has the same effect as the preceding if statement:

$$Words\ (NumWords) := Word\ (1 \mathbin{..} min\ (length\ (Word), MaxWordLen))$$

Although the assignment is shorter than the if statement, it is not necessarily better. Many people understand the if statement more easily than the assignment although it is longer than the assignment.

4.3.1 Initializers

We can declare an array to be a constant or a variable and, in either case, we can provide an initial value for it. The declarations have the standard form

const ☐ : ☐ := ☐

or

var ☐ : ☐ := ☐

in which the first box in each declaration stands for an identifier, the second box stands for a type, and the third box stands for an *initializer*. The initializer for an array consists of the keyword init followed by a list of values. There must be as many values in the list as there are components in the array. We can initialize each component of *Score* to zero by writing

var *MyScore* : *ScoreType* := init $(0, 0, 0, 0, 0)$

Example 4.9   Array Initializers

The following program uses the enumeration *RoseType* of Section 4.2 as the index type of two constant arrays. The array *RoseName* provides a name for each value of *RoseType*, and the array *RoseArea* gives the area required for each kind of rose. The program asks the user to enter the number of roses of each type and it then displays the total area they require.

```
const NameLen := 10
type RoseType : enum (HybridTea, Floribunda, Miniature,
    Climber, Rambler, Shrub)
const RoseName : array RoseType of string (NameLen) :=
    init ("HybridTea", "Floribunda", "Miniature",
        "Climber", "Rambler", "Shrub")
const RoseArea : array RoseType of real :=
    init (2.0, 3.0, 1.5, 2.5, 6.0, 4.5)
```

```
put "Enter the number of roses you have of each type."
var TotalArea := 0.0
for Rose : RoseType
    put RoseName (Rose), repeat (" ", NameLen+2−length (RoseName (Rose))) ..
    var Num : real
    get Num
    TotalArea += RoseArea (Rose) * Num
end for
put "You will need ", TotalArea," square feet for your roses."
```

4.3.2 Two-Dimensional Arrays

The arrays we have seen so far have one dimension. We need the name of the array and one subscript value to access a component of the array. We can also declare arrays with two or more dimensions. An N-dimensional array requires N subscripts to access a component.

In the analogy used at the beginning of Section 4.3, we saw that one number is sufficient to identify a house on a street. In large cities, especially in North America, the streets themselves are numbered, and an address has the form 60 15th Street. This is analogous to a two-dimensional array: the index 15 identifies the street, and the index 60 identifies a particular house on the street.

There are two ways of declaring a two-dimensional array in Turing. To illustrate both of them, we begin with the following declarations.

```
const MaxNameLength := 5
type Name : string (MaxNameLength)
const MaxHouses := 100
type HouseIndex : 1 .. MaxHouses
const MaxStreets := 20
type StreetIndex : 1 .. MaxStreets
```

The simplest way of declaring an array of addresses is

```
var FlatAddress : array StreetIndex, HouseIndex of Name
```

The array *FlatAddress* has two index types. To access a component of the array, we must use two subscripts. For example,

```
FlatAddress (15, 60)
```

corresponds to 60 15th Street. In programming, we usually select larger components before smaller components. Thus, in this case, the street index comes before the house index.

Here is an alternative declaration for an array of addresses:

> var *NestedAddress* : array *StreetIndex* of
> array *HouseIndex* of *Name*

With this declaration, each component of *NestedAddress* is an entire array.

NestedAddress	corresponds to an array of streets.
NestedAddress (15)	corresponds to 15th Street.
NestedAddress (15) (60)	corresponds to 60 15th Street.

The form of the declaration determines the form of the selector expressions. With the above declarations, these selectors would both be illegal:

> *FlatAddress* (15) (60)   ⊘
> *NestedAddress* (15, 60)   ⊘

The advantage of the declaration of *NestedAddress* is that we can access the data at two levels, by street or by house. The declaration of *FlatAddress* provides access by house only. In most situations, we do not need both levels of access, and arrays like *FlatAddress* are simpler and easier to use.

Example 4.10   Two-Dimensional Arrays

The program in this example uses a two-dimensional array, *AllMarks*, of student marks. It is indexed by students and assignments: for example, *AllMarks* (1, 4) is the mark achieved by the first student on the fourth assignment. There is also a one-dimensional array, *Names*, of student names. Since the program is quite long, we interleave the explanation and the code.

The program's first action is to ask the user for the number of students and the number of assignments. After obtaining these values, it declares arrays of the appropriate size. The constant *TableWidth* is used later in the program to draw a rule above and below the table of marks.

```
const MaxNameLen := 10
const FieldWidth := 6
var ClassSize, NumAssign : int
put "How many students are there?   " ..
get ClassSize
put "How many assignments are there?   " ..
get NumAssign
var Names : array 1 .. ClassSize of string (MaxNameLen)
var AllMarks : array 1 .. ClassSize, 1 .. NumAssign of real
const TableWidth := MaxNameLen + FieldWidth * (NumAssign + 1) + 1
```

The next step is to obtain the necessary data. The program does this by asking the user to provide the name and marks for each student. The responses are stored in the arrays *Name* and *AllMarks*.

```
for Student : 1 .. ClassSize
    put skip, "Enter student's name:   " ..
    get Names (Student) : *
    for Assignment : 1 .. NumAssign
        put "Enter mark for #", Assignment, ":   " ..
        get AllMarks (Student, Assignment)
    end for
end for
```

After obtaining all the data, the program displays a report showing the marks each student has obtained. Students' names are extended with blanks to make the columns line up correctly. As the program displays the marks of each student, it accumulates a total mark for the student. The total mark is displayed at the end of each line.

```
put skip, "Name ", repeat (" ", MaxNameLen − length ("Name")) ..
for Assignment : 1 .. NumAssign
    put " #", Assignment : 2, " " ..
end for
put " Total"
put repeat ("-", TableWidth)
for Student : 1 .. ClassSize
    put Names (Student) +
        repeat (" ", MaxNameLen − length (Names (Student))) ..
    var StudentTotal := 0.0
    for Assignment : 1 .. NumAssign
        put AllMarks (Student, Assignment) : FieldWidth : 1 ..
        StudentTotal += AllMarks (Student, Assignment)
    end for
    put StudentTotal : FieldWidth : 1
end for
```

Finally, the program calculates and displays the average mark for each assignment and the average of the totals. The results are displayed as the last row of the report.

```
put repeat ("-", TableWidth)
var GrandTotal := 0.0
put "Averages", repeat (" ", MaxNameLen − length ("Averages")) ..
```

```
    for Assignment : 1 .. NumAssign
      var Average := 0.0
      for Student : 1 .. ClassSize
         Average += AllMarks (Student, Assignment)
      end for
      Average := Average / ClassSize
      put Average : FieldWidth : 1 ..
      GrandTotal += Average
    end for
    put GrandTotal : FieldWidth : 1
```

Here is an example of the use of this program.

```
How many students are there? 4
How many assignments are there? 5

Enter student's name: Amy
Enter mark for #1: 78
Enter mark for #2: 74
Enter mark for #3: .....
```

Name	# 1	# 2	# 3	# 4	# 5	Total
Amy	78.0	74.0	89.0	86.0	91.0	418.0
Brian	90.0	78.0	76.0	77.0	83.0	404.0
Charlotte	92.0	88.0	93.0	76.0	86.0	435.0
David	67.0	71.0	73.0	79.0	81.0	371.0
Averages	81.8	77.8	82.8	79.5	85.3	407.0

Initializers

We can assign initial values to two-dimensional arrays. The init expression must contain as many values as the type of the array requires. The values are not grouped to match the dimensions.

Example 4.11   Initializing a Two-Dimensional Array

The following program declares and initializes a two-dimensional array.

```
type Color : enum (Red, Green, Blue)
const Mix : array Color, Color of string (7) := init (
  "Red", "Yellow", "Magenta", "Yellow", "Green",
  "Cyan", "Magenta", "Cyan", "Blue")
```

The type *Color* has three values. The array *Mix*, which describes the effects of additive color mixing, has $3^2 = 9$ components. The initializer provides nine values.

Functions

The predefined functions *lower* and *upper* work with arrays of two or more dimensions. If the array has more than one dimension, we must specify the dimension whose bounds we need. Dimensions are numbered starting from 1. If we declare

    var *TaxOwed* : array 1980 .. 2000 of real
    var *Table* : array 1 .. 10, 1 .. 100 of string (6)

then

    lower (*TaxOwed*) $\longrightarrow$ 1980
    upper (*TaxOwed*) $\longrightarrow$ 2000
    upper (*Table*, 1) $\longrightarrow$ 10
    upper (*Table*, 2) $\longrightarrow$ 100

The lower bound of each index type of an array is usually 0 or 1, however many dimensions the array has. There are occasional exceptions, such as the array *TaxOwed* in the example above, but these are relatively rare.

Discussion

Initialized arrays can often be used to simplify programs. We can eliminate most of the code of the program in Example 2.5 on page 42, for instance, by declaring a constant array of strings:

    const *Weather* : array 1 .. 12 of *String* (25) := int (
      "Bitterly cold",
      ....)

Other applications of this device are suggested in Exercise 4.10.

4.4 Summary

Numbers in parentheses refer to sections where material appears.

▶ Subranges, enumerations, and arrays are user-defined types.

▶ A *type specifier* is an expression that defines a type (4.1). A type specifier may be a keyword denoting a standard type, an identifier, or an expression such as 1 .. 5.

▶ A subrange type is defined by two constants. The constants may be integers (4.1) or values of an enumeration (4.2).

▶ The values of a subrange type are integers of a consecutive sequence (4.1). Any operation that can be used with integer operands can also be used with operands of a subrange type. An assignment that would give to a subrange variable a value outside its range causes an error at run-time.

▶ An *enumeration* has a set of identifiers as its values (4.2).

▶ The comparison operators and the functions *succ*, *pred*, and *ord* may be used with enumerations (4.2).

▶ An *array* is a collection of indexed components (4.3). An array has an *index type*, which is the type of its subscripts, and a *base type*, which is the type of its components. The index type must be a subrange or an enumeration. The base type can be any type.

▶ The predefined functions *lower* and *upper* return the values of the lower and upper bounds of an array (4.3). If the array has more than one dimension, there must be a second argument specifying the dimension for which the bound is required. The dimensions are numbered from 1.

▶ The initial value of a constant or a variable array may be set by an *initializer* (4.3.1). The initializer must provide exactly one value for each component of the array.

▶ Arrays may have more than one dimension (4.3.2). There is one subscript for each dimension.

4.5   Exercises

4.1   Suppose that we declare the type

> **type** *ShortString* : **string** (30)

Give a suitable declaration for a type whose values are lengths of strings of type *ShortString*.

4.2   Suppose that we have declared

> **type** $A : 1 .. 1$
> **type** $B : 1 .. 0$

What values can A and B have? Are A and B legal types in Turing?

4.3   Dates are sometimes written in the form 5/5/1994, in which both the day and the month are given numerically. Give suitable subrange types for each field of a numeric date.

4.4   Assume that Turing has executed the declarations:

> **type** *Small* : $0 .. 10$
> **type** *Big* : $10 .. 20$
> **var** K : *Small* := 5
> **var** L : *Big* := 15
> **var** M, N : *Small* := 5

For each of the assignment statements below, first decide whether the statement is *statically legal*, that is, whether it is legal for all possible values of the variables K, L, M, and N. Second, decide whether it is *dynamically legal*, that is, whether it is legal for the particular values of the variables given. Finally, if it is legal both statically and dynamically, give the value of the expression on the right-hand side. The assignments are independent of each other; the value of L in (b) is 15, not the value assigned to it in (a).

(a) $L := 2 * K$

(b) $K := L - 2 * K$

(c) $L -= 2 * K$

(d) $L := M + N$

(e) $K := (M + N)$ **div** 2

(f) $L := M * N$ **mod** $10 + 11$

4.5   Write enumerated type declarations suitable for:

(a) days of the week;

(b) months of the year;

(c) coin denominations; and

(d) Turing types.

4.6   Using the declaration

   type *BoxSize* : enum (*Tiny, Small, Medium, Large, ExtraLarge, Colossal*)

decide whether each of the following expressions is legal and, if it is, give its value.

(a) *ord (BoxSize . Large)*

(b) *succ (BoxSize . Small)*

(c) *pred (BoxSize . Colossal)*

(d) *ord (succ (BoxSize . Colossal))*

(e) *succ (ord (BoxSize . Colossal))*

(f) *ord (BoxSize . Small + BoxSize . Large)*

4.7   Suppose that Turing did not have the standard type **boolean**, and we declared

   type *boolean* : enum (*True, False*)

Would this substitution have a significant effect on the programs we can write in Turing?

4.8   Write a program that finds the largest and smallest components of an array of integers.

4.9   Suppose that A is a two-dimensional array of real numbers. Write programs that compute the following values:

(a) the row sums of A;

(b) the column sums of A;

(c) the largest and smallest row sums of A;

(d) the largest and smallest column sums of A;

(e) the largest and smallest components of A.

4.10 Several of the exercises of Chapter 2 are easier to do if we use initialized arrays instead of if or case statements. Write programs that use initialized arrays for Exercises 2.4, 2.7, 2.9, 2.10, 2.11, and 2.12.

4.11 A three-dimensional vector **v** has components v_x, v_y, and v_z. We can represent vectors in Turing programs using declarations such as

> type *Coord* : enum (X, Y, Z)
> type *Vector* : array *Coord* of real
> var U, V, W : *Vector*

Using these declarations, write code corresponding to each of the following vector calculations.

(a) The *magnitude* of a vector **v** is $|\mathbf{v}| = v_x^2 + v_y^2 + v_z^2$.

(b) The *inner product* of two vectors **u** and **v** is the real number
$$\mathbf{u} \cdot \mathbf{v} = u_x v_x + u_y v_y + u_z v_z.$$

(c) The *scalar product* of a real number r and a vector **v** is a vector $\mathbf{w} = r\mathbf{v}$ with components $w_x = rv_x$, $w_y = rv_y$, and $w_z = rv_z$.

(d) The *vector product* of two vectors **u** and **v** is a vector $\mathbf{w} = \mathbf{u} \times \mathbf{v}$ with components
$$w_x = u_y v_z - u_z v_y,$$
$$w_y = u_z v_x - u_x v_z,$$
$$w_z = u_x v_y - u_y v_x.$$

(e) The *triple product* of three vectors **u**, **v**, and **w** is the real number $\mathbf{u} \cdot (\mathbf{v} \times \mathbf{w})$, in which "$\cdot$" is the scalar product and "$\times$" is the vector product defined above.

4.12 Computers are often used to perform statistical analyses of data. The questions below illustrate various statistical calculations.

Assume that there is a collection of real numbers, called the *observations*, $x_1, x_2, \ldots, x_n$, where $n > 1$. Write a program that asks the user for the observations, stores them in an array, and carries out the following statistical calculations.

(a) The *mean*, $\bar{x}$, of the observations is given by
$$\bar{x} = \frac{1}{n} \sum_{i=1}^{n} x_i.$$

(b) The *standard deviation*, σ, of the observations is given by

$$\sigma^2 = \frac{1}{n-1} \sum_{i=1}^{n} (x_i - \bar{x})^2.$$

(c) The *correlation coefficient*, r, between a set of observations $x_1, x_2, \ldots, x_n$ and another set of observations $y_1, y_2, \ldots, y_n$ is given by

$$r = \frac{\sum_{i=1}^{n} (x_i - \bar{x})(y_i - \bar{y})}{\sqrt{\sum_{i=1}^{n} (x_i - \bar{x})^2 \sum_{i=1}^{n} (y_i - \bar{y})^2}}.$$

Chapter 5

Procedures and Functions

Programming is difficult because programs are complex. Almost every line of a program contains important details, and it is easy to become overwhelmed by the mass of detail. It is difficult to write a program without making mistakes; it is more difficult to understand completely a program written by another person; and it is more difficult still to find and correct errors in a large program.

The most important features that a programming language can provide are features that help us to manage complexity. We manage our thoughts about complex ideas by giving names to them. Naming an entity allows us to think about it as a whole, without worrying about its detailed structure. For example, "car" is a name for a complex entity. We can talk about "going there in the car" without having to think about the wheels, the engine, the transmission, or how the car works. Programming languages support this mode of thinking by enabling us to give names to parts of programs.

The simple act of using a name to stand for a computation is a significant step towards simpler programs. We have seen already how to give names to constants, variables, and types. We can also give a name to a sequence of declarations and statements: the result is a *procedure*. Often, the purpose of a sequence is to compute a single value; naming a sequence of this kind yields a *function* that we can use in an expression.

5.1   Predefined Procedures and Functions

Modern programming languages, such as Turing, consist of a small kernel of general-purpose statements and a much larger library of predefined functions and procedures. The statements of Turing discussed in Chapter 2 provide only the rudiments of input and output in the form of get and put statements. These statements do not enable us to perform simple tasks such as clearing the screen or moving the cursor. For these and other actions that ordinary statements cannot perform, Turing provides a collection of predefined procedures and functions. Procedures and functions are collectively called *subprograms*.

In Turing, the expression *sin (Theta)* is a *function call* consisting of a function name and an argument list; "*sin*" is the name of the function and "(*Theta*)" is an argument list containing one argument, *Theta*.

We use subprograms to hide the details of computations. It is not necessary to know how to calculate *sin (Theta)* in order to use the Turing function *sin*. In fact, few programmers know how to calculate *sin (Theta)* accurately. The well-known series $x - x^3/3! + \cdots$, which some programmers might consider using, is neither accurate nor efficient.

Whereas we call a function to obtain a value, we call a procedure to do something, or to have an effect. A procedure call is a kind of statement. For example, the procedure call *locate* (12, 29) is a statement that moves the cursor to row 12 and column 29 of the screen.

5.1.1   Predefined Procedures for Input and Output

The put and get statements provide basic input and output capabilities. Most programs need more control over input and output than put and get can provide. For these programs, Turing provides predefined procedures. In this section, we give a brief description of three useful predefined procedures: *cls*, *locate*, and *getch*.

Procedures *cls* and *locate*

The procedure *cls* clears the screen or, if Turing is running in a window environment, the "run" window. The procedure *locate* positions the cursor in the screen or window. Its two arguments specify the row and column for the cursor.

Example 5.1   Writing on the Screen

The following program clears the screen and writes a message at its center.

```
cls
locate (12, 29)
put "Abstraction is the key" ..
```

The first line calls *cls* to clear the screen. The second line moves the cursor to row 12 and column 29 of the screen. The third line displays a message in the usual way. If the screen has 25 rows and 80 columns, the message will be approximately in the middle of it.

The statement *locate* (12, 29) is a procedure call with two arguments, 12 and 29. The permitted range of values of the arguments depends on the size of the screen. For a PC running DOS or Windows, the first argument must be an integer in the range 1 .. 25 and the second argument must be an integer in the range 1 .. 80.

The Procedure *getch*

The predefined procedure *getch* reads one character from the keyboard. It is useful in interactive programs when we want the computer to respond immediately to a single keystroke such as "y" or "n".

Example 5.2   Reading with **get** and *getch*

The following program uses **get** to read the user's name and *getch* to obtain a one-character response.

```
var Name : string
put "What is your name?   " ..
get Name : *
put "Shall I display your name?   " ..
var Reply : string (1)
getch (Reply)
put ""
if Reply = "y" then
   put "Your name is ", Name, "."
elsif Reply = "n" then
   put "All right, I won't display your name."
else
   put "You should reply 'y' or 'n'."
end if
```

In this program, the effect of the statement

> get *Name* : ∗

is to read an entire line of text from the keyboard. The program does not respond until the user presses the ENTER key. The effect of *getch* is quite different. The program accepts exactly one character from the keyboard and responds immediately, without waiting for the ENTER key to be pressed. The character read by *getch* is assigned to the argument of *getch*, which must be a variable with type **string** (1).

By using *getch*, we make the program more responsive than it would be if we used get. This responsiveness is important for interactive programs, but it has a cost. The user has no chance to correct a mistake because the program does not wait for the ENTER key to be pressed. Consequently, we must validate the character read by *getch*. If the action selected may have serious consequences, such as deleting a file, the program should ask the user for confirmation.

5.1.2   Random Numbers

Turing provides several predefined procedures that generate random numbers. Random numbers have many applications in computing, especially in the area of simulation. We introduce random numbers here partly because Turing provides procedures to generate them and partly because random numbers are a rich source of simple but instructive programs.

Example 5.3   Using Random Numbers in a Simulation

The following program writes 20 numbers, chosen from $1, 2, \ldots, 6$, simulating throws of a die.

```
for : 1 .. 20
   var Score : int
   randint (Score, 1, 6)
   put Score : 2 ..
end for
```

The numbers this program generates look less "random" than we might expect:

> 1 5 1 4 5 3 6 4 1 3 5 6 6 2 3 1 1 2 6 5

When people try to generate random numbers, their attempts are usually "too random". Actual random number lists, such as the one above, contain more repetitions — 6 6 and 1 1 for instance — than we expect.

The statement *randint* (*Score*, 1, 6) assigns a random value to *Score*. The second argument of *randint* gives the smallest permitted number, and the third argument gives the largest permitted number. In this program, each value of *Score* will be a number in the range 1, 2, . . . , 6. Each of these values has the same probability of being chosen.

If we run the program in Example 5.3 several times, we notice that the sequence of "random" numbers is always the same. This is because the numbers are not really random: they are "pseudorandom" numbers generated by a deterministic algorithm. Nevertheless, they have the statistical properties of true random numbers. For example, in a long run of simulated throws, the number 3 will come up one time in six on average.

Sometimes it is useful to have the same sequence of numbers each time we run the program. For instance, we may want consistent results while developing a complicated simulation. In other situations, we may want the sequence of numbers to be unpredictable. This would apply, for example, for a program that plays a game. Turing provides the predefined procedure *randomize* for this purpose. If we include the statement *randomize* at the beginning of the program in Example 5.3, the program will produce a different sequence of throws each time we run it.

Plotting with Characters

If we generate 1,000 random numbers in the range 1 through 10, we would not expect to obtain exactly 100 occurrences of the number 7. Nor would we expect to obtain a significant departure from randomness, such as the absence of the number 7. Example 5.4 displays a distribution of random numbers on the screen, giving us an idea of the properties to expect of such a distribution.

Example 5.4   Plotting a Random Distribution

The following program writes asterisks in the top ten rows of the screen. Initially, all of the rows are blank. During each iteration, the program chooses a row at random and writes an asterisk at the end of it. The program stops when any row contains 80 asterisks.

```
var Histogram : array 1 .. 10 of 0 .. 80
for N : 1 .. 10
    Histogram (N) := 0
end for
cls
randomize
loop
```

```
    var N : int
    randint (N, 1, 10)
    exit when Histogram (N) = 80
    Histogram (N) += 1
    locate (N, Histogram (N))
    put "*" ..
  end loop
```

Figure 5.1 shows the appearance of the screen when the program is about halfway through executing.

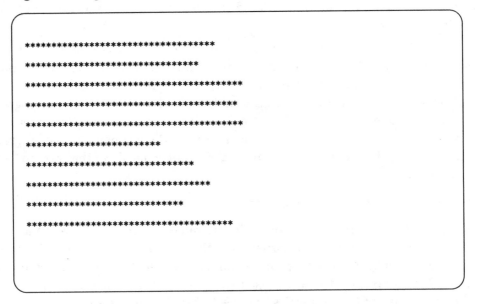

Figure 5.1   Plotting a Random Distribution

Since the program cannot "see" the screen, it needs a way of deciding where to display each asterisk. The method it uses is to maintain an array, *Histogram*, to store the number of asterisks that have been displayed in each row. The key to making such a program work is to ensure that the data structure and the screen image always correspond. In this case, we can express the required correspondence as "the value of *Histogram* (R) must be equal to the number of asterisks displayed in row R".

Random Reals

Another predefined procedure, called *rand*, assigns a real random value to its argument. After Turing has executed the statements

```
var X : real
rand (X)
```

the value of X is a random number that satisfies $0 < X < 1$.

Example 5.5   Generating Random Strings

Suppose we want to generate strings of 50 characters of which, on average, 50% are A's, 30% are B's, and 20% are C's. We begin by constructing an outline for the program. The statement *randomize* initializes the random number generator. The for statement inserts one random letter into the string *Sample* during each iteration. The box stands for the code that assigns a suitable value to *Letter*.

```
randomize
const StringLen := 50
var Sample : string (StringLen) := ""
for : 1 .. StringLen
    [    ]
    Sample += Letter
end for
put Sample
```

To choose a letter, we generate a random number, R, between 0 and 1. Then we use the value of R to determine the value of *Letter*. The following code goes inside the box in the outline above.

```
var R : real
var Letter : string (1)
rand (R)
if R ≤ 0.5 then
    Letter := "A"
elsif R ≤ 0.8 then
    Letter := "B"
else
    Letter := "C"
end if
```

To see why this works, we draw a line of length 1.0 and put marks at 0.5 and 0.8, as in Figure 5.2. This divides the line in the required ratios.

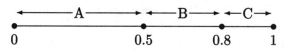

Figure 5.2   Dividing the Line

We mark the line at the position corresponding to R. Since the probability is 50% that the point will lie on the left half of the line, the probability that the program will choose "A" is also 50%. Similarly, since the probability is 30% that the point will lie between 0.5 and 0.8, the probability that the program will choose "B" is also 30%. Finally, the probability that the point will lie between 0.8 and 1.0, and that the program will choose "C", is 20%.

Here is a string generated by the program.

ACAAAAABAAACBAACAAAACAABBBBBABAAABCABBCACBBABAACBBB

It consists of 26 "A"s (52%), 16 "B"s (32%), and 8 "C"s (16%). These proportions are quite close to the desired proportions, given the small size of the sample.

Using Random Numbers

Random numbers are often used in the study of complex processes, such as weather, economic systems, and evolution. The use of random numbers enables us to discover general properties of such systems by allowing us to examine selected variables in isolation. For example, to demonstrate that a particular combination of temperature and humidity leads to rain, we can run a weather simulation program with assigned values of temperature and humidity and random values for the other variables. The next example uses random numbers to simulate a simple evolutionary process.

Example 5.6   Using Random Numbers to Simulate Evolution

The program below simulates a population of 100 individuals called *Memes*. Each Meme has two genes, its *left gene* and its *right gene*. The gene pair of a Meme determines the probability that the Meme dies. Whenever a Meme dies, another is born, so the population remains constant. A newborn Meme has two parents, and it inherits one gene from each parent.

There are three kinds of gene, *Red*, *Green*, and *Blue*. The program uses an enumeration, *GeneType*, to represent genes. The array *MortProb* contains the mortality statistics: the value of $MortProb(L, R)$ is the probability that a Meme with left gene L and right gene R will die during the current simulated time unit. Since the time unit is arbitrary, the rows and columns of the matrix do not have to add up to 1.

```
type GeneType : enum (Red, Green, Blue)
var MortProb : array GeneType, GeneType of real := init (
    0.4, 0.6, 0.9,
    0.6, 0.8, 0.9,
    0.9, 0.9, 0.7)
```

Next, we introduce a population of 100 Memes, each with two genes. Since many of the variables in the program refer to Memes, we declare the type *PopIndex* to index them.

```
const Population := 100
type PopIndex : 1 .. Population
var LeftGene, RightGene : array PopIndex of GeneType
```

We use the random number generator to assign a random pair of genes to each Meme. The array *GeneVals* translates the integers 1, 2, and 3 to the corresponding genes, *Red*, *Green*, and *Blue*.

```
const GeneVals : array 1 .. 3 of GeneType :=
   init (GeneType.Red, GeneType.Green, GeneType.Blue)
randomize
for Meme : PopIndex
   var G : int
   randint (G, 1, 3)
   LeftGene (Meme) := GeneVals (G)
   randint (G, 1, 3)
   RightGene (Meme) := GeneVals (G)
end for
```

As the program runs, it displays the gene pool. Since each Meme has two genes and each gene has one of three possible colors, there are nine kinds of Meme. Accordingly, the gene pool has three rows and three columns. The number in the second row and third column, for example, gives the number of Memes with a green left gene and a blue right gene. The next piece of code initializes the screen with row and column headings for the gene pool.

```
cls
put "⎵⎵⎵⎵R⎵⎵⎵G⎵⎵⎵B"
put "R"
put "B"
put "G"
```

The main loop of the program simulates the evolution of the population. For each Meme, the program generates a random number, M. If the value of M is greater than the mortality coefficient of the Meme, the Meme dies and is replaced by another one. To simulate the "birth" of a new Meme, we use the random number generator to select parents, *Mom* and *Dad*, and take one gene from each.

There are two points to note about the simulation of birth. First, we do not want either of the parents to be the Meme who just died, and we do not want both parents to be the same Meme. The program generates parents at random until both conditions are satisfied. Second, the new Meme's right gene is its mother's left gene and its left gene is its father's right gene. Without this reversal, there would be two entirely independent gene pools (left and right), and half of the effort of the simulation would be wasted.

The simulation runs until the user presses a key. The function *hasch*, which is described in detail in Section 6.1, detects this event.

```
loop
    exit when hasch
    for I : PopIndex
        var M : real
        rand (M)
        if M > MortProb (LeftGene (I), RightGene (I)) then
            % An individual has died and a new one is born.
            var Mom, Dad : int
            loop
                randint (Mom, 1, Population)
                randint (Dad, 1, Population)
                exit when I ≠ Mom and I ≠ Dad and Mom ≠ Dad
            end loop
            LeftGene (I) := RightGene (Mom)
            RightGene (I) := LeftGene (Dad)
        end if
    end for
```

After the funerals and birth ceremonies, the program counts the number of each kind of Meme and displays the gene pool.

```
    var GeneCounts : array GeneType, GeneType of int :=
        init (0, 0, 0, 0, 0, 0, 0, 0, 0)
    for I : PopIndex
        GeneCounts (LeftGene (I), RightGene (I)) += 1
    end for
    for I : GeneType
        locate (ord (I) + 2, 2)
        for G : GeneType
            put GeneCounts (I, G) : 4  ..
        end for
    end for
end loop
```

By choosing different values for the components of the array *MortProb*, we can use the program to demonstrate properties of genetic evolution. Sometimes the populations in the nine cells reach a stable equilibrium, but more often, one or two gene combinations become dominant and the other combinations die out.

5.1.3 Measuring and Displaying Time

Turing provides several procedures for measuring and displaying time. Figure 5.3 summarizes the time management procedures.

Procedure	Effect
clock (*c*)	Set integer *c* to the time in milliseconds since the process began.
delay (*d*)	Wait for integer *d* milliseconds.
date (*d*)	Set string *d* to today's date (DD MMM YY).
sysclock (*c*)	Set integer *c* to time used by process (milliseconds).
time (*t*)	Set string *t* to time now (HH:MM:SS).
wallclock (*c*)	Set integer *c* to time since 1/1/1970 (seconds).

Figure 5.3 **Procedures for Measuring and Displaying Time**

The precise effects of the procedures depend on the kind of computer and operating system on which Turing is running. In particular, although some of the results are given in milliseconds (thousandths of a second), PCs and Macintoshes are not as accurate as the choice of unit suggests. The time on a PC may be off by as much as 55 milliseconds (1/18 seconds), and the time on a MacIntosh may be off by as much as 17 milliseconds (1/60 seconds).

A simple application of the data and time procedures is to display the date and time on the screen.

Example 5.7 Displaying the Date and Time

The following program displays the current date and time at the top of the screen. To avoid flicker, the display is updated only when the time changes. The variable *OldTime* stores the previous value of *Time* so that the program can tell when the time changes.

```
setscreen ("nocursor")
cls
var Date : string
date (Date)
locate (1, 31)
put Date ..
loop
  var OldTime, Time : string := ""
  loop
    time (Time)
    if Time ≠ OldTime then
      locate (1, 43)
      put Time ..
      OldTime := Time
    end if
  end loop
end loop
```

The predefined procedure *clock* gives the number of milliseconds that have elapsed since the program was started. We can use *clock* to measure how much time Turing takes to perform operations.

In principle, we can use complexity theory to predict the time that a program requires to complete a given computation. Such predictions are difficult if the program is complex; it may not be feasible to obtain precise results. By measuring the time that a program actually takes to solve a small problem, we can predict the time that it will require to solve large problems.

Example 5.8   Timing a Program

Suppose we want to find the time required to multiply two real numbers. Since this time is very short, we should do a large number of multiplications to obtain an accurate value. This means that we must write a loop, but we do not want to measure the time required to manage the iterations. The solution is to write two loops, one with a multiplication and one without. We time both loops, and the final result is the difference between the two times. Each loop cycles 10,000 times, and the time returned by *clock* is in milliseconds. We divide the result by 10, obtaining the result in microseconds (millionths of a second).

```
var Start, Middle, Finish : int
clock (Start)
const X := 99.9
const Y := 123.4
```

```
for : 1 .. 10000
    const Z := 0.0
end for
clock (Middle)
for : 1 .. 10000
    const Z := X * Y
end for
clock (Finish)
const FirstLoopTime := Middle − Start
const SecondLoopTime := Finish − Middle
put "Real multiply requires ",
    (SecondLoopTime − FirstLoopTime) div 10, " microseconds."
```

When run on a computer with an Intel 80486 processor running at 33 MHz, this program displayed

```
"Real multiply requires 45 microseconds."
```

5.2   Declaring New Procedures

Although the predefined subprograms provide useful services, the most important feature of subprograms is that we can define our own. When we declare subprograms, we are extending the language to match our own particular requirements.

The ability to declare new subprograms is an important step towards writing large programs. We cannot manage a sequence of thousands of statements, but we can manage thousands of statements that have been divided into small groups. The key to successful management is to give a name to each group. Subprograms enable us to abstract from the low level of statements to the higher level of procedure names.

5.2.1   Declaring a Procedure

The simplest form of procedure declaration consists of a *header* and a *body*. The header declares the name of the procedure and its parameters. The body contains declarations and statements that determine the effect of the procedure.

Example 5.9   Declaring a Procedure

Interactive programs often need to ask the user a question that requires the answer "yes" or "no". The procedure *Ask*, defined below, displays a message, obtains a response from the user, and returns a Boolean value.

```
procedure Ask (Message : string, var Reply : boolean)
  var Ch : string (1)
  loop
    put Message ..
    getch (Ch)
    put ""
    if Ch = "y" or Ch = "Y" then
      Reply := true
      exit
    elsif Ch = "n" or Ch = "N" then
      Reply := false
      exit
    else
      put "Please answer 'y' or 'n'."
    end if
  end loop
end Ask
```

The procedure *Ask* reads only one character. If the character is **"y"** or **"Y"**, we assume that the user means "yes". If the character is **"n"** or **"N"**, we assume that the user means "no". If the character has any other value, the procedure displays an error message and repeats the question.

The preceding code is a declaration of the procedure *Ask*. Nothing happens until we call the procedure. The second line in the body of the following loop statement calls the procedure *Ask*.

```
loop
  var DoIt : boolean
  Ask ("Do you want to continue?   ", DoIt)
  if DoIt then
    put "Continuing ..."
    exit
  end if
end loop
```

Running the program produces a dialogue such as the following.

```
Do you want to continue?   x
Please answer 'y' or 'n'.
Do you want to continue?   y
Continuing ...
```

Example 5.9 illustrates most of the important ideas involved in writing a procedure. The line beginning with keyword **procedure** is the *header* of the procedure. It introduces the name of the procedure, *Ask*, and its two parameters, *Message* and *Reply*. The parameter declarations resemble variable declarations and, in fact, play a similar role.

The first declaration, *Message* : string, introduces *Message* as a string parameter. The effect is as if we had declared

> const *Message* : string := " . . . . . "

In other words, *Message* has the properties of a constant within the body of the procedure. The value of the constant is provided by the caller of the procedure. In Example 5.9, the value is "Do you want to continue?   ".

The second declaration introduces *Reply* as a Boolean variable. The keyword **var** in the parameter list indicates that it is a variable parameter, which can be changed within the body of the procedure. When the procedure is called, *Reply* may or may not have a well-defined value. A procedure with variable parameters should contain assignment or other statements that change the value of these parameters. If the user enters Y or y, procedure *Ask* sets *Reply* to true, and if the user enters N or n, it sets *Reply* to false.

The header is followed by the *body* of the procedure. The body is similar to a program in that it consists of declarations and statements. The last statement of the body of procedure *Ask* is followed by end *Ask*, indicating the end of the procedure. The last line of a procedure always consists of the keyword end and the name of the procedure.

Example 5.9 includes the *procedure call*

> *Ask* ("Do you want to continue?   ", *DoIt*)

Turing executes the procedure call by executing the declarations and statements within the body of *Ask*. The effect is as if we had executed a program consisting of the declarations

> const *Message* := "Do you want to continue?   "
> var *Reply* : bool

followed by the declarations and statements in the body of *Ask*. The procedure loops until the user has entered one of the keys y, Y, n, or N. When the loop terminates, the procedure also terminates with the value of *Reply* set appropriately. In Example 5.9, we can think of *Reply* as a second name for the argument *DoIt*. An assignment of a value to *Reply* in the body of the procedure *Ask* gives *DoIt* the same value.

In the header of the procedure *Ask*,

> procedure *Ask* (*Message* : string, var *Reply* : boolean)

the variables *Message* and *Reply* are *parameters* or *formal parameters*. In the procedure call

> *Ask* ("Do you want to continue?   ", *DoIt*)

the string "Do you want to continue?   " and the variable *DoIt* are *arguments* or *actual parameters*.

Four rules relate arguments to parameters.

- The number of arguments in the call must be the same as the number of parameters in the procedure heading.
- The type of each argument must be the same as the type of the corresponding parameter.
- If the parameter name is preceded by var, the corresponding argument must be a variable.
- If the parameter name is not preceded by var, the corresponding argument may be an expression or a variable.

5.2.2   The return Statement

As the procedure *Ask* in Example 5.9 shows, a procedure returns control to the caller after executing its last statement. Turing also provides a return statement that causes the procedure to return immediately. We can sometimes use the return statement to reduce the amount of code we have to write in a procedure.

Example 5.10   Using the return Statement

The procedure *ToUpper* converts the lower case letters in a string to the corresponding upper case letters. If, however, the string already contains an upper case letter, the procedure returns immediately, leaving the string unchanged. Given the argument "banana", the procedure constructs the string "BANANA", executes the assignment *OldString* := *NewString*, and returns. Given the argument "falling Coconuts", the procedure scans the input string until it reaches "C" and then executes the return statement, leaving the parameter *OldString* unchanged.

> procedure *ToUpper* (var *OldString* : string)
>   var *NewString* := ""
>   const *CaseDiff* := *ord* ("A") − *ord* ("a")
>   for *Pos* : 1 .. *length* (*OldString*)

```
    if index ("ABCDEFGHIJKLMNOPQRSTUVWXYZ", OldString (Pos)) > 0 then
        return
    elsif index ("abcdefghijklmnopqrstuvwxyz", OldString (Pos)) > 0 then
        NewString += chr (ord (OldString (Pos)) + CaseDiff)
    else
        NewString += OldString (Pos)
    end if
end for
OldString := NewString
end ToUpper
```

It is always a good idea to test a new procedure, especially if it is at all complex. The program that performs the tests should be as simple as possible so that we have confidence in the results of the tests. Here is a program that tests the procedure *ToUpper*:

```
loop
    put "Enter string:   " ..
    var TrialString : string
    get TrialString : *
    exit when TrialString = ""
    toupper (TrialString)
    put TrialString, skip
end loop
```

Here are some of the results:

```
Enter string: banana
BANANA
Enter string: falling Coconuts
falling Coconuts
Enter string:
```

Style

We could have avoided the return statement in Example 5.10 by using a Boolean variable. This would have made the program easier to read at the expense of a few extra lines of code. The problem with the version given is that it is easy to overlook the return statement hidden in the for statement; we might assume that the statement *OldString := NewString* is always executed. The return statement is not often necessary. It is best to use it only when there is no simpler alternative.

5.2.3   Program Development

Subprograms play an important role in program development. They help us to manage complexity by separating the concerns of *what* we need to do from the details of *how* we do it. The next example demonstrates the use of simple procedures in the development of a program that exhibits quite complex behavior.

Example 5.11   Developing Programs with Procedures

The program generates primitive random sentences. Each sentence has three parts: a subject part, a verb part, and an object part. In the following sentences, which the program might generate, the parts are separated by slashes:

```
Ann / eats / the small hippopotamus .
The thirsty person / plays with / the red car .
```

First, we declare a type for the words of a sentence. A word has at most 20 letters.

> const *MaxWordLength* := 20
> type *WordType* : string (*MaxWordLength*)

The program needs words from which to build sentences. The next group of declarations sets up initialized constant arrays of words in several categories. The arrays given here have a small number of words; it is easy to add more words to increase the vocabulary of the program. Each word is followed by a blank character, so it will not be necessary to insert blanks later.

> const *Adjectives* : array 1 .. 7 of *WordType* :=
>   init ("dusty ","red ","young ","small ",
>   "thirsty ","ferocious ","slow ")
> const *Nouns* : array 1 .. 6 of *WordType* :=
>   init ("locomotive ","hippopotamus ","person ",
>   "lollipop ","car ","computer ")
> const *ProperNames* : array 1 .. 6 of *WordType* :=
>   init ("Ann ","Bill ","Carl ","Denise ","Emily ","Feng ")
> const *VerbForms* : array 1 .. 5 of *WordType* :=
>   init ("bumps ","eats ","plays with ",
>   "goes to ","points at ",)

In the program that follows, the first procedure, *GenWord*, appends a word to the current sentence. The first parameter, *Store*, is an array of words, and the second parameter, *Sentence*, is a partial sentence. When *GenWord* is called, the parameter *Store* receives an array of words of the appropriate kind.

The index type of the parameter *Store* is 1 .. ∗. This means that the array *Store* will have as many components as the corresponding argument. Within *GenWord*, we can use *upper* (*Store*) to find out how many components there actually are. In fact, we use *upper* (*Store*) in the call to *randint* to choose a word from *Store*. The principal action of the procedure is to append this random word to the sentence. The parameter name *Sentence* is preceded by var because the procedure alters its value.

procedure *GenWord* (*Store* : array 1 .. ∗ of *WordType*, var *Sentence* : string)
   var *WordPos* : int
   randint (*WordPos*, 1, *upper* (*Store*))
   Sentence += *Store* (*WordPos*)
end *GenWord*

The next few procedures use *GenWord* to build the sentence. The procedure *GenArticle* generates one of the strings "The", "the", "A", or "a", and appends it to the current sentence. The parameter *Caps* is true if the article is the first word of the sentence, in which case the first letter of the article should be capitalized. The procedure uses a random number to generate "The" or "the" in about 60% of the calls and "A" or "a" in the other 40%.

procedure *GenArticle* (*Caps* : boolean, var *Sentence* : string)
   var *RandArticle* : real
   rand (*RandArticle*)
   if *RandArticle* < 0.6 then
     if *Caps* then
       Sentence += "The "
     else
       Sentence += "the "
     end if
   else
     if *Caps* then
       Sentence += "A "
     else
       Sentence += "a "
     end if
   end if
end *GenArticle*

The procedure *GenAdjectives* generates zero or more adjectives and appends them to the sentence. It uses a loop that uses a random number to choose between exiting and generating an adjective. There is a probability of one half that it will generate no adjectives at all, a probability of one quarter that it will generate one adjective, and so on.

```
procedure GenAdjectives (var Sentence : string)
  var RandAdj : real
  loop
    rand (RandAdj)
    exit when RandAdj < 0.5
    GenWord (Adjectives, Sentence)
  end loop
end GenAdjectives
```

The procedure *GenNounPhrase* is similar to the other generators. Roughly 70% of the noun phrases that it generates consist of an article, some adjectives, and a noun. The other 30% consist of a proper name only. It is easy to understand *GenNounPhrase* because it uses the procedures previously declared. It would be harder to understand if it did all the work by itself.

```
procedure GenNounPhrase (Caps : boolean, var Sentence : string)
  var RandNoun : real
  rand (RandNoun)
  if RandNoun < 0.7 then
    GenArticle (Caps, Sentence)
    GenAdjectives (Sentence)
    GenWord (Nouns, Sentence)
  else
    GenWord (ProperNames, Sentence)
  end if
end GenNounPhrase
```

Finally, the main program consists of a loop that generates one sentence and then waits for one second to allow the user to read the sentence. The call to *randomize* ensures that it will generate different sentences each time it is run.

```
randomize
loop
  exit when hasch
  var Sentence := ""
  GenNounPhrase (true, Sentence)
  GenWord (VerbForms, Sentence)
  GenNounPhrase (false, Sentence)
  put Sentence, "."
  delay (1000)
end loop
```

Here are some typical sentences generated by the program. A considerable amount of additional programming would be required to create interesting prose.

```
The slow slow lollipop plays with a computer .
The locomotive points at the dusty car .
A car plays with a ferocious lollipop .
A lollipop bumps Carl .
Denise plays with a thirsty red young computer .
Carl points at a hippopotamus .
A hippopotamus goes to the small red young slow car .
```

Local Declarations

The body of a procedure can include declarations. For example, the procedure *GenWord* declares the variable *WordPos* and the procedure *GenArticle* declares the variable *RandArticle*. The constants and variables declared inside a procedure cannot be used outside the procedure. They are called *local variables*. Similarly, a constant declared within a procedure is called a *local constant*.

A procedure can use constants and variables declared outside it provided that the declarations appear before the procedure declaration in the program text. For example, the procedures *GenWord*, *GenArticle*, and so on, can make use of the arrays containing words: *Adjectives*, *Nouns*, *ProperNames*, and *VerbForms*. These are called *nonlocal* variables.

5.3 New Functions

Function declarations look similar to procedure declarations, but there are three differences that reflect the different roles of functions and procedures. First, we introduce the declaration with the keyword **function** instead of **procedure**. Second, functions must not have variable parameters. Third, a function must yield a result. We indicate the type of the result by writing it at the end of the function header. We use a **result** statement within the function to return the value of the result.

Example 5.12   Declaring a Boolean Function

The function *Even* returns the Boolean value **true** if its argument is an even integer and **false** otherwise.

```
function Even (N : int) : boolean
    result N mod 2 = 0
end Even
```

The following simple program illustrates the use of *Even*.

```
loop
  put "Enter a number (0 terminates):   "
  get Num
  exit when Num = 0
  if Even (Num) then
    put Num," is even."
  else
    put Num," is odd."
  end if
end loop
```

Example 5.12 illustrates the crucial differences between functions and procedures. A procedure call is a kind of statement; we call a procedure to cause an effect. In contrast, a function call is a kind of expression; we call a function to compute a value.

The function *Even* in Example 5.12 has an integer parameter and computes a Boolean value. The function *CenterString* in the next example has two parameters, a string and an integer, and it computes a string.

Example 5.13   A Function with Two Parameters

The function *CenterString* returns a string centered in a field of given width.

```
function CenterString (Str : string, Width : int) : string
  const Gap := ( Width − length (Str)) div 2
  if Gap > 0 then
    result repeat (" ", Gap) + Str
  else
    result Str
  end if
end CenterString
```

For example, the following code displays the string **"HELP"** approximately at the center of the screen. We assume that the screen has 25 rows and 80 columns.

```
cls
locate (12, 1)
put CenterString ("HELP", 80)
```

Referential Transparency

An important property of functions in mathematics is that the value of an application depends only on the value of the arguments. If x and y are valid arguments for a function f, then $x = y$ implies $f(x) = f(y)$. This principle, called *referential transparency*, underlies numerous algebraic identities such as

$$f(x) - f(x) \;=\; 0$$
$$f(x) + f(x) \;=\; 2f(x)$$

Using nonlocal variables, it is possible to write Turing functions that do not have this property.

```
var NonLocal := 0

function Bad (Local : int) : int
    NonLocal += 1
    result 2 * Local + NonLocal
end Bad

put Bad (3) + Bad (3)
```

Looking at the last line of this program, we would predict that the number displayed would be even. Whatever the value of $Bad\,(3)$, if we compute it twice and add the results, we should get $2 \times Bad\,(3)$, which must be an even number. But, if we run the program, it actually displays 15. What has happened?

The first time $Bad\,(3)$ is evaluated, $NonLocal$ is zero. Within the body of Bad, Turing adds 1 to $NonLocal$ and adds this value to the result, giving $2 \times 3 + 1 = 7$. At the second call, $NonLocal$ is 1, and it is this value that is incremented, giving 2, and added to the result, giving 8. Consequently, the program displays $7 + 8 = 15$. We say that the function Bad has *side effects*.

Style

Functions such as Bad cause confusion and are likely to introduce errors into programs. In almost all circumstances, the functions we use in a program should behave like mathematical functions. There are a few situations in which it may be desirable for a function to use the value of a nonlocal variable, but a function should never change the value of a nonlocal variable.

5.4 Recursive Subprograms

A recursive subprogram is a subprogram that calls itself. Recursion is a simple idea with profound consequences. In principle, any programming task can be performed without recursion. In practice, we can often use recursive subprograms to obtain simple and elegant solutions to difficult problems.

5.4.1   Recursive Definitions

Suppose that we write $S(n)$ to stand for the sum of the first n natural numbers. For example, $S(4) = 1+2+3+4 = 10$. There are several ways in which we could define the function S. For instance, we could use as a definition the equation

$$S(n) = 1 + 2 + \cdots + n.$$

Although the meaning of this equation is intuitively clear, its exact meaning depends on a precise interpretation of the three dots. In attempting to eliminate the dots, we might notice that

$$S(n-1) = 1 + \cdots + (n-1)$$

and

$$S(n) = 1 + \cdots + (n-1) + n.$$

From these, we can deduce that

$$S(n) = S(n-1) + n$$

but this is not sufficient for a definition. For instance:

$$
\begin{aligned}
S(3) &= S(2) + 3 \\
&= S(1) + 2 + 3 \\
&= S(0) + 1 + 2 + 3 \\
&= ?
\end{aligned}
$$

To obtain a complete definition, we need a value for $S(0)$:

$$S(n) = \begin{cases} 0, & \text{if } n = 0; \\ S(n-1) + n, & \text{if } n > 0. \end{cases}$$

The definition gives the expected value for $S(n)$ whenever $n \geq 0$. We can therefore accept it as a definition of the function S. It is a *recursive* definition because S appears both on the left and on the right of "=". It is not a circular definition because one of the phrases on the right does not mention S.

It is important to realize that we may have to apply the definition several times to obtain a single value. For example, one application of the definition gives the value of $S(2)$ as $S(1) + 2$. We now need a second application to obtain $S(1) = S(0) + 1$ and a third to obtain $S(0) = 0$. Putting these together gives $S(2) = 0 + 1 + 2 = 3$.

5.4.2   Recursion in Programs

It is straightforward to translate a recursive definition into a Turing function. The following Turing function, called *Sum*, computes values of the mathematical function S.

```
function Sum (N : int) : int
   if N = 0 then
      result 0
   else
      result Sum (N − 1) + N
   end if
end Sum
```

The function *Sum* yields the results we expect:

$$Sum\,(0) \longrightarrow 0$$
$$Sum\,(4) \longrightarrow 10$$

The function *Sum* is recursive because its body contains a call to *Sum* itself. It has three properties that are shared by all recursive subprograms. First, there is a simple case that is solved without a recursive call. In *Sum*, the simple case is the **then** part of the if statement. Second, there is also a more complicated case that is solved with a recursive call. In *Sum*, the complicated case is the **else** part of the if statement. Third, the problem the recursive call solves is always "smaller" or "simpler" in some sense than the original problem. Function *Sum* computes the value of $Sum\,(N-1)$ to obtain the value of $Sum\,(N)$; $Sum\,(N-1)$ is a smaller problem than $Sum\,(N)$ because $N-1$ is smaller than N. If the recursive problem was not simpler than the original problem, the function would go on calling itself forever.

There is a resemblance between recursion and mathematical induction. For example, we can prove by induction that $Sum\,(N) = N\,(N+1)/2$ by proving first that $Sum\,(0) = 0$. Then, assuming the result for $Sum\,(N-1)$, we can derive it for $Sum\,(N)$. In both the recursive function and the inductive proof, there is a simple *base case* and an *inductive step* from one value to the next.

Example 5.14   Using Recursion in Program Design

In Example 3.4, we considered the problem of determining whether a string was a palindrome. This is a problem we can solve easily by recursion provided that we start by defining "palindrome" in a recursive way. The first important property of a palindrome is that its first and last letters are the same. The second property is that the letters between the first and last letters *also form a palindrome*. The first version of the recursive definition is as follows: A string is a palindrome if its first and last letters are the same and the letters in between them form a palindrome.

This is not quite good enough because it has no "simple" case. The simple case for palindromes is that every string with fewer than two characters is a palindrome. The complete recursive definition is: A string is a palindrome if either (a) it has zero or one characters or (b) its first and last letters are the same and the letters in between them form a palindrome. This definition is all we need to write a recursive function that tests for palindromes.

```
function IsPalindrome (S : string) : boolean
    result length (S) ≤ 1
        or S (1) = S (∗) and IsPalindrome (S (2 .. ∗ −1))
end IsPalindrome
```

The function *IsPalindrome* depends on the fact that Turing does not evaluate the second operand of "or" if the first operand is true, as we saw in Section 3.3.2. In the function *IsPalindrome*, if the length of the string S is 0 or 1, the expressions after "or" do not get evaluated. We can use the following code to test *IsPalindrome*.

```
var TrialString : string
loop
    put "Enter a string:   " ..
    get TrialString : ∗
    exit when TrialString = "stop"
    if IsPalindrome (TrialString) then
        put TrialString," is a palindrome."
    else
        put TrialString," is not a palindrome."
    end if
end loop
```

Here are some results from this program:

```
Enter a string:    level
level is a palindrome.
Enter a string:    palindrome
palindrome is not a palindrome.
Enter a string:    amanaplanacanalpanama
amanaplanacanalpanama is a palindrome.
Enter a string:    stop
```

If we add the statement

```
put "Testing " S
```

to the function *IsPalindrome* before the **result** statement, the program displays each application of the function. Displays of this kind provide useful insight into the mechanism of recursion.

Recursive Tricks

It is easy to understand the principle of a recursive function, but it is sometimes hard to see how the function works. This is because the program uses intermediate results that do not appear explicitly in the code. For example, we might paraphrase the computations involved in the evaluation of *IsPalindrome* (`"level"`) as follows:

$$length \, (\texttt{"level"}) = 5 \geq 1$$
$$\texttt{"level"} \, (1) = \texttt{"level"} \, (5) = \texttt{"l"}$$
$$length \, (\texttt{"eve"}) = 3 \geq 1$$
$$\texttt{"eve"} \, (1) = \texttt{"eve"} \, (3) = \texttt{"e"}$$
$$length \, (\texttt{"v"}) = 1$$
$$\Rightarrow \texttt{"v"} \text{ is a palindrome}$$
$$\Rightarrow \texttt{"eve"} \text{ is a palindrome}$$
$$\Rightarrow \texttt{"level"} \text{ is a palindrome}$$

The hidden intermediate values sometimes give rise to puzzling behavior, as the following example shows.

Example 5.15   A Recursive Trick

The procedure *Backwards* reads numbers until the user enters zero. It then displays the numbers in reverse order.

```
procedure Backwards
    var N : int
    get N
    if N > 0 then
        Backwards
        put N, " " ..
    end if
end Backwards
```

To use *Backwards*, we write a program that calls it:

```
put "Enter numbers:   " ..
Backwards
```

When we run the program and enter the data *4 7 5 2 0*, the results look like this:

```
Enter numbers: 4 7 5 2 0
2 5 7 4
```

To understand how *Backwards* works, we start by *assuming* that it works correctly. In other words, it reads numbers until it reads a zero and it then displays the numbers in reverse order. Next, look at the body of *Backwards* and assume that the number read by the **get** statement is not zero. In this case, *Backwards* performs three actions:

> get *N*
> *Backwards*
> put *N*

Since we are assuming that *Backwards* works, the effect of these three statements is to read a number *N*, read numbers until zero and display them in reverse order, and display *N*. Thus the number read first is displayed last. This accounts for the reverse order. Furthermore, when *Backwards* reads zero, it does nothing, which is why zero terminates the process.

5.4.3   Simplifying by Recursion

Recursion, used appropriately, is a flexible tool with many applications. Programming tasks that initially appear quite difficult often have straightforward recursive solutions. The crucial step is to recognize the pattern that leads to a recursive solution.

Example 5.16   Recursive Definition of a Counter

Cars have an odometer that indicates the number of miles or kilometers the car has traveled. The odometer looks something like Figure 5.4, which shows the odometer of a car that has traveled 15,724 kilometers.

The problem we consider in this example is how to increment the display. Since we can represent the display as an array of digits, the problem is to write a procedure that alters such an array. The difficulty is that, when the last digit is a 9, a carry is necessary, and the carries may propagate. For example, if the current reading

6	5	4	3	2	1
0	1	5	7	2	4

Figure 5.4   The Odometer of a Car

is 15,999, the procedure must change it to 16,000. The problem is not easy to solve with loops, but it is straightforward if we use recursion.

First, we declare a suitable type for the counter. As the small numbers at the top of the diagram suggest, the components of the counter are numbered from right to left. The first component corresponds to the rightmost box of the display:

> const *MaxDigits* := 6
> type *CounterType* : array 1 .. *MaxDigits* of 0 .. 9

Next, we write a procedure that increments a particular column of the counter. The call *Increment* (*Counter*, *Digit*) adds 1 to component *Digit* of the counter and performs a carry if necessary. If the current value of *Counter* (*Digit*) is less than 9, *Increment* simply adds 1 to it. If the value is 9, *Increment* sets it to zero and executes the recursive call *Increment* (*Counter*, *Digit* + 1).

> procedure *Increment* (var *Counter* : *CounterType*, *Digit* : 1 .. 6)
>   if *Digit* ≤ *MaxDigits* then
>   if *Counter* (*Digit*) = 9 then
>   *Counter* (*Digit*) := 0
>   *Increment* (*Counter*, *Digit* + 1)
>   else
>   *Counter* (*Digit*) += 1
>   end if
>   end if
> end *Increment*

When the counter reaches 999999, the carry will propagate all the way across and call *Increment* (*Counter*, 7). In this case, *Increment* does nothing because there is no digit in the seventh position. The effect is that the counter resets to 000000.

The next procedure displays a value of a counter:

> procedure *Display* (*Counter* : *CounterType*)
>   for decreasing *Digit* : *MaxDigits* .. 1
>   put *Counter* (*Digit*) : 2 ..
>   end for
>   put ""
> end *Display*

Finally, the main program initializes a counter and then calls the procedures *Display* and *Increment* to show the changing value of the counter.

> var *Kilometers* : *CounterType*
> for *Digit* : 1 .. *MaxDigits*
>   *Kilometers* (*Digit*) := 0

```
    end for
    loop
```
     Display (*Kilometers*)
     Increment (*Kilometers*, 1)
     delay (200)
     exit when *hasch*
    end loop

In this example, we have used recursion to solve a tricky problem in a simple and elegant way. The key to understanding the procedure *Increment* is to focus on what it says rather than how it works. Its purpose is to increment the current digit; if the current digit is 9, it is necessary to increment the next digit. That is all there is to it.

5.5 Rules for Subprograms

The first four sections of this chapter provide a general introduction to subprograms but do not describe the precise rules for declaring and calling subprograms. In this section, we present subprograms from a more formal point of view, with complete explanations of the rules that govern their use.

5.5.1 Declarations and Scopes for Subprograms

Turing does not allow subprogram declarations inside statements or subprograms. Subprogram declarations are allowed in the main program and in modules. (Section 10.1 describes modules.)

Subprogram declarations may be interleaved with other declarations and statements in the main program. It is usually best, however, to put all of the subprogram declarations before any of the statements of the main program. Programs are easy to understand if they have a simple structure.

The freedom to declare subprograms between statements is sometimes useful, but it must be used with care. Initialization statements, for instance, might be included with declarations at the beginning of the program.

The declaration of a subprogram must appear before any calls to the subprogram, in accordance with Turing's general "declaration before use" rule. For this purpose, Turing considers the header of the subprogram to be its declaration. Consequently, recursive calls are allowed. The rule does not allow mutually recursive subprograms to be declared. These require "forward" declarations, described in Section 5.5.2.

Within a subprogram, we can use the names of any constants, variables, types, or subprograms that are declared before the subprogram. When a name is declared outside a subprogram and used inside it, we say that the name is *imported* into the subprogram. The more imported names there are in a subprogram, the harder it is to understand. Although some names must be imported, we should try to keep the number of imported names as small as possible.

Turing allows, but does not require, a subprogram to have an *import list*. The import list consists of the keyword "import" followed by a list of the names declared outside the subprogram but used inside it. If there is an import list, it must appear immediately after the subprogram header. An import list is a form of documentation; it provides a reader with a list of the names that a subprogram uses but does not declare.

Example 5.17   Using an Import List

The following declarations occur near the beginning of a large program:

```
var Entries := 0
type Item : real
var Store : array 1 .. 10 of Item
```

Later in the program, we write a procedure, *Insert*, that refers to the variables *Store* and *Entries*. Turing does not require the import list that we include in the following declaration of *Insert*, but it warns anybody reading the declaration that these names are declared elsewhere.

```
procedure Insert (This : Item)
  import Store, var Entries
  var I := 1
  loop
    if I > Entries then
      Entries += 1
      Store (Entries) := This
      exit
    elsif Store (I) = This then
      put "Error:  duplicate entry."
      exit
    else
      I += 1
    end if
  end loop
end Insert
```

If an imported variable is altered within the subprogram, its name should be preceded by var in the import list. If the name of an imported variable is not preceded by var, the variable can be accessed but not altered within the subprogram. In Example 5.17, the procedure *Insert* alters the variable *Entries*. The import list therefore contains the item "var *Entries*".

If an import list contains a name that has not yet been declared, the name must be preceded by the keyword forward. A name in an import list cannot be preceded by both var and forward.

5.5.2   Forward Declarations for Subprograms

The "declare before use" rule of Turing requires us to declare an entity — constant, variable, type, procedure, or function — before we use it. Sometimes this rule is too restrictive. Suppose that procedure P calls procedure Q and that Q calls P. This situation is called *indirect recursion* or *mutual recursion*. It is clear that we cannot declare P and Q without violating the "declare before use" rule. Turing provides *forward declarations* for mutually recursive procedures.

A forward declaration separates the two parts of a subprogram, its header and its body. As soon as the Turing compiler has read the header of a subprogram, it can validate calls to the subprogram. It does not need to read the body of the subprogram until the calls are executed.

Example 5.18   Mutual Recursion with Forward Declarations

Suppose we need a function that checks the format of a string. The string must represent an expression consisting of a letter and an argument. The argument is the empty string or else it is an expression enclosed in parentheses. Legal strings include `"f"`, `"f(x)"`, `"f(g(x))"`, and so on. We declare two functions, *IsExpr* and *IsArg*, to recognize expressions and arguments. Since an expression may have an argument, *IsExpr* must call *IsArg*. Also, since an argument may contain an expression, *IsArg* must call *IsExpr*. We write a forward declaration for *IsArg*, a normal declaration for *IsExpr*, and finally we provide the body of *IsArg*.

```
forward function IsArg (S : string) : boolean
   import forward IsExpr

function IsExpr (S : string) : boolean
   const Letters := "abcdefghijklmnopqrstuvwxyz"
   result length (S) ≥ 1 and index (Letters, S (1)) > 0 and IsArg (S (2 .. *))
end IsExpr
```

```
body function IsArg
  result S = "" or
    length (S) ≥ 3
    and S (1) = ",("
    and S(*) = ")"
    and IsExpr (S (2 .. * −1))
end IsArg
```

The forward declaration in Example 5.18 consists of the keyword **forward** followed by the header of *IsArg*. Although Turing does not normally require an import list for a subprogram, it does require an import list in a forward declaration. In this case, the only thing that *IsArg* imports is *IsExpr*, but *IsExpr* has not yet been declared. Consequently, it appears in the import list as "forward *IsExpr*", indicating that its declaration comes later.

Consider the evaluation of

$IsExpr$ ("f(g(x))")

The string "f(g(x))" has more than one character, and the first character is a letter. Consequently, *IsExpr* calls

$IsArg$ ("(g(x))")

The string "(g(x))" is not empty, but it satisfies the first three conditions after the **or** in *IsArg*. Therefore, *IsArg* calls *IsExpr* to check that "g(x)" is an expression. Evaluation continues with the calls:

$IsExpr$ ("g(x)")
$IsArg$ ("(x)")
$IsExpr$ ("x")
$IsArg$ ("")

The last call returns **true**. The other calls — there are five of them altogether — are waiting for a reply. Each in turn receives the reply **true** and passes it back up the chain. Finally, the original call returns **true**.

5.5.3 Type Equivalence and Assignability

There are two situations in which Turing must check that two types are equivalent. In an assignment statement, the type of the variable on the left must be equivalent to the type of the expression on the right. In a subprogram call, the type of the argument must be equivalent to the type of a **var** parameter.

There are six situations in which types are equivalent.

- The types are the same standard type.
- The types are subranges with equal first and last values.
- The types are strings with equal maximum lengths.
- The types are arrays with equivalent index types and equivalent base types.
- The types both name the same type.
- One type names the other.

The following declarations illustrate the type equivalence rules for arrays.

```
type T1 : array 1 .. 3 of real
type T2 : array 1 .. 3 of real
type T3 : T1
type T4 : T1
```

The types $T1$ and $T2$ are equivalent because they are arrays with the same index and base types. The types $T1$ and $T3$ are equivalent because $T3$ is a name for $T1$. The types $T3$ and $T4$ are equivalent because they are names for the same type.

Assignability

Assignability is another relationship between types. The statement $V := E$ is legal if the type of E is assignable to the type of V. Similarly, the call $P(E)$ is legal if the type of the argument E is assignable to the type of the corresponding constant parameter.

The relationships of equivalence and assignability are the same except in one situation. Suppose that T_V is the type of V and T_E is the type of E, then $V := E$ is legal if either T_V is equivalent to T_E or T_V is **real** and T_E is **int**. In the second case, Turing implicitly converts the expression E to **real** before performing the assignment. Similarly, when an **int** argument is passed to a **real** parameter, Turing implicitly converts the argument to **real** before passing it to the subprogram.

5.6   Preconditions and Postconditions

Subprograms may have preconditions and postconditions. These are similar to the assertions and invariants described in Section 3.3.3. Preconditions and postconditions, like assertions and invariants, are useful in two ways. They help us to detect errors quickly, and they provide useful documentation.

A precondition consists of the keyword "**pre**" and a Boolean expression that must be true on entry to the subprogram. A postcondition consists of the keyword "**post**" and a Boolean expression that must be true on exit from the subprogram.

Example 5.19   Using Preconditions and Postconditions

The procedure *Divide* below is based on Example 3.3 on page 84. Given integers *Dividend* and *Divisor*, it computes the quotient *Quot* and the remainder *Rem* that are obtained when *Dividend* is divided by *Divisor*. It has a precondition that requires the arguments to be positive and a postcondition that formally expresses the result of the division.

```
procedure Divide (Dividend, Divisor : int, var Quot, Rem : int)
    pre Dividend ≥ 0 and Divisor > 0
    post Dividend = Quot * Divisor + Rem and 0 ≤ Rem and Rem < Divisor
    Quot := 0
    Rem := Dividend
    loop
        invariant Dividend = Quot * Divisor + Rem
        exit when Rem < Divisor
        Quot += 1
        Rem -= Divisor
    end loop
end Divide
```

A precondition places a requirement on the caller of the procedure. The precondition of *Divide* says, in effect: If you provide me with two positive integers, I will perform my designated task. The postcondition places a requirement on the procedure itself. The postcondition of *Divide* says, in formal language, that the values of *Quot* and *Rem* are the correct results of division.

Turing evaluates the precondition on entry to the procedure and the postcondition before returning from the procedure. If either condition is false, Turing stops and issues an appropriate error message.

The postcondition for a function usually says something about the result of the function. The result of a Turing function does not usually have a name but, for the purpose of writing a postcondition, we declare the name of the result in the header of the function. This result name can be used in the postcondition but nowhere else in the body of the function.

Example 5.20   A Postcondition for a Function

The function *GCD* computes the greatest common divisor of its integer arguments M and N. Both arguments must be positive.

```
function GCD (M, N : int) G : int
    pre M > 0 and N > 0
    post M mod G = 0 and N mod G = 0
```

```
         var Mc := M
         var Nc := N
         loop
            const T := Mc mod Nc
            exit when T = 0
            Mc := Nc
            Nc := T
         end loop
         result Nc
      end GCD
```

Variables in Preconditions and Postconditions

The preconditions and postconditions of a subprogram must come before the declarations of local variables. It follows from Turing's "declaration before use" rule that the only variables we can use in a precondition or postcondition are parameters and imported variables. From the point of view of style, it is best to use only parameters in preconditions and postconditions.

The value of a variable parameter of a procedure may change during execution of the procedure. When the postcondition is evaluated, parameters have their final values. In the following program, the parameter N has the value 1 when the postcondition is executed.

```
      procedure P (var N : int)
         post N > 0
         N += 1
      end P
      var S := 0
      P (S)
```

Sometimes we need to mention both the initial and the final values of a parameter in a postcondition. Turing provides the init statement for this purpose. The init statement has the form:

```
      init  ▭  :=  ▭
```

The first box stands for a variable name that is not declared anywhere else in the procedure. The second box stands for a parameter name. The statement assigns the initial value of the parameter to the variable. The variable can be used only in a postcondition.

The following version of the procedure P has a postcondition that says that the value of the parameter N must increase when the subprogram is called.

```
procedure P (varN : int)
   init OldN := N
   post N > OldN
   N += 1
end P
var S := 0
P (S)
```

There may be one or more init statements in a procedure. They must all precede the postcondition. We can use the variables declared in an init statement only in the postcondition.

Limitations

There are some limitations of preconditions and postconditions. Consider the following version of the function GCD from Example 5.20.

```
function GCD (M, N : int) G : int
   pre M > 0 and N > 0
   post M mod G = 0 and N mod G = 0
   result 1
end GCD
```

This version of GCD will always satisfy its postcondition but it is clearly useless for computing a greatest common divisor. The problem is that the postcondition of GCD says only that G divides M and N; it does not say that G is the *greatest* common divisor of M and N. The postcondition that we would like to write is: G is a divisor of both M and N and, if K is also a divisor of both M and N, then $K \leq G$. The technical problem that prevents us from doing this is that we cannot write quantifiers in Turing expressions.

A similar problem arises with the invariant of the loop in GCD. The invariant on which the loop is based is actually

$$GCD (M, N) = GCD (Mc, Nc)$$

but if we included this invariant in the declaration, the function would loop forever.

A further problem is that it may be impossible to formalize the concepts we want to express. The postcondition of a procedure that displays the value of an array on the screen, for example, might be: The array can easily be read from the screen.

5.7   Summary

Numbers in parentheses refer to sections where material appears.

▶ A procedure has an effect (5.1).

▶ A function returns a value (5.1).

▶ Procedures and functions are collectively called *subprograms* (5.1).

▶ A subprogram has a declaration consisting of a *header* and a *body* (5.2). After a subprogram has been declared, it can be *invoked* or *called*.

▶ A subprogram starts with a *header* (5.2). The header of a subprogram declaration includes the name of the subprogram and the name and type of each of its parameters. There can be any number of parameters, and a parameter may have any type.

▶ A constant parameter is a constant initialized by the value of the corresponding argument within the subprogram body (5.2). It may not be altered within the body of the subprogram.

▶ A variable parameter is another name for the corresponding argument (5.2). It may be altered within the body of the subprogram.

▶ Arguments must match parameters in number and type (5.2).

▶ The return statement may be used within the body of a procedure (5.2).

▶ The header of a function declaration must include the type returned by the function (5.3).

▶ The result statement must occur at least once within the body of a function (5.3).

▶ Import lists are required in forward declarations (5.5.2).

▶ A subprogram may have a precondition and a postcondition (5.6).

▶ A precondition contains a Boolean expression that must be true on entry to the subprogram (5.6).

▶ A postcondition contains a Boolean expression that must be true on exit from the subprogram (5.6).

▶ The header of a function may name the result of the function (5.6). The result name can be used in the postcondition but nowhere else.

▶ A procedure may contain init statements between the header and the postcondition (5.6). Each init statement declares a variable whose value is the initial value of a var parameter. The variable can be used in the postcondition but not elsewhere in the procedure.

5.8 Exercises

5.1 Use random number generators in programs that simulate:

(a) tossing a coin;

(b) throwing a pair of dice;

(c) shuffling a deck of 52 playing cards.

5.2 There are many ways in which we can improve the simulation of Example 5.6. Here are some suggestions.

(a) Try varying the population and the mortality probabilities.

(b) Record the ages at which Memes die. The program should display a matrix showing life expectancy for each gene combination. The values should be related to the probabilities in the mortality matrix.

(c) Assume that the left gene controls "attraction" between Memes. For example, Memes with the same left gene might be more likely to produce offspring. What effect does this have on the gene pool?

5.3 It is sometimes convenient to store dates in the form YYMMDD, using six digits. This representation is compact and easy to sort. Write a function that converts dates to this form from the form provided by the predefined procedure *date*. For example, the date **24 May 94** would be converted to **940524**.

5.4 Write a function that converts the time returned by the predefined procedure *time* into the number of seconds since midnight.

5.5 Write a procedure that, given integers *Low* and *High*, obtains an integer *N* from the user and checks that *N* satisfies the condition $Low \leq N \leq High$. The procedure should display a message of the form

    `"Please enter a number between 0 and 100:"`

and should loop until it obtains an acceptable reply.

5.6 Write a procedure that has the same effect as *ToUpper* in Example 5.10. Do not use a `return` statement.

5.7   The primitive sentence generator of Example 5.11 can be improved in various ways. Try some of the following ideas.

    (a) Add more words to the word stores.

    (b) Add to the program's repertoire of sentence structures.

    (c) Qualify the verbs with adverbs such as "quickly" and "probably".

    (d) Experiment with the constants that determine the probability of various events.

    (e) Enhance the program so that it uses "An" or "an" when appropriate, and include some words that begin with vowels.

5.8   Write a program that drills the user in arithmetic. The program should display a simple arithmetic problem with random operands, ask the user for the correct solution, and then tell the user whether the solution was correct. A typical problem might be: $5 \times 13 = ?$.

5.9   Write a function that changes the extension of a file name. The first argument is a file name and the second is the desired extension. The result returned by the function is the new file name. Here are some examples of the function in use.

    ChangeExt (`"results.dat"`, `"bak"`) $\longrightarrow$ `"results.bak"`
    ChangeExt (`"simpname"`, `"txt"`) $\longrightarrow$ `"simpname.txt"`

5.10   The value of $N!$ (N factorial) is $N! = 1 \times 2 \times \cdots \times N$. Write two functions that compute $N!$, one using a loop or for statement and the other using recursion. Compare the execution times of the two functions.

5.11   The Fibonacci sequence $1, 1, 2, 3, 5, 8, 13, \ldots$ is defined by

$$F_0 = 1$$
$$F_1 = 1$$
$$F_n = F_{n-1} + F_{n-2}$$

Write two functions that compute F_n, one using a loop or for statement and the other using recursion. Compare the execution times of the two functions.

5.12 Complete each of the following functions with a body that satisfies the postcondition.

(a) function $ExtendName\,(R,E:\text{string})\,S:\text{string}$
post $index(R,".")=0$ and $S=R+"."+E$ or $S=R$

. . . .

end $ExtendName$

(b) function $Bigger\,(M,N:\text{int})\,R:\text{int}$
post $M\geq N$ and $R=M$ or $M<N$ and $R=N$

. . . .

end $Bigger$

(c) function $Abs\,(X:\text{real})\,Y:\text{real}$
post $X\geq 0$ and $Y=X$ or $X<0$ and $Y=-X$

. . . .

end Abs

(d) function $Quadratic\,(A,B,C:\text{real})\,X:\text{real}$
pre $B\neq 0$
post $B*B<4.0*A*C$ or $A*X*X+B*X+C=0.0$

. . . .

end $Quadratic$

(e) function $IntSqrt\,(S:\text{int})\,R:\text{int}$
pre $S\geq 0$
post $R=floor(sqrt(S))$
. . . .   % Do not use $floor$ and $sqrt$ here!
end $IntSqrt$

Chapter 6

Input and Output

The basic tools for accomplishing input and output in Turing are the **get** and **put** statements. These statements suffice for small programs that need no more than **get** to read from the keyboard and **put** to display results on the screen.

There are various ways in which we can enhance this simple behavior. A well-written program should validate its input. Validation ensures that the program will not behave unpredictably or crash when it receives erroneous input.

In addition, there are situations in which **get** and **put** are inadequate. In such situations, for input, Turing provides subprograms to read one character at a time and to tell whether a key has been pressed. For output, Turing provides subprograms that clear the screen, change colors, and display characters anywhere on the screen. We can use these subprograms to construct programs that make full use of the interactive capabilities of the computer.

As well as reading from the keyboard and writing to the screen, many programs access disk files. Since the operations of reading from and writing to a disk file are conceptually similar to using keyboards and screens, Turing uses modified forms of the **get** and **put** statements. Other Turing statements "open" files before we use them and "close" them when we have finished with them. Section 6.3 describes the use of disk files.

6.1 Managing the Keyboard

The keyboard is the principal input device for most applications. It is also the only input device that is described in this book. There are other input devices, such as mice and joysticks, but current versions of Turing do not support them.

6.1.1 Validating Input

A program can ask the user to enter a number, or a name, or another kind of value, but it cannot force the user to press particular keys. For example, the user might enter !@# instead of 123 in response to a request for a number. Consequently, a program should always check as thoroughly as possible that the user's response is acceptable. This is called *validating the input*.

There are limits to the amount of validation a program can do. If the user intends to enter 12.34 but actually enters 13.24, the program cannot detect the error and the results will probably be incorrect. Our objective in this section is to ensure that the program can never fail as a result of incorrect input.

In the next example, we consider the possibility that the user might enter data that is unacceptable to the program. The program must perform validation before making further use of the data provided.

Example 6.1   Validating the Input

A program stores part descriptions as strings of 20 characters. Here is an extract from the program:

```
const DescLength := 20
var PartDesc : string (DescLength)
put "Enter part description:  " ..
get PartDesc : *
```

This is a bad piece of code. If the user responds to the request with

```
"copper plated frying pan"
```

the program fails because the input string contains more than 20 characters. There are several alternative ways of writing the code. One way is to accept a long reply but to copy at most 20 characters into the variable *PartDesc*. The predefined function *min* provides a convenient way of doing this. The value of $min(x, y)$ is the smaller of x and y.

```
const DescLength := 20
var PartDesc : string (DescLength)
var Reply : string
put "Enter part description:  " ..
get Reply : *
PartDesc := Reply (1 .. min (length (Reply), DescLength))
```

An alternative approach is to reject a reply that is too long and to ask the user to try again:

```
const DescLength := 20
var PartDesc : string (DescLength)
var Reply : string
loop
  put "Enter part description:  " ..
  get Reply : *
  if length (Reply) ≤ DescLength then
    PartDesc := Reply
    exit
  else
    put "Please choose a description with no more than ",
      DescLength," characters."
  end if
end loop
```

We cannot decide which of these methods is better without knowing more about the ways in which the program will be used. Truncating the reply to twenty characters is convenient for the user, who does not have to choose abbreviations, but truncation might lead to ambiguities. For example, the program would not be able to tell the difference between "stainless steel plated teaspoons" and "stainless steel plated cauldrons".

A program that rejects descriptions with more than twenty characters has moved some responsibility back to the user. This is permissible, but it should be avoided when possible. Making routine decisions is an appropriate task for a computer. In this case, the best solution would be a program that accepts descriptions of any length and stores all the characters. The second best solution would be a program that stores only some of the characters and reports ambiguous descriptions to the user.

Reading Numbers Safely

Validation of numbers is particularly difficult. It is easy enough to check that a number falls within a permitted range — that is the point of Exercise 5.5 on page 163. Range checking is of no use, however, if the user presses the letter "O" instead of the digit "0", or the letter "l" instead of the digit "1", or enters something unanticipated, such as "help". Any of these will make the program fail. Turing provides no easy solution for this problem, and other languages are no better.

We can avoid failure by writing **get** statements that read only strings. These **get** statements accept any keystrokes apart from a few special control characters. The price to pay for added security is that the programmer must do more work. Since Turing does not know what the input string represents, it cannot perform implicit conversions. Consequently, we must write the conversion code ourselves.

Example 6.2   Reading Numbers Safely

It is useful to have a procedure that reliably returns either an integer entered by the user or an indication that the user does not want to provide an integer. The procedure *GetInt*, declared below, prompts for input and reads a string. It accepts the ESC character or a string that can be converted to a positive integer, but nothing else.

```
procedure GetInt (Prompt : string, var IntReady : boolean, var IntValue : int)
   const ESC := chr (27)
   loop
      var Reply : string
      put Prompt ..
      get Reply : *
      if Reply = ESC then
         IntReady := false
         exit
      else
         var Pos := 1
         IntValue := 0
         loop
            exit when Pos > length (Reply)
            if index ("0123456789", Reply (Pos)) > 0 then
               IntReady := true
               IntValue := 10 * IntValue + ord (Reply (Pos)) − ord ("0")
               Pos += 1
            else
```

```
            IntReady := false
               exit
            end if
         end loop
         if IntReady then
            exit
         else
            put "Invalid number: please try again."
         end if
      end if
   end loop
end GetInt
```

When *GetInt* is called, it displays the parameter *Prompt* as a request on the screen. When *GetInt* returns, *IntReady* is true if the user entered a number and false otherwise. If *IntReady* is true, *IntValue* holds the number entered; otherwise it is undefined. A typical application of *GetInt* might be coded in the following way.

```
loop
   var GotIt : boolean
   var Height : int
   GetInt("How high is it?  ", GotIt, Height)
   exit when not GotIt
   put Height
end loop
```

A typical dialogue with *GetInt* would look like this:

```
How high is it? &*
Invalid number: please try again.
How high is it? 78
78
How high is it? ^]
```

The user responded to the third question by pressing the ESC key, which has the same effect as holding down the CTRL key and pressing "]". This is why Turing displays ESC as "^]".

The interesting thing about *GetInt* is its complexity. It is not unusual for interactive programs to have more code devoted to input validation and screen management than to the actual calculations. The exercises at the end of the chapter suggest that further improvements are possible.

6.1.2   Interactive Programming

For many applications, we need finer control of the keyboard than **get** can provide. Sometimes, we need a program that can respond to a single keystroke, such as "y" or "n". On other occasions, we need a program that performs calculations, or displays an image, until the user presses a key. The **get** statement is not suitable for either of these tasks because it suspends the program until the user has pressed the ENTER key. The predefined procedure *getch* solves both problems by responding to a single keystroke.

A typical use of *getch* looks like this:

```
var Ch : string (1)
getch (Ch)
```

When Turing executes this code, it suspends the program until the user presses a key. The value of *Ch* when *getch* returns depends on the key pressed. The program makes a decision based on the value of *Ch*. If the user is supposed to press "y" for "yes" or "n" for "no", the appropriate code would be

```
if Ch = "y" then
    ┌──────┐
    └──────┘
elsif Ch = "n" then
    ┌──────┐
    └──────┘
else
    put "Please enter 'y' or 'n'!"
```

The procedure *getch* provides more flexibility than this example suggests because it recognizes almost all of the keys of the keyboard, including ESC, BACKSPACE, the "F" command keys, and combinations such as shift–F4. The value of *ord* (*Ch*) is a number in the range $0 \ldots 255$ that identifies the keys pressed. The possible values of *ord* (*Ch*) are listed in Appendix E.

Example 6.3   Reading Special Keys

Suppose that we are writing a program that must respond to the ESC key, the F2 key, and the ENTER key but may ignore all other keys. Normally, Turing will display a symbol whenever a key is pressed. If the key is not one of the usual letter or digit keys, the symbol may confuse the user. To avoid the appearance of unexpected symbols on the screen, we use the predefined procedure *setscreen* with the argument "noecho". If the user may press any one of a number of keys, the program should use a **case** statement to choose an appropriate response. In the following program, the boxes stand for code that will be executed after the user has pressed the corresponding key.

```
const ESC := 27
const ENTER := 10
const F2 := 188
var Ch : string (1)
setscreen ("noecho")
getch (Ch)
case ord (Ch) of
  label ESC :
      ┌──────┐
      └──────┘
  label ENTER :
      ┌──────┐
      └──────┘
  label F2 :
      ┌──────┐
      └──────┘
  label :
      ┌──────┐
      └──────┘
end case
```

Detecting Keystrokes

The procedure *getch*, like the statement **get**, has an important limitation: it suspends the program and waits for the user to press a key. We cannot use *getch* or get if we are writing a program that continues to run until the user presses a key. The predefined Boolean function *hasch* is provided for just this purpose: it returns true if a key has been pressed.

Example 6.4   Using *hasch*

The following program tiles the screen of a PC with randomly colored rectangles. When the user presses a key, the program stops and clears the screen.

```
cls
loop
  exit when hasch
  var Row, Column, Shade : int
  randint (Row, 1, maxrow − 1)
  randint (Column, 1, maxcol)
  randint (Shade, 1, maxcolor)
  locate (Row, Column)
  color (Shade)
  put chr (219) ..
end loop
cls
```

The program also uses three other new functions. The predefined function *maxrow* returns the number of usable rows of characters on the screen; the predefined function *maxcol* returns the number of columns in a row; and the predefined function *maxcolor* returns the largest integer that can be used as a color on the system.

Turing does not discard the keystroke detected by *hasch*. Instead, the key pressed is made available to the next get statement or *getch* call. In the following code, the box stands for some action that the program performs repeatedly.

```
loop
    exit when hasch
    [        ]
end loop
var Reply : string
put "What next?   " ..
get Reply
```

This code contains two undesirable features. The character entered to stop the loop appears on the screen. To prevent this, we can write *setscreen* ("noecho"). In addition, the character will become the first character of *Reply*, which is not what the user expects. To prevent this, we use *getch* to "capture" the unwanted character. The following code incorporates these improvements:

```
setscreen ("noecho")
loop
    exit when hasch
    [        ]
end loop
var Ch : string (1)
getch (Ch)
var Reply : string
put "What next?   " ..
setscreen ("echo")
get Reply
```

6.2 Managing the Screen

If we want people to use our programs, we have to make them easy to use. Making a program easy to use is part of designing the user interface. Screen management is an important part of user interface design. The tools that Turing provides for managing the screen include the put statement and the predefined procedures *cls*, *locate*, and *setscreen*. The predefined procedures *color* and *colorback* control the colors of text and background, respectively.

The key to good screen management is careful use of the put and get statements and the predefined procedures *getch* and *locate*. Although we have discussed the put and get statements in previous sections, we briefly review their effects when they are used in conjunction with *locate*.

6.2.1 Screen Layout for Input

A get statement or a call to *getch* reads characters from the current cursor position. We can, for example, choose a particular area of the screen for input and read all information from that area. It is best *not* to choose the last row of a PC screen for input, however, because pressing the ENTER key when the cursor is on the bottom row makes all of the text on the screen scroll upwards.

Example 6.5   Reading Real Numbers

A program is required to read a positive real number from the keyboard. If the user enters a negative number, the program should display an error message and ask for another number. The bottom two rows of the screen are to be used for the dialogue with the user.

The procedure *GetReal* performs this task. It uses a loop that exits when the user has entered a positive real number. If the screen or window has 25 rows, the program will use row 24 to read the number and row 25 to report errors.

```
procedure GetReal (Message : string, var RealValue : real)
  const ErrorMessage := "Please enter a positive number."
  loop
    locate (maxrow − 1, 1)
    put ""
    locate (maxrow − 1, 1)
    put Message ..
    get RealValue
    exit when RealValue ≥ 0.0
    locate (maxrow, 1)
    put ErrorMessage ..
  end loop
  locate (maxrow, 1)
  put repeat (" ", length (ErrorMessage)) ..
end GetReal
```

The following code provides a simple test for *GetReal*.

```
loop
   var X : real
   GetReal ("Enter:   ", X)
   locate (10, 35)
   put X
end loop
```

In procedure *GetReal*, the statement

```
put ""
```

deletes all text to the right of the cursor on row *maxrow* − 1. We cannot use the same statement on row *maxrow* because it would cause text on the screen to scroll up. Instead, we use put statements that write only the text required, followed by " .. " to prevent scrolling.

Monitoring Input Characters

The **get** statement does not allow us to limit the length of an input string. However carefully we design the screen layout, a mischievous user can always make a mess of it by responding to **get** statements with very long strings. The only way to avoid this is to use *locate* and *getch* to control the precise position of every character displayed on the screen.

Example 6.6   Restricting the Length of an Input String

The procedure *GetString* reads a string of bounded length from the keyboard. As the user enters the string, it is displayed at a particular position on the screen.

The program indicates the length limit by shading the screen of the PC with ASCII character 176. We must ensure that the string returned by the program is exactly the same as the string displayed on the screen when ENTER is pressed.

The ASCII graphic characters have codes from 32 to 126. The procedure *GetString* ignores nongraphic characters and any characters entered after the specified length has been reached. It exits whenever the user presses ENTER.

```
const ENTER := chr (10)
const Shading := chr (176)
const MinGraphic := chr (32)
const MaxGraphic := chr (126)
```

```
procedure GetString (Row, FirstCol, Len : int, var Reply : string)
  locate (Row, FirstCol)
  put repeat (Shading, Len)
  Reply := ""
  var Col := FirstCol
  var Ch : string (1)
  loop
    locate (Row, Col)
    getch (Ch)
    exit when Ch = ENTER
    if MinGraphic ≤ Ch and Ch ≤ MaxGraphic
        and length (Reply) < Len then
      locate (Row, Col)
      put Ch ..
      Reply += Ch
      Col += 1
    end if
  end loop
end GetString
```

Before using the procedure, we call *setscreen* (`"noecho"`) to prevent the user's keystrokes from being echoed on the screen. The following code illustrates the use of *GetString*.

```
setscreen ("noecho")
loop
  var MyString : string
  GetString (10, 35, 10, MyString)
  locate (1, 1)
  put MyString
  put length (MyString)
end loop
```

Simplifying Data Entry

People tend to make mistakes when entering data. We can reduce the likelihood of mistakes by simplifying the task of data entry. For example, it is easier to select an option from a menu than it is to enter the name or number of the option. It often happens, however, that making things easier for the user has the opposite effect on the programmer. There is much more work involved in writing a user-friendly, menu-driven program than in writing a program that provides only a simple dialogue.

Example 6.7   A Simple Menu

The major feature of this example is the procedure *SelectOption*. We provide *SelectOption* with a position on the screen and an array of strings. The procedure returns with the number of the menu item selected by the user or with -1 if the user did not make a choice.

The first step is to declare constants for the keys we need. The user presses the up and down arrow keys to move the highlighting up and down the menu display, the ENTER key to indicate a selection, and the ESC key to exit without making a selection. The following codes for the arrow keys apply to PCs and compatibles:

```
const DownArrow := 208
const UpArrow := 200
const ENTER := 10
const ESC := 27
```

Next, we introduce a constant array that simplifies management of the screen colors. There are two modes for a displayed menu item: normal and highlighted. At any time, one item is highlighted. The program responds to the arrow keys by moving the highlighted area up and down over the items. For each mode, there are two fields: foreground and background. We therefore need a total of four colors, which we store in *ScreenColors*. The procedure *SetColors* calls the predefined procedures *color* and *colorback* to set the foreground and background colors.

```
type ModeType : enum (Normal, HiLite)
type FieldType : enum (Foreground, Background)
const ScreenColors : array ModeType, FieldType of int := init (15, 11, 15, 12)

procedure SetColors (Mode : ModeType)
    color (ScreenColors (Mode, FieldType . Foreground))
    colorback (ScreenColors (Mode, FieldType . Background))
end SetColors
```

The next procedure, *PutOption*, displays a menu item. Its purpose is to encapsulate three small operations that are frequently performed together: setting the screen colors, moving the cursor to a particular position, and displaying a string.

```
procedure PutOption (Mode : ModeType, Row, Col : int, Option : string)
    SetColors (Mode)
    locate (Row, Col)
    put Option ..
end PutOption
```

The procedure that does most of the work is called *SelectOption*. Its parameters are: *Row* and *Col*, which specify a position on the screen; *Menu*, which is an array of strings; and *Option*, which is the number of the item selected by the user when the procedure returns. An example of a menu array appears on page 180. The important point to notice is that both the number and length of the items are determined by the argument corresponding to *Menu* rather than by *SelectOptions* itself. Thus we can use *SelectOption* to select from any menu up to the maximum size of the screen.

The first action of the procedure is to display the menu at the correct position on the screen, using normal colors. The lower bound of the for statement is 1 because we do not display the first item. The first item is displayed at the beginning of the loop statement that follows the for statement. It is left to the caller to ensure that the menu fits on the screen.

```
procedure SelectOption (Row, Col : int,
     Menu : array 0 .. * of string (*), var Option : int)
  SetColors (ModeType . Normal)
  for Item : 1 .. upper (Menu)
     locate (Row + Item, Col)
     put Menu (Item) ..
  end for
```

The rest of the procedure is a loop that maintains the following invariant: The menu item *Option* is highlighted. The value of *Option* changes as the user presses the arrow keys. Each time it changes, the current item is redrawn with normal colors and the newly selected item is redrawn with highlighted colors.

The effect of the down arrow is to increase the value of *Option*. This corresponds to the convention of numbering the items from the top to the bottom of the menu. If the user presses the down arrow key with the final item highlighted, the highlight moves up to the first item. Similarly, pressing the up arrow key with the first item highlighted moves the highlight down to the last item.

If the ESC key is pressed, the loop terminates with $Option = -1$, indicating that the user does not want to make a selection. The ENTER key terminates the loop with the current value of *Option* unchanged. The procedure ignores keys other than the up and down arrows, ESC, and ENTER.

```
Option := 0
loop
  var Ch : string (1)
  PutOption (ModeType . HiLite, Row + Option, Col, Menu (Option))
  getch (Ch)
```

```
case ord (Ch) of
    label DownArrow :
        PutOption (ModeType . Normal, Row+Option, Col, Menu (Option))
        if Option = upper (Menu) then
            Option := 0
        else
            Option += 1
        end if
        PutOption (ModeType . HiLite, Row + Option, Col, Menu (Option))

    label UpArrow :
        PutOption (ModeType . Normal, Row+Option, Col, Menu (Option))
        if Option > 0 then
            Option −= 1
        else
            Option := upper (Menu)
        end if
        PutOption (ModeType . HiLite, Row + Option, Col, Menu (Option))

    label ESC :
        Option := −1
        exit

    label ENTER :
        exit
    label :

    end case
end loop
end SelectOption
```

The array *Menu*, declared below, is an example of the kind of data we should pass
to *SelectOption*. The blanks before and after the items make the menu easier to
read. The blanks following the items are important: if they were omitted, the
displayed item bars would have different lengths and the menu would have a
ragged right edge.

```
var Menu : array 0 .. 4 of string (10) :=
    init ("␣Jump␣␣␣␣␣", "␣Step␣␣␣␣␣", "␣Walk␣␣␣␣␣",
          "␣Leapfrog␣", "␣Swim␣␣␣␣␣")
```

Here is a simple loop that uses *SelectOption*. Each time the user makes a selection
or presses ESC, it displays the number of the selection near the bottom left of the
screen.

```
setscreen ("noecho")
setscreen ("nocursor")
loop
  var Option : int
  SelectOption (10, 30, Menu, Option)
  locate (20, 1)
  color (maxcolor)
  colorback (0)
  put Option
  exit when Option = −1
end loop
```

The code in Example 6.7 is only part of a menu system. A complete menu system requires the program to maintain a data structure that accurately represents the screen so that parts of the display can be erased and redisplayed as required. Graphical user interfaces are further extensions of these techniques.

6.3 Text Files

A *text file* is a sequence of characters stored on a disk. A program can read characters from a text file or write characters to a text file. From the point of view of the program, reading characters from a file is much like reading characters from the keyboard, and writing characters to a file is much like displaying characters on the screen. The get statement, used for reading from the keyboard, is used also for reading from a file. Similarly, the put statement is used to write characters to a file.

6.3.1 Reading Files

We can interact with the keyboard or screen at any point in the program. With text files, the situation is slightly different. Before we can use a file, we must *open* it, and after we have finished using the file, we must *close* it.

Example 6.8 Displaying the Contents of a File

The following program opens a file called `"astronom.dat"`, displays its contents on the screen, and then closes it.

The first step is to open the input file. In this example the file name is included as part of the program. In addition to the file name, we need a number for it. The number, called *Stream* in this case, is assigned by the open statement.

```
const FileName := "astronom.dat"
var Stream : int
var Line : string
open : Stream, FileName, get
if Stream = 0 then
    put "I cannot open ", FileName
    return
end if
```

The rest of the program consists of a loop that reads one line of the file at a time:

```
loop
    exit when eof (Stream)
    get : Stream, Line : *
    put Line
end loop
close : Stream
```

The statement

```
open : Stream, FileName, get
```

calls the operating system to determine whether the required file, `astronom.dat`, exists. If it does, the **open** statement gives it a *stream number* and assigns the stream number to the variable *Stream*. If the file cannot be opened, *Stream* will be set to zero, otherwise it will be set to a small nonzero value. The last argument of the **open** statement, **get**, says that we are opening the file in order to read information from it. Technically, we are opening `astronom.dat` in *input mode*.

If the program is unable to open the file, it displays a message and stops. The **open** statement may fail for any of the following reasons: the file is not in the current working directory; the file does not exist at all; too many files have been opened. The last failure occurs because Turing limits the number of files that may be open at one time to a small number, such as 10.

As long as it is not zero, the value of *Stream* is of no interest to the programmer. It is usually a small positive integer but it may occasionally be negative. After Turing executes the **close** statement, the stream number has no significance at all, although it remains an integer variable in the current scope.

If the **open** statement succeeds, the program uses a modified form of the **get** statement to read data from the file. The keyword **get** is followed by a colon, the stream number, a comma, and the variable list. In Example 6.8, the variable list consists of the single item, *Line* : *, indicating that we want an entire line of the file to be read into the variable *Line*.

The loop continues to read and display lines of the file until the Boolean expression *eof (Stream)* becomes true, indicating that we have reached the end of the file. After leaving the loop, the program uses the **close** statement to close the file. The keyword **close**, like **open**, is followed by a colon and the stream number.

It is important to remember that *all* operations performed on a file must include the stream number as an operand. The colon immediately following **get** or **put** tells Turing that the first item is a stream number.

6.3.2 Writing Files

Writing to a file is similar to reading from a file. The **open** statement has **put** instead of **get** as its third argument. Turing creates a new file with the given name. If a file with that name exists, Turing erases it. The stream number returned by **open** is zero only if a new file cannot be created.

Example 6.9   Copying a File

The program in this example copies the contents of one file to another file, one line at a time. The first step is to ask the user for the names of the input and output files. The second step is to attempt to open them.

```
var InFileName, OutFileName : string
var InStream, OutStream : int

put "Enter input file name:   " ..
get InFileName
open : InStream, InFileName, get
if InStream = 0 then
   put "I cannot open ", InFileName
   return
end if

put "Enter output file name:   " ..
get OutFileName
open : OutStream, OutFileName, put
if InStream = 0 then
   put "I cannot open ", OutFileName
   return
end if
```

The heart of the program is a loop that reads the input file, one line at a time, and writes the lines to the output file. The loop terminates at the end of the input file.

If we wanted to perform any processing on the file during the copying process, we would insert code at the point indicated by the box.

```
loop
    exit when eof (InStream)
    var Line : string
    get : InStream, Line : *
    [        ]          % Put code that processes the line here.
    put : OutStream, Line
end loop
close : InStream
close : OutStream
```

When the copy is complete, we close both files. If the **close** statements are omitted, Turing will close the files when the program finishes executing.

Style

It is good programming practice to close files as soon as we have finished using them. One reason for closing files is that open files occupy valuable space in memory. A more important reason is that if a power failure or other disaster occurs while files are open, their contents may be lost.

File Processing

The processing we perform on a line may be simple or complex, depending on the application. The next example illustrates a simple form of processing.

Example 6.10   Displaying Line Numbers

The following loop creates an output file that has a line number at the beginning of each line of text. Code for opening and closing the input and output files, which is the same as in Example 6.9, is not shown.

```
var LineNumber := 0
loop
    exit when eof (InStream)
    var Line : string
    get : InStream, Line : *
    LineNumber += 1
    put : OutStream, LineNumber : 4, " ", Line
end loop
```

Character Processing

Sometimes we need to process a file character by character. In many cases, the relationship between input lines and output lines is not simple. For example, a program might read lines of text, extract words, and write each word on a separate line of the output file.

Example 6.11 Copying by Characters

The following loop copies an input file to an output file character by character. Since the loop performs no additional processing, it has the same effect as the loop in Example 6.9. Code for opening and closing the files is omitted. The **get** statement in this loop reads exactly one character from the input file, and the **put** statement writes that character to the output file.

```
loop
   var Ch : string (1)
   exit when eof (InStream)
   get : InStream, Ch : 1
   [_____]            % Put code that processes the character here.
   put : OutStream, Ch ..
end loop
```

Examples 6.9 and 6.11 demonstrate that we can process files either line by line or character by character. When we read a file line by line, we do not have to process line breaks. When we read a file character by character, however, we must process line breaks.

For line by line copying, the relevant statements are

```
get : InFile, Line : *
put : OutFile, Line
```

The **get** statement copies the contents of an entire line into the variable *Line*. The end-of-line character, \n, is *not* copied into *Line*. The **put** statement writes all of the characters in *Line* to the output file and then, because there is no " .. ", writes \n to finish the line.

For character by character copying, the statements we require are

```
get : InFile, Ch : 1
put : OutFile, Ch ..
```

The **get** statement reads exactly one character. At the end of the line, it reads the character \n and assigns that value to *Ch*. The **put** statement writes exactly one character and, because " .. " is present, does *not* write \n. At the end of each line, however, $Ch = $ \n, and this character is written to the output file.

For example, suppose that the input file contains

```
A Robin Redbreast in a Cage
 Puts all Heaven in a Rage.
```

If we copy this file line by line, the values of *Line* are

```
Line = A Robin Redbreast in a Cage
Line = Puts all Heaven in a Rage.
```

Note that the lines do not contain end-of-line (\n) characters. If we copy the file character by character, the values of *Ch* are

```
A ␣ R o b i n ␣ R e d b r e a s t ␣ i n ␣ a ␣ C a g e ␣ \n
P u t s ␣ a l l ␣ H e a v e n ␣ i n ␣ a ␣ R a g e \n
```

Note that the ends of lines appear as \n characters. A program that processes characters must recognize ends of lines and handle them appropriately.

Example 6.12   Processing Each Character of a File

Suppose that we want to change each lower case letter in a file to the corresponding upper case character. We process the file character by character. Once again, we assume that the files are opened and closed as in Example 6.9.

```
const CaseDiff := ord ("A") − ord ("a")
loop
   var Ch : string (1)
   exit when eof (InStream)
   get : InStream, Ch : 1
   if index ("abcdefghijklmnopqrstuvwxyz", Ch) > 0 then
      Ch := chr (ord (Ch) + CaseDiff)
   end if
   put : OutStream, Ch ..
end loop
```

Some programs read a file to extract particular information or statistics from it. These programs usually display their results on the screen rather than writing them to a file.

Example 6.13   Counting the Words in a File

It is often useful to count the words in a file. The following loop provides an approximate count by assuming that a word is any group of characters that does not contain a blank, a tab character, or a line break. The program simulates a simple finite state machine with two states.

```
var WordCount := 0
var State := 0
loop
    var Ch : string (1)
    exit when eof (InStream)
    get : InStream, Ch : 1
    case State of
        label 0 :
            if index (" \t\n", Ch) > 0 then
                State := 1
                WordCount += 1
            end if
        label 1 :
            if index (" \t\n", Ch) = 0 then
                State := 0
            end if
    end case
end loop
```

6.4 Summary

Numbers in parentheses refer to sections where material appears.

▶   The **get** statement reads text from the keyboard one token or one line at a time (6.1).

▶   Programs should validate their input whenever this is feasible (6.1.1).

▶   The predefined procedure *getch* reads one character from the keyboard (6.1.2).

▶   The predefined procedure *hasch* returns **true** if the user has pressed a key (6.1.2).

▶   The predefined functions *maxrow* and *maxcol* return the number of rows and the number of columns available for text (6.1.2).

▶   The predefined procedures *locate* and *getch* support precise control for input (6.2.1).

▶   The **open** statement opens a file (6.3).

▶   Turing allows only a small number of files, typically ten, to be open at one time (6.3).

▶   Files should be closed as soon as they have been processed (6.3).

▶   The "get :" statement, with a stream number as its first argument, reads data from a text file (6.3.1).

▶   The "put :" statement, with a stream number as its first argument, writes data to a text file (6.3.2).

6.5 Exercises

6.1 Write a procedure that draws the outline of a rectangle on the screen. The parameters of the procedure should determine the size and position of the rectangle. Use the character "*" as the border character.

6.2 The PC provides special characters that we can use to draw the borders of a rectangle. Their codes appear in Appendix E on page 368. Write a procedure, similar to the procedure of the preceding exercise, that draws a rectangle on the screen using border characters.

6.3 Using the border characters specified in Exercise 6.2, modify the procedure *SelectOption* in Example 6.7 on page 178 so that it displays the menu in a bordered box.

6.4 Modify the procedure *GetString* in Example 6.6 on page 176 so that the user can edit the input string.

(a) It is quite easy to process the BACKSPACE character; the program should move the cursor one position left and erase the character most recently entered.

(b) It is more difficult but also more interesting to allow the use of the left and right arrow keys to move the cursor within the string. Amongst other things, you have to decide what the program should do when the user presses a character key: should the new character overwrite the current character or be inserted into the string?

6.5 Write a program that presents the user with a form to complete. For example, the program might display **Name**, **Street**, **City**, **Province** or **State**, and **Postal Code** or **Zip Code**, each followed by a shaded box indicating the number of characters required. When the user has completed the form successfully, the program should write the data to a text file.

6.6 Write a program that finds occurrences of a specified string in a file. The program should ask the user for the name of a file, then for a string. It should display each line of the file that contains the string.

6.7   Use the procedure *locate* to plot character graphs on the screen. You can use the formulas suggested below, but you should also design others for yourself. In each of the following, values of X lie between 1 and 80 and values of Y lie between 1 and 25.

(a) $Y = 12 - 10 * \sin(2\pi X/80)$.

(b) $Y = 23(1 - e^{-((x-40)/20)^2})$.

(c) $Y = 25 + \dfrac{24(1 - x^2)}{6399}$.

6.8   The procedure *GetInt* in Example 6.2 can be improved in several ways. Write versions of *GetInt* that incorporate the following improvements.

(a) The caller should be able to specify the minimum and maximum values of the integer that the user provides.

(b) The procedure should be able to read signed integers. If the first character of the user's response is "+" or "−", the procedure should record it. After converting the digits as before, the procedure should negate the value (multiply it by −1) if the first character was "−".

(c) The procedure can be generalized to read real numbers. The revised version should allow at most one decimal point in a string of digits and should scale the result according to the position of the decimal point.

6.9   By now, you probably have plenty of files containing Turing programs. Programs that extract information from these files may improve your productivity. Write programs that:

(a) list the subprograms used by a program;

(b) check to see whether a given subprogram is used in a program;

(c) make a list of all the identifiers used in a program;

(d) extract the comments from a program.

Chapter 7

Sound and Graphics

Turing provides predefined subprograms for creating simple sounds and images. These subprograms provide the basis for entertainment, simple programming exercises, and effective ways of analyzing complex data. The material about sound in this chapter demonstrates a close relationship between two seemingly unrelated objects — a computer program and a musical form. This relationship is not coincidental. Similar structures, or patterns, occur in many different areas. Repetition, for instance, occurs in wallpaper as repeated instances of a design, in music as repeated passages, and in programming as loops.

Graphics provides a useful example of an important principle in programming: choose a simple set of basic procedures that can be combined in different ways. Writing simple procedures that work together is more effective than writing complex procedures that are useful for only a small number of applications.

Most Turing programs are *portable*, which means they can be run on any computer with a Turing compiler or interpreter and give essentially the same results. If a program uses specialized features of a particular computer's hardware, it cannot be completely portable, whatever language we use to write it. The programs we describe in this chapter use special features of the computer on which Turing is running. Consequently, these programs may not behave in exactly the same way on all computers. For example, graphics procedures work on all computers, but the results depend on the resolution and color capabilities of the screen, and procedures that generate sound work only on PCs.

7.1 Sound

Sound generation brings the concept of *time* into programming in a particular way. A sound-producing program must not only generate the right sound, it must generate the right sound at the right time. Usually, we want the computer to perform calculations as quickly as possible, but there is no point in reproducing music or speech as quickly as possible.

The general problems of *real-time control*, as this area of computing is known, are complex. By providing several predefined procedures that control the built-in loudspeaker of a PC, Turing enables us to obtain results without exposure to the complexity of real-time programming.

7.1.1 The Procedures *play* and *playdone*

The predefined procedure *play* translates a string into a sequence of notes that are sounded through the loudspeaker of a PC. A complete description of the procedure *play* appears in Appendix H on page 372.

The argument of *play* is a string that represents a melody. A number in the string specifies the duration of the notes that follow it. For example, 4 introduces quarter-notes, and 8 introduces eighth-notes.

The letters a, b, . . . , g correspond to the musical notes $A, B, \ldots, G$. The letter p indicates a pause. The symbol + raises a note by a semitone, and the symbol – lowers a note by a semitone. For example, g+ stands for the note $G\sharp$.

The symbol < lowers the pitch of the notes that follow it by one octave. The symbol > operates in a similar fashion but raises the pitch one octave.

Example 7.1   Using the *play* Procedure

The following program produces an approximation of the first nine bars of "The Harmonious Blacksmith" by George Frideric Handel.

```
play ("4 p 8 eg+f+bg+ 6 f+e")
play ("8 f+bg+ > 6 c+ < e 8 d+ 6 bd+ 8 c+a+")
play ("4 b 8 eg+f+bg+ 6 f+e")
play ("8 f+bg+ > 6 c+ < e 8 d+ 6 bd+ 8 c+a+")
play ("4 b 8 b > 6 e < b > 8 c+ < b 6 g+b > e < b")
play (" > 8 c+ < b 6 g+b > ed+d+c+c+ < bbag+ab")
play ("4 f+ 8 bef+e 6 bg+f+e")
play ("f+d+ 8 eb 6 ef+d+ag+f+ 8 g+ 6 f+e")
play ("4 e p")
```

Each call to *play* performs one bar of the melody. The program is not quite finished because it does not play the last note correctly. Any program that uses *play* must finish with

```
loop
    exit when playdone
end loop
```

The predefined function *playdone* returns true if the last call to *play* has completed its task. If *play* has not finished, *playdone* returns false. Thus the final loop statement of the program ensures that the program does not terminate before the performance is complete.

7.1.2 The Procedures *sound* and *delay*

The procedure *play* is limited in two respects. First, it generates only the pitches of a keyboard instrument. Second, the duration of each note must be a simple fraction of a whole note. The procedure *sound* is more general; it generates a sound of any pitch and any duration. As arguments to *sound*, we provide a frequency in Hertz, or cycles per second, and a duration in milliseconds. For example, *sound* (440, 2000) plays 440 Hertz (concert *A*) for 2 seconds. Both arguments are integers.

When we use the *play* procedure, we choose the pitch and duration of a note from a restricted range of options. The *sound* procedure requires us to do more work to obtain a sound, but it provides greater control over the precise characteristics of the sound.

Example 7.2 Playing a Sequence of Sounds

The following program generates a sequence of sounds at $100, 200, 300, \ldots$ Hertz.

```
for Harmonic : 1 .. 20
    sound (100 * Harmonic, 200)
end for
delay (500)
```

Since *playdone* does not work in conjunction with *sound*, we use the predefined procedure *delay* to pause for 500 milliseconds (half a second) after Turing has begun to play the final note.

Musical Frequencies

The sounds created by the program in Example 7.2 constitute a *harmonic series* in which the frequency of each note is 100 Hertz higher than that of its predecessor. We do not hear the harmonic series as a regular scale because our perception of the relationship between two notes is determined by the ratio of their frequencies rather than by the difference between their frequencies. The conventional scale for Western music is called the *equitempered scale*: the ratio between consecutive tones, called a *semitone*, is $\sqrt[12]{2}$, or about 1.059.

Example 7.3   Generating Musical Frequencies

The following program creates an array containing integer approximations to the frequencies of the 88 notes of a standard piano keyboard. The frequency $A = 440$ Hertz is exact. The frequency of a note n semitones above A is $440 \times 2^{n/12}$. For notes below A, n is negative.

```
type PianoKeys : −39 .. 48
var Freqs : array PianoKeys of int
for Key : PianoKeys
    Freqs (Key) := round (440 * 2 ** ((Key − 9)/12))
end for
```

The array *Freqs* stores the frequencies of all the notes of a piano. It is arranged so that *Freqs* (0) is the frequency of middle C, nine semitones below A. The frequencies are computed as real numbers and then rounded to obtain an integer value suitable for *sound*. As a result of rounding, the piano is slightly out of tune.

7.1.3   Common Structures

People can play and sing popular songs together without practice or rehearsal because most songs have a simple rhythmic and melodic structure. We can express the structure of simple musical forms using loops and procedures. It is not surprising that we can express musical structures with program structures. The building blocks that are common to both music and programs — sequence, repetition, and grouping — appear in many different contexts. In the following example, we exploit the simplicity of a 12-bar blues.

Example 7.4   Using Procedures to Create Structure

A blues is a musical structure consisting of twelve bars with four beats in each bar. The first two bars and the last two bars are in a particular key, called the *tonic key*. The intervening bars are in keys with a fixed relationship to the tonic.

The program uses the array *Freqs* computed in Example 7.3. Intervals are therefore expressed in semitones rather than in conventional musical terms.

The constant *NoteLen* determines the tempo of the performance. A reasonable value for it is 150 milliseconds. Smaller values speed up the performance, and larger values slow it down.

Each beat consists of two notes, the second an octave higher than the first. To give a little life to an otherwise dull performance, the first note is twice as long as the second.

```
const NoteLen := 150
procedure OneBeat (Note : int)
    sound (Freqs (Note), 2 * NoteLen)
    sound (Freqs (Note + 12), NoteLen)
end OneBeat
```

The rhythmic pattern is a two-bar unit, consisting of eight beats. The pitch of each beat is determined by the argument *Base*.

```
procedure TwoBars (Base : int)
    OneBeat (Base + 0)
    OneBeat (Base + 4)
    OneBeat (Base + 7)
    OneBeat (Base + 9)
    OneBeat (Base + 10)
    OneBeat (Base + 9)
    OneBeat (Base + 7)
    OneBeat (Base + 4)
end TwoBars
```

A 12-bar blues is a specific sequence of chords, but there are a number of variations. The sequence we use here is the basic pattern:

```
procedure TwelveBars (Tonic : int)
    TwoBars (Tonic)
    TwoBars (Tonic)
    TwoBars (Tonic + 5)
    TwoBars (Tonic)
    TwoBars (Tonic + 7)
    TwoBars (Tonic)
end TwelveBars
```

The program calls *TwelveBars* repeatedly until the user presses a key. The key in this example is E♭, which is 21 semitones below middle C:

```
loop
    TwelveBars (−21)
    exit when hasch
end loop
```

7.2 Graphics

Each of Turing's graphics procedures performs a simple, well-defined task. There are predefined procedures for displaying dots, lines, boxes, arcs, and ovals. There are also procedures that fill closed areas with a particular color. In this section, we introduce each procedure and give an example of its use.

Although the examples of this chapter are quite simple, we can use the graphic capabilities of Turing to generate elaborate images. Of course, a program that creates a complex picture will usually be longer than the example programs given here. The ideas are the same, however. We can use graphics procedures in combinations to construct rich and varied images.

7.2.1 Drawing with Pixels

There are two ways in which a Turing program can control the appearance of the screen. The simplest way is to write *characters* on the screen. The other way, which we discuss in this section, is to write single dots, or *pixels*, on the screen. With pixel graphics, we can achieve a wide range of useful and interesting effects, at the expense of some programming effort.

In character mode, the screen is organized into rows and columns of characters. In graphics mode, we use a system in which a coordinate (X, Y) determines a position on the screen. The minimum values of both X and Y are zero. The point $(0, 0)$ is at the bottom left of the screen. The maximum values of X and Y depend on several factors, including the type of computer and operating system on which Turing is running. The predefined functions *maxx*, *maxy* provide these values, however, enabling us to write graphics programs that produce similar results on a variety of systems. In all cases, the point $(maxx, maxy)$ is at the top right corner of the screen.

The values returned by *maxx* and *maxy* depend on several factors, including the resolution of the display and the size of the viewing window. Typical values

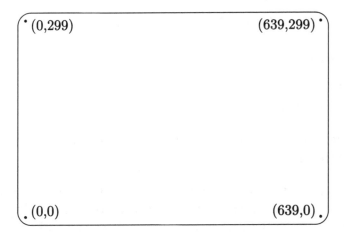

(0,299)   (639,299)

(0,0)   (639,0)

Figure 7.1   The Coordinate System for Pixel Graphics

for a PC are $maxx = 639$ and $maxy = 299$. Assuming these maximum values, Figure 7.1 shows the position and coordinates of four points at the corners of the screen. Note that Y values increase up the screen, according to the conventions of science and mathematics. This distinguishes graphics mode from text mode, in which row numbers increase down the screen.

Since $maxx$ and $maxy$ are odd numbers, there is no pixel exactly at the center of the screen. The coordinate $maxx$ div 2 is just left of the center, and the coordinate $(maxx+1)$ div 2 is just right of center. Although the distance between these pixels is not great, it is sometimes critical if we want an image to fit exactly on the screen.

7.2.2   Drawing Dots

The procedure *drawdot* draws a single dot, or pixel, on the screen. Drawing one dot is a simple operation. In computer graphics, however, all pictures are composed of dots. Thus *drawdot* is the most fundamental operation, the one from which we can derive all other operations necessary for elaborate images. A call to *drawdot* has the form

$$drawdot\,(X, Y, C)$$

in which X specifies the X-coordinate, Y specifies the Y-coordinate, and C specifies the color.

The color will be a small integer, usually chosen from $0, 1, \ldots, 15$. The predefined function *maxcolor* returns the maximum permitted value of the color argument, which will depend on the video equipment of the computer.

The arguments of *drawdot* satisfy the following relations:

$$0 \le X \le maxx$$
$$0 \le Y \le maxy$$
$$0 \le C \le maxcolor$$

If the arguments do not satisfy these relations, Turing does not report an error, but nothing appears on the screen.

Color values 1 through *maxcolor* give different colors, but the color 0 always produces the background color. The predefined procedure *colorback* changes the background color. Note that, when we call *colorback*, the background color does not change immediately; the change takes effect only after the next call to *cls*.

Example 7.5   Plotting a Curve with *drawdot*

The following program plots the graph of the sine function for two complete cycles. We plot values of $sin(X)$, in which X is a real variable that varies from 0 to 4π. The graph is plotted as a sequence of points. Each point is drawn by a call to the predefined procedure *drawdot*.

```
const PlotColor = 1
const XScale := 4.0 * 3.14159/maxx
var Yi : int
var X, Y : real
for Xi : 0..maxx
    X := Xi * XScale
    Y := sin (X)
    Yi := round (maxy div 2 * (Y + 1.0))
    drawdot (Xi, Yi, PlotColor)
end for
```

The pixel coordinate Xi that corresponds to X must be an integer that varies from 0 to $maxx$. The values of X and Xi are related by the equation $X = Xi \times XScale$, where $XScale = 4\pi/maxx$. This value is declared as a constant in the program.

The value of $sin(X)$ varies between -1 and $+1$. The value of the pixel coordinate Yi varies between 0 and $maxy$. The curve will use the full height of the screen if $Yi = maxy$ when $Y = 1$ and $Yi = 0$ when $Y = -1$. Section 7.2.5 describes a general way of obtaining formulas for coordinate transformations.

7.2.3   Color and Structure

Color adds interest to a picture and sometimes provides insight into a complex structure. We can use the random number generator to introduce random colors into a picture.

Example 7.6   Displaying Colored Dots

The following equations generate a sequence of points called an *orbit*. $|X_n|$denotes the absolute value of X_n.

$$X_{n+1} \;=\; 1 - Y_n + k|X_n|;$$
$$Y_{n+1} \;=\; X_n.$$

For $k = 1$, values of X and Y lie between -9 and 16. To plot a value of X, we first add 9 to it, obtaining a value between 0 and 25, and then multiply this value by *maxx* div 25, obtaining a coordinate between 0 and *maxx*. The transformation for Y values is similar but uses *maxy*. The constant *Factor*, which corresponds to k in the equations above, changes the size and other properties of the image. Values close to 1 give good results.

```
const Factor := 1.05
const ColorCycle := 1000
const XScale := maxx div 25
const YScale := maxy div 25
var X := −0.1
var Y := 0.0
var Count := 0
var Col : int
loop
    if Count mod ColorCycle = 0 then
        randint (Col, 1, maxcolor)
    end if
    Count += 1
    drawdot (round (XScale * (X + 9)), round (YScale * (Y + 9)), Col)
    const XNew := 1 − Y + Factor * abs (X)
    Y := X
    X := XNew
end loop
```

The constant *ColorCycle* determines how often the color changes. Different values produce different patterns on the screen.

7.2.4   Drawing Lines

The procedure *drawline* draws a straight line. The call

$$drawline\,(X1, Y1, X2, Y2, C)$$

joins the points $(X1, Y1)$ and $(X2, Y2)$ with a line in color C. If the points $(X1, Y1)$ and $(X2, Y2)$ are both within the screen limits, all of the line will appear on the screen. If one or both of the points is outside the screen limits, only the visible part of the line will be drawn.

In the general case, if we try to draw any object that is partly off the screen, Turing plots the part that is on the screen. We can use this property of the plotting procedures to simplify graphics programs. The action of deleting the invisible part of the object, performed by the predefined procedures, is called *clipping*.

Example 7.7   Approximating a Curve with Straight Lines

We can use *drawline* to join the dots in a point plot such as the sine function. The following program has the same structure as the program of Example 7.5. The difference is that we plot a new value at pixels $0, 5, 10, \ldots$ rather than at every pixel. Connecting these points with straight lines yields a curve that is almost indistinguishable from the more accurate line of dots.

```
const PlotColor = 1
const XScale := 4.0 * 3.14159/maxx
var Xi, Yi : int
var YOld := round (maxydiv2 * (0.0 + 1.0))
var XOld := 0
var X, Y : real
loop
    Xi := XOld + 5
    X := Xi * XScale
    Y := sin (X)
    Yi := round (maxydiv2 * (Y + 1.0))
    drawline (XOld, YOld, Xi, Yi, PlotColor)
    XOld := Xi
    YOld := Yi
end loop
```

The program must store the coordinates of both the current point, (Xi, Yi), and the previous point, $(XOld, YOld)$, to plot the line joining them.

7.2.5   Scaling Transformation

In each of the preceding examples of graphics programming, we have used a scaling transformation to obtain X and Y coordinate values suitable for plotting. Graphics programming can be quite tedious if we work out scaling factors and coordinate transformations for every picture. The art of graphics programming is to devise procedures that do the tedious part of the work automatically.

Suppose that the real arrays $XVals$ and $YVals$ contain the coordinates of points on a curve. That is, the Ith point on the curve has coordinate $(XVals(I), YVals(I))$. We want to plot the curve using the entire screen. To do this, we start by finding the minimum and maximum values of $XVals$ and $YVals$. From these, we can compute a coordinate transformation that we can use to plot the curve.

Suppose that the variables $XMin$, $XMax$, and $YMin$, $YMax$ are the minimum and maximum values in the arrays $XVals$ and $YVals$, respectively. We need a scaling transformation that takes values between $XMin$ and $XMax$ to values between 0 and $maxx$, and a similar transformation for Y values. Figure 7.2 shows the point P at (X_r, Y_r) in the original coordinate system and the corresponding point P' at (X_i, Y_i) in the screen coordinate system.

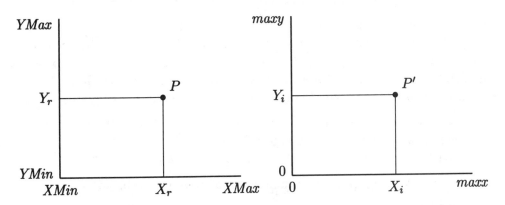

Figure 7.2   **Coordinate Systems for Scaling Transformation**

Since the transformation must be linear, it has the form $X_i = AX_r + B$ in which X_r is a real value, X_i is an integer value between 0 and $maxx$, and A and B are constants. Substituting the values we know gives the equations

$$0 = A \times XMin + B$$

and

$$maxx = A \times XMax + B$$

from which we can infer

$$A = \frac{maxx}{XMax - XMin}$$

and

$$B = -\frac{XMin \times maxx}{XMax - XMin}.$$

Substituting these values of A and B gives the required transformation for X values:

$$X_i = maxx \times \left(\frac{X_r - XMin}{XMax - XMin} \right).$$

It is easy to see that the result is correct: if we set $X_r = XMin$, we have $X_i = 0$ and, if $X_r = XMax$, then $X_i = maxx$. The transformation for Y values is similar:

$$Y_i = maxy \times \left(\frac{Y_r - YMin}{YMax - YMin} \right).$$

These equations are often useful in graphics programming, and it is worthwhile remembering them.

Example 7.8   Using Transformations to Plot Mathematical Functions

We can use the scaling transformations to plot a curve from data provided in arrays. The parameters of the procedure *Plot* are two arrays with open upper bounds and a color. The precondition of *Plot* requires each of the arrays to have at least one component. The procedure does not require the arrays to have the same length, but it uses the shorter array to determine the number of points plotted.

```
procedure Plot (XVals, YVals : array 0 .. * of real, Color : int)
    pre upper (XVals) ≥ 1 and upper (YVals) ≥ 1
    const Num := min (upper (XVals), upper (YVals))
```

The first step is to compute the minimum and maximum values in each array:

```
var XMin := XVals (0)
var XMax := XVals (0)
var YMin := YVals (0)
var YMax := YVals (0)
for I : 1 .. Num
    XMin := min (XMin, XVals (I))
    XMax := max (XMax, XVals (I))
    YMin := min (YMin, YVals (I))
    YMax := max (YMax, YVals (I))
end for
```

We then calculate the ranges of the arrays to avoid unnecessary computation during the plotting process, and the initial values of the pixel coordinates, *XOld* and *YOld*, using the transformation equations derived above.

```
const XRange := XMax − XMin
const YRange := YMax − YMin
var XOld := round (maxx * (XVals (0) − XMin)/XRange)
var YOld := round (maxy * (YVals (0) − YMin)/YRange)
```

The rest of the procedure consists of a for loop that plots the remaining coordinate pairs:

```
for I : 1 .. Num
    var XNew := round (maxx * (XVals (I) − XMin)/XRange)
    var YNew := round (maxy * (YVals (I) − YMin)/YRange)
    drawline (XOld, YOld, XNew, YNew, Color)
    XOld := XNew
    YOld := YNew
end for
end Plot
```

The following program uses procedure *Plot* to draw the graph of $y = xe^{-x^2}$ for the interval $-2.5 \le x \le 2.5$.

```
var X, Y : array 0 .. 100 of real
const pi := 3.14159
for N : 0 .. 100
    X (N) := (N − 50)/20
    Y (N) := X (N) * exp (−X (N) ** 2)
end for
Plot (X, Y, maxcolor)
```

7.2.6 Drawing Boxes

The procedure *drawbox* draws a rectangular outline on the screen. The call

> *drawbox* (*XLeft*, *YBottom*, *XRight*, *YTop*, *Color*)

draws a box with its left side at *XLeft*, its right side at *XRight*, its bottom at *YBottom*, and its top at *YTop*. Alternatively, we can say that the bottom left corner is at (*XLeft*, *YBottom*) and the top right corner is at (*XRight*, *YTop*). The outline is drawn using the indicated color. If the coordinates of the box are off the screen, Turing draws only the part of the box that is on the screen.

The procedure *drawfill* fills an area of the screen with a color. The call

$$drawfill\,(X,\,Y,\,FillColor,\,BorderColor)$$

is best understood by way of an analogy. Imagine that we start pouring paint with color *FillColor* at the point $(X,\,Y)$ on the screen. The paint spreads across the screen in all directions, but it is stopped whenever it encounters the color *BorderColor*. The effect is that the area surrounding the point $(X,\,Y)$ out to the border colored *BorderColor* is filled with the color *FillColor*. If the border is not closed, paint leaks through it, and the entire screen gets painted. The edges of the screen behave as borders.

Example 7.9   Plotting and Filling Colored Rectangles

The program in this example draws random filled rectangles, producing the effect of an unimaginative abstract painting. The minimum and maximum dimensions of the rectangles are determined by the constants *XMin*, *XMax*, *YMin*, and *YMax*. In its main loop, the program chooses random sizes within these limits and then picks a point at random on the screen for the center of the rectangle. Finally, it draws the rectangle and fills it with a random color. The loop terminates when the user presses a key.

```
randomize
const XMin := 5
const XMax := maxx div 4
const YMin := 5
const YMax := maxy div 4
loop
   var Xsize, Ysize, Xcenter, Ycenter, Color : int
   randint (Xsize, XMin, XMax)
   randint (Ysize, YMin, YMax)
   randint (Xcenter, 0, maxx)
   randint (Ycenter, 0, maxy)
   randint (Color, 1, maxcolor)
   const XLeft := Xcenter − Xsize div 2
   const XRight := Xcenter + Xsize div 2
   const YBottom := Ycenter − Ysize div 2
   const YTop := Ycenter + Ysize div 2
   drawbox (XLeft, YBottom, XRight, YTop, Color)
   drawfill (Xcenter, Ycenter, Color, Color)
   exit when hasch
end loop
```

7.2.7   Drawing Ovals and Arcs

In contrast to the procedures described above, the predefined procedures *drawoval* and *drawarc* draw curves. The call

$$drawoval\,(XCenter,\,YCenter,\,XRadius,\,YRadius,\,Color)$$

draws the outline of an oval, or ellipse, with center at $(XCenter,\,YCenter)$, horizontal radius *XRadius*, vertical radius *YRadius*, and color *Color*. All the arguments are integers.

The procedure *drawarc* is similar to *drawoval* but has two additional arguments. The call

$$drawarc\,(XCenter,\,YCenter,\,XRadius,\,YRadius,\,Start,\,Finish,\,Color)$$

draws part of the oval defined by the first four arguments. The arguments *Start* and *Finish* specify the angles at which the arc must start and finish.

As in coordinate geometry, the zero angle is in the direction of the increasing X-axis, and angles increase in a counterclockwise direction. These conventions are illustrated in Figure 7.3.

Example 7.10   Plotting and Filling Complex Shapes

The following program draws 15 phases of the moon. When the moon is full, we see it as a circle. When it is not full, we see a shape bounded by a semicircle and an ellipse. The semicircle is part of the outline of the full moon, and the ellipse marks the transition from light to darkness on the surface of the moon.

There are three phases that are easy to plot: the new moon is a semicircular arc, the half moon is a filled semicircle, and the full moon is a filled circle. For the phases between, we draw a semicircular arc and an ellipse with a horizontal radius smaller than the radius of the moon. When the ellipse faces in the same direction

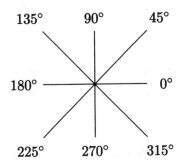

Figure 7.3   Conventions for Angles

as the semicircle, the image resembles a crescent moon, and when the ellipse faces in the opposite direction, the oval image resembles a gibbous moon.

We begin by choosing constants for the color of the moon; the dimensions that partition the screen into fifteen areas, five horizontal and three vertical; and the radius of the moon image:

> const *Color* := *maxcolor*
> const *Xdist* := *maxx* div 10
> const *XRadius* := *round*(0.7 * *Xdist*)
> const *Ydist* := *maxy* div 6
> const *YRadius* := *XRadius*

The phases are numbered $0, 1, \ldots, 14$. For each phase, we calculate the coordinates of the center of the image and draw a semicircular arc for one side:

> for *Phase* : 0 .. 14
>   const *XCenter* := *Xdist* + 2 * (*Phase* mod 5) * *Xdist*
>   const *YCenter* := *Ydist* + 2 * (*Phase* div 5) * *Ydist*
>   *drawarc* (*XCenter*, *YCenter*, *XRadius*, *YRadius*, 90, 270, *Color*)

The opposite arc depends on the phase. For phases $0, 1, \ldots, 6$, the arc has the same start and finish angles as the semicircle; for phase 7, it is a straight line; and for phases $8, 9, \ldots, 14$, it is an arc with the start and finish angles reversed.

> if *Phase* ≤ 6 then
>   *drawarc* (*XCenter*, *YCenter*, *round* ((7 − *Phase*) * *XRadius*/7),
>   *YRadius*, 90, 270, *Color*)
> elsif *Phase* = 7 then
>   *drawline* (*XCenter*, *YCenter* + *YRadius*, *XCenter*,
>   *YCenter* − *YRadius*, *Color*)
> else
>   *drawarc* (*XCenter*, *YCenter*, *round* ((*Phase* − 7) * *XRadius*/7),
>   *YRadius*, 270, 90, *Color*)
> end if

Finally, we must turn the outline into a solid. For the new moon, phase 0, there is nothing to do. For the other phases, we choose a point inside the outline and fill it with the chosen color:

> if *Phase* > 0 then
>   *drawfill* (*XCenter* − *XRadius* + 1, *YCenter*, *Color*, *Color*)
> end if
> end for

7.2.8 Displaying Text in Graphics Mode

We can use both the put statement and the *locate* procedure in graphics mode. They both work in the usual way. The predefined procedure *locatexy* positions text in graphics mode. The arguments are graphics coordinates X and Y. For example, the program

> *locatexy* (*maxx* div 2, *maxy* div 2)
> put "Hi!" ..

displays the message "Hi!" just to the right of the center of the screen. The advantage of *locatexy* over *locate* is that it allows us to work with the same coordinate system for both text and graphics. There is a small catch, however. The call *locatexy* (X, Y) does not put text *exactly* at the point (X, Y). Instead, it finds and uses the closest position that is consistent with text placement on the 25×80 character grid. Thus we cannot rely on precise positioning of text in graphics mode.

Example 7.11 Labeling the Axes of a Graph

The following code is intended to write labels on the Y-axis of a graph.

> for *YMark* : 0 .. 10
>   *locatexy* (0, (*YMark* + 1) $*$ *maxy* div 12)
>   put *YMark*/10 : 3 : 1
> end for

Unfortunately, the labels are not spaced evenly. This is because *locate* and *locatexy* use different coordinate systems. The arguments of *locate* are a row and a column, with the first row at the top and the first column at the left of the screen. The arguments of *locatexy* are coordinates X and Y with $(0,0)$ at the bottom left of the screen, as in Figure 7.1.

7.3 Animation

An *animation* is a sequence of images. An animation program alternately erases an image and draws the next one in the sequence. If this is done fast enough, we may create the illusion that an object is moving across the screen. The amount of animation we can do is limited by the speed of the computer we are using. To be fully convincing, an animation program should redisplay the screen 30 times per second, which requires computing and displaying $640 \times 480 \times 30 = 9,216,000$ pixels each second. Even with a fast computer, programming for animation requires careful management of resources.

Example 7.12   Animating a Pixel

The program below moves a single pixel in a "random walk". The initial position of the pixel is the center of the screen. From its current position, (X, Y), we calculate a new position, $(XNew, YNew)$, by adding a random integer to each coordinate and checking that the new position is on the screen. The statement $drawdot(X, Y, 0)$ erases the pixel by drawing it in the background color. The following statement, $drawdot(XNew, YNew, maxcolor)$, draws the new pixel at the next position.

If we erase the pixel, calculate the new position, and draw the pixel at its new position, the image will flicker. To reduce flicker, we leave the old image on the screen until we are ready to draw the new image.

```
var X := maxx div 2
var Y := maxy div 2
loop
   exit when hasch
   % Calculate the next X position.
   var Dx, XNew : int
   randint (Dx, -1, 1)
   XNew := X + Dx
   if X < 0 then
      X := maxx
   elsif X > maxx then
      X := 0
   end if
   % Calculate the next Y position.
   var Dy, YNew : int
   randint (Dy, -1, 1)
   YNew := Y + Dy
   if Y < 0 then
      Y := maxy
   elsif Y > maxy then
      Y := 0
   end if
   % Erase the old point and plot the new one.
   drawdot (X, Y, 0)
   drawdot (XNew, YNew, maxcolor)
   X := XNew
   Y := YNew
end loop
```

Animating an Image

To animate an image larger than a single pixel, we need a way of erasing and redrawing images rapidly. The predefined procedures *takepic* and *drawpic* make this easy to do. The procedure *takepic* makes a "snapshot" of a rectangular area of the screen and stores the result in an array. The procedure *drawpic* draws the recorded image either at the same place on the screen or elsewhere.

Suppose that we want to capture a rectangular area with bottom left corner $(X1, Y1)$ and top right corner $(X2, Y2)$. The first step is to declare an array large enough to store the pixels. We use the predefined function *sizepic* to determine the size of the array:

   var *Buffer* : array 1 .. *sizepic* $(X1, Y1, X2, Y2)$ of int

The next step is to store the image by executing

   takepic $(X1, Y1, X2, Y2, Buffer)$

We can now display the image at a point (X, Y) on the screen by calling

   drawpic $(X, Y, Buffer, 0)$

The coordinates (X, Y) of *drawpic* give the position of the bottom left corner of the image. In Figure 7.4, the rectangle with a solid outline shows the effect of the call *takepic* $(20, 20, 60, 40, Buffer)$. The boxes with dashed outlines show the effects of the calls *drawpic* $(80, 100, Buffer)$ and *drawpic* $(100, 40, Buffer)$.

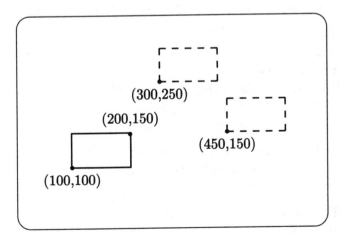

Figure 7.4   Using *takepic* **and** *drawpic*

There are two ways in which *drawpic* can draw an image. It can simply draw the image on the screen or it can superimpose the image on the background in such a way that the background information is not lost. If we draw the picture twice in the same place using the superimposition mode, the image first appears and then disappears, leaving the background unchanged. The last argument of *drawpic* determines the drawing mode. The call

$$drawpic\,(X, Y, Buffer, 0)$$

displays the image in *Buffer* in normal mode, and the call

$$drawpic\,(X, Y, Buffer, 1)$$

displays it in superimposition mode.

Using *takepic* and *drawpic*

Those of us who have seen animated scenes from scientific visualizations or computer games may not find a ball moving around the screen an exciting image. As is often the case in computer science, advanced applications have their roots in simple beginnings. Striking images and animated scenes are created in programs of greater complexity by using the same basic principles as those used in the following example to move a ball.

Example 7.13   Animating a Ball

The following program uses *takepic* and *drawpic* to move the image of a ball around the screen. We begin by using *drawoval* and *drawfill* to draw a filled yellow circle at the bottom left of the screen. The array *Ball* stores the image of the ball.

```
const Yellow := 14
const Radius := 10
const Diameter := 2 * Radius
drawoval(Radius, Radius, Radius, Radius, Yellow)
drawfill (Radius, Radius, Yellow, Yellow)
var Ball : array 1 .. sizepic (0, 0, Diameter, Diameter) of int
```

Now we have an image. The next step is to take a picture of it. Immediately after taking the picture, we call *drawpic* to erase it. The screen goes blank, but we have recorded the image we need:

```
takepic (0, 0, Diameter, Diameter, Ball)
drawpic (0, 0, Ball, 1)
```

We start the ball rolling near the bottom left of the screen. Initially, both the X and Y directions are positive. We draw the ball in its initial position:

var $X := maxx$ div 3
var $Y := maxy$ div 3
var $XDir := 1$
var $YDir := 1$
$drawpic\,(X, Y, Ball, 1)$

The main loop computes the new position of the ball, erases the old image, and redraws the ball at the new position. The ball travels diagonally across the screen, with $XDir$ and $YDir$ controlling its direction. When it reaches a boundary of the screen, it bounces, and we draw a line indicating the point of impact. As the program runs, more and more lines appear on the screen, but the ball appears to move over them, illustrating the superimposition technique.

```
loop
    exit when hasch
    if X = 0 or X + Diameter = maxx then
        drawline (0, Y, maxx, Y, 12)
        XDir := −XDir
    end if
    const XNew := X + XDir
    if Y = 0 or Y + Diameter = maxy then
        drawline (X, 0, X, maxy, 11)
        YDir := − YDir
    end if
    const YNew := Y + YDir
    drawpic (X, Y, Ball, 1)
    drawpic (XNew, YNew, Ball, 1)
    X := XNew
    Y := YNew
end loop
```

7.4   Summary

Numbers in parentheses refer to sections where material appears.

- ▶ The predefined procedures *play*, *playdone*, and *sound* create sounds (7.1).

- ▶ The procedure *play* translates the characters of a string into notes (7.1.1).

- ▶ The procedure *playdone* returns **true** if the sound generated by *play* has finished (7.1.1).

- ▶ The procedure *sound* makes a sound using the loudspeaker of a PC (7.1.2).

- ▶ The predefined procedure *delay* pauses the program for the specified number of milliseconds (7.1.2).

- ▶ The predefined functions *maxx* and *maxy* return the maximum values of graphics screen coordinates (7.2.1).

- ▶ The predefined function *maxcolor* returns the maximum color code (7.2.2).

- ▶ The predefined procedure *drawdot* draws one colored pixel on the screen (7.2.2).

- ▶ The predefined procedure *drawline* draws a colored line on the screen (7.2.4).

- ▶ It is usually necessary to scale values before they are plotted (7.2.5). General-purpose scaling transformations avoid the need to compute formulas for each graph separately.

- ▶ The predefined procedure *drawbox* draws a rectangle on the screen (7.2.6).

- ▶ The predefined procedure *drawfill* fills an area on the screen (7.2.6).

- ▶ The predefined procedures *drawoval* and *drawarc* draw curved lines on the screen (7.2.7).

- ▶ The predefined procedure *locatexy* positions text using graphical coordinates (7.2.8). Text can be displayed only at character boundaries.

- ▶ The predefined procedures *drawpic*, *sizepic*, and *takepic* are used to erase and draw images rapidly (7.3).

7.5   Exercises

7.1   Many Scottish folk songs, such as *Auld Lang Syne*, use the pentatonic scale. Pentatonic melodies can be played on the black notes of a piano. The frequencies of notes of the pure pentatonic scale have simple arithmetic relationships to the tonic. Taking $C = 1$, the relative frequencies of the other notes are $D = 9/8$, $F = 4/3$, $G = 3/2$, and $A = 5/3$. Find integers with these ratios and use them to play a pentatonic scale.

7.2   Write a program that displays the words of a song as it plays the corresponding notes. The program should read a file that contains both the music and the words for the song.

7.3   Write a program, like the one that appears in Example 7.4 on page 194, that uses initialized arrays rather than procedures to store relative pitch information.

7.4   Describe the effect of each of the following calls:

   (a) *drawline* $(0, maxy, maxx, 0, 1)$;
   (b) *drawline* $(maxx$ div $3, maxy$ div $2, 2 * maxx$ div $3, maxy$ div $2, 1)$;
   (c) *drawbox* $(0, 0, maxx, maxy, 1)$;
   (d) *drawoval* $(maxx$ div $2, maxy$ div $2, maxx$ div $2, maxy$ div $2, 1)$;
   (e) *drawarc* $(30, 20, 30, 20, 180, 270, 1)$.

7.5   Write a procedure that draws a rectangle of width w and height h tilted at an angle θ to the horizontal. If one corner is at (x, y), the coordinates of the four corners are:

$$P_1 \quad = \quad (x, y);$$
$$P_2 \quad = \quad (x + w \cos \theta, y + w \sin \theta);$$
$$P_3 \quad = \quad (x + w \cos \theta - h \sin \theta, y + w \sin \theta + h \cos \theta);$$
$$P_4 \quad = \quad (x - h \cos \theta, y + h \sin \theta).$$

7.6   The formula $P_n = KP_{n-1}(1 - P_{n-1})$ is a simplified model of population growth. The formula gives the current year's population, P_n, as a function of the previous year's population, P_{n-1}. The population is scaled so that $0 < P_n < 1$. For different values of the constant K, the population is stable, oscillatory, or chaotic. Write a program that asks for a value of K, chooses a random initial population, and plots population change for *maxx* years. Values of K between 1.5 and 3 give interesting results.

7.7   The program in Example 7.9 on page 204 can be improved in various ways.

   (a) Although the program calls *drawfill*, it occasionally draws an unfilled rectangle. Explain why this happens, and suggest a way to correct it.

   (b) After the user has pressed a key to terminate the program, Turing displays a message that spoils the effect. Modify the program so that the user can admire the finished product.

   (c) Extend the program to paint random ovals, or a mixture of rectangles and ovals, instead of just rectangles.

7.8   Another way of creating "abstract paintings" is to use recursion. Write a recursive procedure *Split* with four parameters that define two corners of a rectangle. The procedure works as follows.

   (a) If the rectangle is too small to split, color it with a random color.

   (b) Otherwise, choose a random point on the longest side of the rectangle, draw a line across it, and call *Split* for each of the two subrectangles.

The "splitting" action is explained in the figure below. Suppose that *Split* has been called with points A and B and it is big enough to split. The procedure chooses the point P at random. It then makes two recursive calls: one with the points A and P, and the other with the points Q and B.

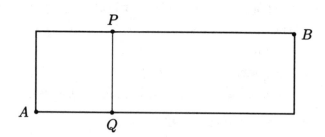

7.9   The lines drawn by the program in Example 7.13 on page 210 have a short blue segment at the end. Can you explain this?

7.10 Write a program that uses the formula given in Exercise 3.7 on page 101 to plot depth of field curves for a lens.

7.11 Use *sizepic* and *takepic* to store images of the two square "tiles" shown below. Store only the arcs, not the outlines of the tiles. Write a program that covers the screen with these tiles and then enters a loop. Each cycle of the loop chooses a tile at random and "flips" it to the other pattern.

7.12 Suppose that the screen represents your view from the front window of a spacecraft moving with velocity v. A star at distance d appears at time t_0 at position (x, y) on the screen. At time $t > t_0$, the star will appear to have moved to (x', y') on the screen, where $x' = rx$, $y' = ry$, and

$$ r = \frac{d}{d - v(t - t_0)}. $$

Use these equations to simulate the view from the spacecraft of a number of stars. New stars should appear at random points on the display.

7.13 A stretched string can vibrate in several modes. When a string of length L is vibrating in mode n, its shape at maximum deflection is given by the equation

$$ y = A \sin\left(\frac{n\pi x}{L}\right) $$

and the frequencies of vibration are given by $f = nk$ for $n = 1, 2, \ldots$. The constant k is given approximately by

$$ k \approx \frac{1}{2}\sqrt{\frac{T}{LM}}. $$

In this formula, M is the mass of the string and T is its tension.

Write a program that displays the shape of the string and plays a tone at the corresponding frequency for a given mode. Assume that $M = 0.01$ kilograms, $L = 1$ meter, and $T = 10^4$ Newtons.

7.14 Write a program that allows the user to draw simple pictures on the screen. Pressing an arrow key should move the cursor one pixel in the corresponding direction. To move faster, say ten pixels at a time, the user presses SHIFT and an arrow key. The user must also be allowed to select a color.

Chapter 8

Sets, Records, and Unions

The memory of a computer has little formal structure. Typically, it consists of a large number of identical cells. On most modern computers, each cell contains eight bits and is called a *byte*. Some supercomputers have memories with a larger cell size, such as 2, 4, or 8 bytes. Whatever the cell size, each byte may contain a meaningful value, such as a character, or it may be part of a larger entity, such as a real number or a string.

Data structures in programming languages are abstractions imposed on the memory of the computer. They create the illusion that the memory has a structure that is matched to the needs of a particular program. In fact, an array, which consists of many components of the same size, has a structure that is quite similar to the memory used to store it. The close correspondence between the structure of an array and the structure of the underlying memory reflects the history of programming languages; arrays were the first data structure to be introduced into programs.

Modern programming languages allow us to think in terms of the problem we are trying to solve rather than the machine we are using to solve it. When we are solving a problem, we do not want to think about the memory of the computer but about the structure of the data in the problem domain. The data structures we discuss in this chapter, sets, records, and unions, allow us to match the forms of programs to the requirements of their applications.

8.1   Sets

Sets are the fundamental "data structure" of mathematics. A set is a collection of objects called the *elements* or *members* of the set. The elements are chosen from a *universe* or *universal set*. For example, from the universe of natural numbers $0, 1, 2, \ldots$ we can construct finite sets such as $\{\,1, 2, 4, 8\,\}$ and infinite sets such as the set of all odd numbers: $\{\,1, 3, 5, 7, \ldots\,\}$.

8.1.1   Defining Sets

We can define sets in Turing, but there are some limitations. The total number of elements in the universe must be less than 31, and the elements of a set must be chosen from either a subrange or an enumeration type. The declarations

> type *Small* : 0 .. 20
> type *SmallSet* : set of *Small*

introduce two new types. The first is a subrange type, which we have already discussed in Section 4.1, and the second is a set type. We say that *Small* is the *base type* of *SmallSet*. Values of type *Small* are small numbers. Values of type *SmallSet* are *sets* of small numbers. The set $\{\,0, 5, 10, 15, 20\,\}$ is a value of the type *SmallSet*. In Turing, we write it as *SmallSet* $(0, 5, 10, 15, 20)$. We can also use this form as an initializer in constant and variable declarations:

> const *M4* := *SmallSet* $(0, 4, 8, 12, 16, 20)$
> var *M5* := *SmallSet* $(0, 5, 10, 15, 20)$

The set *M4* contains multiples of 4. Since it is a constant, we cannot change its value. The set *M5* contains multiples of 5. Since it is a variable, we can change its value using the operations described below.

There are two special values of the type *SmallSet*. The constant

> const *Empty* := *SmallSet* $()$

is the *empty set*, which has no elements, and the constant

> const *Universe* := *SmallSet* (all)

is the *universal set*, which contains every value of the base type. In this example, *Empty* represents the set $\{\,\}$ or $\emptyset$ and *Universe* represents the set $\{\,0, 1, \ldots, 20\,\}$. In mathematics, the empty set is the *unique* set that has no members. In Turing, each set type T has its own empty set, $T\,()$.

8.1.2 Set Operations

For each of the common mathematical operations on sets, there is a corresponding operation in Turing. The connection between mathematical expressions and Turing expressions is shown in Figure 8.1.

Expression	Mathematical Notation	Turing Notation
Empty set	$\emptyset$	$T\,()$
Universal set	$\mathcal{U}$	$T\,(\text{all})$
Number of elements in A	$|A|$	
The union of A and B	$A \cup B$	$A + B$
The intersection of A and B	$A \cap B$	$A * B$
The set difference between A and B	$A \backslash B$	$A - B$
x is a member of A	$x \in A$	x in A
x is not a member of A	$x \notin A$	x not in A
A is a subset of B	$A \subseteq B$	$A \leq B$
A is a proper subset of B	$A \subset B$	$A < B$
A is a superset of B	$A \supseteq B$	$A \geq B$
A is a proper superset of B	$A \supset B$	$A > B$

Figure 8.1   Set Operations and Predicates

Two set types are equivalent if they have equivalent base types. The operands of the binary set operators "+", "*", "−", "≤", "<", "≥", and ">" must be sets with equivalent types.

The operator "in", which tests for set membership, has the same precedence as the comparison operators. Using the declarations of $M4$ and $M5$ given above, we can evaluate the following expressions.

$$10 \text{ in } M5 \quad \longrightarrow \quad \text{true}$$
$$10 \text{ in } M4 \quad \longrightarrow \quad \text{false}$$
$$M5 + M4 \quad \longrightarrow \quad \{\, 0, 4, 5, 10, 12, 15, 16, 20 \,\}$$
$$M5 * M4 \quad \longrightarrow \quad \{\, 0, 20 \,\}$$
$$M5 - M4 \quad \longrightarrow \quad \{\, 5, 10, 15 \,\}$$
$$M5 \leq M4 \quad \longrightarrow \quad \text{false}$$

Turing does not have an operator corresponding to $|A|$, the number of elements in a set. It is straightforward, however, to write a function that counts the members of a set:

```
function Size (S : SmallSet) : Small
   var Count := 0
   for I : Small
      if I in S then
         Count += 1
      end if
   end for
   result Count
end Size
```

8.1.3 Classifying with Sets

Sets are often useful for representing nonexclusive properties. For example, we might classify kinds of food by a number of properties. Four foods and six properties are shown in Figure 8.2. Since a particular food may have more than one property, an enumerated type is not sufficient, but a set type is appropriate.

Example 8.1   Using Sets for Classification

To express the table that appears in Figure 8.2 in Turing, we declare two enumerations corresponding to the rows and columns of the table:

```
type Prop : enum (HiProtein, Fatty, Tasty, Dark, Available, Expensive)
type Food : enum (Brie, Broccoli, Caviar, Chocolate)
```

Each row and column of Figure 8.2 is a set. If we are interested in the set of properties associated with a food, the columns are the sets of interest:

```
type PropSet : set of Prop
```

Property	Food Brie	Broccoli	Caviar	Chocolate
High in protein	•		•	
High in fat	•			•
Strong taste	•		•	•
Dark color		•	•	•
Widely available	•	•		•
Expensive	•		•	

Figure 8.2   Properties of Food

With these declarations, we can represent the table as an array of sets of properties indexed by foods:

const *FoodProps* : array *Food* of *PropSet* := init (
  PropSet (*Prop.HiProtein*, *Prop.Fatty*, *Prop.Tasty*,
    Prop.Available, *Prop.Expensive*),
  PropSet (*Prop.Dark*, *Prop.Available*),
  PropSet (*Prop.HiProtein*, *Prop.Dark*, *Prop.Expensive*),
  PropSet (*Prop.Fatty*, *Prop.Tasty*, *Prop.Dark*, *Prop.Available*))

8.1.4   Structuring Data

Arrays, sets, and initializers, used in combination, enable us to build useful structures without writing any statements. The example of representing bridge hands shows how much we can do with type and constant declarations alone.

Example 8.2   Using Sets to Represent Bridge Hands

A standard deck of playing cards has 52 cards divided into four suits. There are also two jokers, which we ignore. The cards in a suit, in order of rank, are 2, 3, 4, 5, 6, 7, 8, 9, 10, Jack = 11, Queen = 12, King = 13, and Ace = 14. At the beginning of each round of a bridge game, one of the four players deals 13 cards from a shuffled deck to each player. Since the only interesting feature of a bridge hand is the presence or absence of a particular card, we can use sets to simulate bridge deals.

We declare the rank of a card as a subrange type and the cards of a particular suit as a set type:

    type *RankType* : 2 .. 14
    type *CardSet* : set of *RankType*

A hand consists of four such sets, one for each suit:

    type *SuitType* : enum (*Spades, Hearts, Diamonds, Clubs*)
    type *HandType* : array *SuitType* of *CardSet*

Bridge players are generally known by the compass directions North, East, South, and West, whether or not they actually sit in these positions. A game begins when each player has received a hand:

    type *PlayerType* : enum (*North, East, South, West*)
    type *GameType* : array *PlayerType* of *HandType*

A variable of type *GameType* is an array with four components, one for each player. Each component of the array is a variable of type *HandType*, which in turn is an array of four components, each one a set of cards in a particular suit.

Using Turing's ability to declare structured constants, we can declare some useful constant values of these types. An empty hand contains no cards and a fresh deck of cards contains every card.

    const *Empty* : *HandType* :=
       init (*CardSet* (), *CardSet* (), *CardSet* (), *CardSet* ())
    const *Deck* : *HandType* :=
       init (*CardSet* (all), *CardSet* (all), *CardSet* (all), *CardSet* (all))

To display hands, we need symbols and colors for the suits. The character codes we use here for the suit symbols are suitable for the PC. For other computers, we would use the letters "S", "H", "D", and "C" to stand for spades, hearts, diamonds, and clubs.

    const *SuitChars* : array *SuitType* of string (1) :=
       init (*chr* (6), *chr* (3), *chr* (4), *chr* (5))
    const *SuitColors* : array *SuitType* of 0 .. 15 := init (*black, red, red, black*)

We display the hands on the screen with north at the top. Each player position has a name and a position on the screen. The screen position is specified as a row and a column.

    const *Positions* : array *PlayerType* of string (5) :=
       init ("North", "East", "South", "West")
    const *Rows* : array *PlayerType* of 1 .. 25 := init (3, 9, 15, 9)
    const *Cols* : array *PlayerType* of 1 .. 80 := init (31, 51, 31, 11)

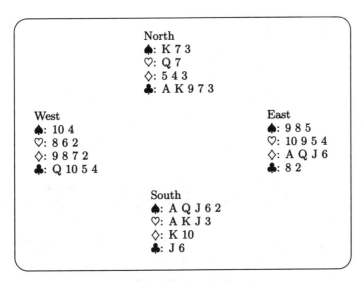

Figure 8.3   Displaying a Bridge Hand

We use a constant array to map card ranks into names:

```
type RankType : 2 .. 14
const CardName : array RankType of string (2) := init (
    "2", "3", "4", "5", "6", "7", "8",
    "9", "10", "J", "Q", "K", "A")
```

The procedure *ShowHands* displays the hands of all four players. It consists of three nested loops: one for the players, one for the suits, and one for the cards within a suit. Since it is conventional in bridge to list the cards in descending rank order, from Ace down to 2, we use decreasing in the for loop.

Since *Game* is an array of arrays, we can give it two subscripts. *Game* denotes four hands; *Game* (*Player*) denotes one player's hand, and *Game* (*Player*) (*Suit*) denotes the set of cards in a particular suit of that player's hand. Figure 8.3 shows the result of executing *ShowHands*.

```
procedure ShowHands (Game : GameType)
    for Player : PlayerType
        color (blue)
        locate (Rows (Player), Cols (Player))
        put Positions (Player) ..
        for Suit : SuitType
            color (SuitColors (Suit))
            locate (Rows (Player) + ord (Suit) + 1, Cols (Player))
```

```
        put SuitChars (Suit), ":    " ..
        for decreasing Rank : 14 .. 2
          if Rank in Game (Player) (Suit) then
            put CardName (Rank), "  " ..
          end if
        end for
      end for
    end for
  end ShowHands
```

Procedure *Deal* uses Turing's random number generator to simulate dealing. We begin with two arrays. The first array, called *Cards*, is initialized with a full deck of cards. The second array, called *Game*, is initialized with four empty hands. There are two nested loops: the outer loop cycles once for each card in the hand, and the inner loop cycles once for each player.

We use the random number generator to generate random suits and ranks. Using random numbers presents the problem that the generator might choose a card that has already been dealt. We avoid this problem by calling the random generator in a loop, exiting only after obtaining a valid suit or rank. The statements

```
    Cards (Suit) −= CardSet (Rank)
    Game (Player) (Suit) += CardSet (Rank)
```

use the set difference and sum operators, abbreviated into assignments, to move the chosen card from the dealer's deck to the player's hand. The procedure contains additional statements to display the progress of the deal.

```
    procedure Deal (var Game : GameType)
      color (blue)
      locate (24, 10)
      put "Dealing " ..
      var Cards := Deck
      for Player : PlayerType
        Game (Player) := Empty
      end for
      for Cycle : RankType
        for Player : PlayerType
          var Suit : SuitType
          loop
            var Trial : int
            randint (Trial, 1, 4)
            case Trial of
```

```
            label 1 : Suit := SuitType . Spades
            label 2 : Suit := SuitType . Hearts
            label 3 : Suit := SuitType . Diamonds
            label 4 : Suit := SuitType . Clubs
          end case
          exit when Cards (Suit) ≠ CardSet ()
        end loop
        color (SuitColors (Suit))
        put SuitChars (Suit) . .
        var Rank : int
        loop
          randint (Rank, 2, 14)
          exit when Rank in Cards (Suit)
        end loop
        Cards (Suit) −= CardSet (Rank)
        Game (Player) (Suit) += CardSet (Rank)
      end for
    end for
  end Deal
```

The main program is a loop that alternately deals a hand and displays it on the screen. The program stops when the user presses the ESC key.

```
const Escape := chr (27)
randomize
setscreen ("nocursor")
setscreen ("noecho")
loop
  var Game : GameType
  Deal (Game)
  for Player : PlayerType
    ShowHands (Game)
  end for
  var Ch : string (1)
  getch (Ch)
  cls
  exit when Ch = Escape
end loop
```

Although it is a large step from dealing a random hand to playing a game of bridge, the data structures we have declared for this example might well serve as a basis for a program that plays bridge.

8.2   Records

Most objects have many different properties of which only some are relevant for a particular application. For example, a person is associated with a name, an age, and a credit rating, among other properties. Similarly, a car is associated with a manufacturer, a model, a price, and so on. The common feature of properties like these is that we are usually interested in a small number of items of different types. We cannot use arrays to encode the information because arrays store many items of the same type. The appropriate data structure for these applications is the *record*.

8.2.1   Programming with Records

A record declaration introduces the components of a record. Each component has a name and a type. Having declared a record type, we can declare variables of the type and use them.

Example 8.3   Using Records

In Example 4.3 on page 107, we used the following declarations to describe roses:

> const *NameLength* := 10
> type *RoseType* : enum (*HybridTea, Floribunda, Miniature,*
>   *Climber, Rambler, Shrub*)
> const *RoseName* : array *RoseType* of string (*NameLength*) :=
>   init ("hybridtea", "floribunda", "miniature",
>   "climber", "rambler", "shrub")

A careful gardener who decides to keep a history of the rose garden might use a data type like the one below.

> type *RoseRecord* :
>   record
>   *Kind* : *RoseType*
>   *YearPlanted* : int
>   *Location* : string (30)
>   *Height* : int
>   *Color* : string (15)
>   end record

The declaration of *RoseRecord* introduces a new type. To maintain information about actual roses, we must declare some variables of this type. Here, a suitable declaration is followed by statements that assign values to the record components:

var *BigRose* : *RoseRecord*
BigRose.*Kind* := *RoseType*.*Rambler*
BigRose.*YearPlanted* := 1989
BigRose.*Location* := "Front, left of porch"
BigRose.*Height* := 60   % inches.
BigRose.*Color* := "Wine red"

A variable of type *RoseRecord* has five components, called *fields*. Each field has a name: *Kind*, *YearPlanted*, and so on. Each field also has a type and behaves like a variable of that type. For example, the type of *YearPlanted* is int, and the component *BigRose*.*YearPlanted* is an integer variable. Since it is an integer variable, we may use it in expressions, assign values to it, pass it as an argument to subprograms, and so on. A diagrammatic representation of a record appears in Figure 8.4.

To use a field of a record, we must identify both the record and the field. We do this by writing a *selector* consisting of the record name, a dot, and the field name. The expression *BigRose*.*YearPlanted* selects a field of the record *BigRose*.

In a record type declaration, the names of the fields must be distinct. Field names do not, however, have to be different from other names in the program. This is because field names are always used after the dot in a selector. We can think of the field name in the declaration of *RoseRec* as being in a hidden scope that is revealed by the phrase "*RoseRec*.".

The dot notation is related to the index notation used for arrays. If A is the name of an array, then $A(I)$ is the name of its Ith component. Similarly, if R is a record, then $R.F$ is the name of its field F. The names A and R are labels for *composite variables* or *structured variables*. The terms $A(I)$ and $R.F$ select components of these variables.

BigRose

Kind	Rambler
YearPlanted	1989
Location	"Front, left of porch"
Height	60
Color	"Wine red"

Figure 8.4   A Value of the Type *RoseRecord*

We can declare a constant or variable record with an initializer. The initializer has the same form as an array initializer: the keyword init is followed by a list of field values.

The following declaration achieves the effect of the assignments to the fields of *BigRose* in Example 8.3.

> var *BigRose* : *RoseRecord* :=
>   init (*RoseType*.*Rambler*, 1989, "Front, left of porch", 60, "Wine red")

A record can have fields that are arrays, and an array can have components that are records. We can use records and arrays to build data structures as complex as we need. Arrays are useful for aggregations with many components of the same type. Records are useful for aggregations of a few variables of different types.

Example 8.4   Storing Records in Arrays

An inventory containing a single rose is of little use. The gardener would be better served by an array of rose records:

> const *RoseMax* := 50
> type *RoseIndex* : 0 .. *RoseMax*
> var *RoseData* : array *RoseIndex* of *RoseRecord*

The procedure *ShowRose* uses selection to display the components of the rose record *Rose* at position (*Row*, *Col*) on the screen. The display requires five lines, one for each component of the record.

> procedure *ShowRose* (*Row*, *Col* : int, *Rose* : *RoseRecord*)
>   *locate* (*Row*, *Col*)
>   put "Kind: ", *RoseName* (*Rose*.*Kind*) ..
>   *locate* (*Row* + 1, *Col*)
>   put "Year planted: ", *Rose*.*YearPlanted* ..
>   *locate* (*Row* + 2, *Col*)
>   put "Location: ", *Rose*.*Location* ..
>   *locate* (*Row* + 3, *Col*)
>   put "Height: ", *Rose*.*Height*," inches" ..
>   *locate* (*Row* + 4, *Col*)
>   put "Color: ", *Rose*.*Color* ..
> end *ShowRose*

Assuming that the array *RoseData* has been filled with useful data, we could write a simple "rose browser" along the following lines.

```
cls
loop
   locate (1, 1)
   put "Please enter rose number:   " ..
   var Num : int
   get Num
   exit when Num = 0
   if 1 ≤ Num and Num ≤ RoseMax then
      ShowRose (3, 10, RoseData (Num))
   else
      put "Invalid number."
   end if
end loop
```

8.2.2   Rules for Records

We have seen, in Example 4.7 on page 112 for instance, that the size of an array can be determined at run-time. If the array is a component of a record, however, this is not possible. Each component of a record must have a size that is known at compile-time. Consequently, a record type must not include variable-length arrays or strings.

A record type declaration introduces a unique type that is not equivalent to any other type. The types *Point* and *Position* are not equivalent, although they have identical structures:

```
type Point :
   record
      X, Y : real
   end record
type Position :
   record
      X, Y : real
   end record
```

Merely renaming, however, does not introduce a new type. The type *Coordinate*, declared as

```
type Coordinate : Position
```

is simply another name for *Position* and is therefore equivalent to it.

We can use the assignment operator to copy the components of one record to another. If A and B are records with the same type, the statement $A := B$ copies the components of B into the corresponding fields of A.

We cannot compare records using the comparison operators. If it is meaningful to compare records for equality, or to decide whether one record is bigger than another in some sense, we can write a function that explicitly compares fields.

The reason that Turing does not provide comparison operators for records is that the meaning of a comparison depends on the application. Suppose that *Rose1* and *Rose2* are variables of type *RoseRecord*. What does it mean to say *Rose1* = *Rose2*? A reasonable definition might be: Two roses are equal if they are of the same kind and they are growing in the same place. In other words, we do not consider the age, height, or color of roses in the comparison. But there is no way that a programming language can decide which fields of the record to include in the comparison and which to ignore. Consequently, we must define special functions if we want to compare records. The following function would be suitable for comparing roses.

```
function EqualRoses (Rose1, Rose2 : RoseRecord) : boolean
    result Rose1.Kind = Rose2.Kind
        and Rose1.Location = Rose2.Location
end EqualRoses
```

8.2.3   Combining Records and Arrays

In this section, a simple program demonstrates several aspects of record processing. In the example, unlike in previous examples in this book, we introduce parts of the program in the order in which they would normally arise during program development. Before the program can be executed, the parts must be reordered to satisfy Turing's "declare before use" rule.

Example 8.5   Storing Information in Records and Arrays

We choose between records and arrays on the basis of the kind of data that we need to store. The information that a teacher needs about a student might include the student's name, identification number (ID), numerical marks, and letter grade. The heterogeneous nature of this data suggests that we use a record for each student. The class as a whole has a homogeneous structure because the teacher needs the same information about each student. This suggests that we use an array to represent the class. We declare

```
const MaxStudents := 50
type StudIndex : 1 .. MaxStudents
var Class : array StudIndex of StudentRec
```

This code cannot be compiled by Turing because we have not yet declared the type *StudentRec*.

A student record contains the name, ID, test scores, and total score for a student. We restrict names to 30 characters and IDs to 8 characters. If we use default strings with 255 characters, the name and ID alone would require more than 500 characters in each record.

```
const NameLen := 30
const IDLen := 8
const MaxTests := 20
type TestIndex : 1 .. MaxTests
type StudentRec :
  record
    Name : string (NameLen)
    ID : string (IDLen)
    Marks : array TestIndex of real
    Total : real
  end record
```

The first action of the program is to determine the number of students in the class and the number of tests they will take. If these numbers exceed the capacity of the program, it issues an apologetic message and quits. The statement quit is defined in OOT but not in Turing; its effect is to halt the program immediately.

```
var NumStudents : int
put "Enter class size:  " ..
get NumStudents
if NumStudents > MaxStudents then
  put "Sorry, I can't process that many students."
  quit
end if

var NumTests : int
put "Enter number of tests:  " ..
get NumTests
if NumTests > MaxTests then
  put "Sorry, I can't process that many tests."
  quit
end if
```

Next, the program asks the user to enter the name and ID of each student:

```
put skip, "Please enter the name and ID of each student."
for St : 1 .. NumStudents
    GetName (Class (St))
    put ""
end for
```

The procedure *GetName* obtains the information required for a single student. It also initializes the test scores for the student. An entire student record is passed as a variable parameter to the procedure. Within the procedure, we can access fields of the record because its declaration is in scope. The code given here does not perform any validation.

```
procedure GetName (varStudent : StudentRec)
    put "Name:    " ..
    get Student.Name
    put "ID: " ..
    get Student.ID
    for Test : TestIndex
        Student.Marks (Test) := 0.0
    end for
end GetName
```

The next step is to read the scores for all the tests. The program uses a nested loop to do this; the outer loop cycles through the tests and the inner loop cycles through the students:

```
for Test : 1 .. NumTests
    put skip, "Please enter results for test ", Test
    for St : 1 .. NumStudents
        GetMark (Class (St), Test)
    end for
end for
```

After reading all the scores, the program computes the total score for each student:

```
for St : 1 .. NumStudents
    Class (St).Total := 0.0
    for Test : 1 .. NumTests
        Class (St).Total += Class (St).Marks (Test)
    end for
end for
```

The procedure *GetMark* asks the user to enter the score for a particular student. Its parameters are a student record and a test number:

```
procedure GetMark (varStudent : StudentRec, Test : TestIndex)
    put ShowName (Student), " :    " ..
    get Student. Marks (Test)
end GetMark
```

Finally, the program asks if the user wants a report. If so, the program displays the total mark, followed by individual test marks, for each student.

```
var Reply : string (1)
put "Do you want a report?    " ..
getch  (Reply)
put ""
if Reply = "y" or Reply = "Y" then
   for St : 1 .. NumStudents
       Report (Class (St), NumTests)
   end for
end if
```

The procedure *Report* prints the report for each student. It uses two subsidiary functions, *ShowName* and *ShowId*, to convert the name and ID of a student to fixed length strings.

```
function ShowName (Student : StudentRec) : string (NameLen)
    result Student. Name + repeat (" ", NameLen − length (Student. Name))
end ShowName

function ShowID (Student : StudentRec) : string (IDLen)
    result Student. ID + repeat (" ", IDLen − length (Student. ID))
end ShowID

procedure Report (Student : StudentRec, NumTests : TestIndex)
    put ShowName (Student), " ", ShowID (Student) ..
    put Student. Total : 6 : 1 ..
    for Test : 1 .. NumTests
       put Student. Marks (Test) : 6 : 1 ..
    end for
    put skip
end Report
```

Discussion

Examples 8.2 and 8.5 both illustrate the importance of developing data structures at an early stage in program construction. If the data structures are suited to the application, it is straightforward to write the code. Conversely, it is often the case when coding proves difficult that the data structures are not appropriate.

8.3   Unions

Although the rule that a variable has a unique type contributes to the readability and security of a program, occasionally it is a nuisance. There are situations in which we actually want to use a variable to store values of different types. For these occasions, Turing provides *union* types.

8.3.1   Using Unions

We use a union type when we need a variable that can play different roles in different situations. The union variable has a *tag* that determines its role each time it is used.

Example 8.6   Variable Data Formats

A sensor in a factory measures and reports two real values corresponding to the temperature and pressure of water in a boiler. Occasionally, the sensor is unable to measure the values and, instead of sending the values, it sends a string explaining why the measurement could not be made. A record stores the information sent by the sensor:

```
type MeasureRecord :
   record
      Valid : boolean
      Temperature, Pressure : real
      Explanation : string (60)
   end record
```

If the field *Valid* is true, the values of *Temperature* and *Pressure* are reliable. Otherwise, the program should not access these values but instead should use the field *Explanation*.

The union type provides an alternative way of representing the information provided by the sensor. Here is the union declaration:

```
type MeasureUnion :
   union Valid : boolean of
      label true :
         Temperature, Pressure : real
      label false :
         Explanation : string (60)
   end union
```

Suppose that M is a variable of type *MeasureUnion*. If M. *Valid* is true, Turing allows us to access the fields M. *Temperature* and M. *Pressure* but not the field M. *Explanation*. Conversely, if M. *Valid* is false, Turing allows us to access M. *Explanation* but not M. *Temperature* or M. *Pressure*.

The union declaration has significant advantages over the record declaration. It is safe, because Turing prevents access to fields that have not been initialized. It may also save memory; since the fields *Temperature* and *Pressure* can never be active at the same time as the field *Explanation*, they can be overlaid in memory.

A union declaration resembles a **case** statement. The resemblance is intentional; **case** statements provide an obvious way of processing union variables. The following procedure shows how we could display a report from the sensor.

```
procedure Show (M : MeasureUnion)
   case M . Valid of
      label true :
         put "Temperature = ", M . Temperature : 8 : 2
         put "Pressure = ", M . Pressure : 8 : 2
      label false :
         put "Temperature and pressure unknown:   ", M . Explanation
   end case
end Show
```

The field *Valid* of *MeasureUnion* is called the *tag field*. The type of the tag must be a subrange or an enumeration. Turing does not permit assignment to the tag value; instead, we use a **tag** statement to set the value of a tag. Procedure *GetPumpData* illustrates the use of **tag** statements to initialize a measurement.

```
procedure GetPumpData (var M : MeasureUnion)
   if [____] then   % A measurement has been made
   tag M , true
   M . Pressure := 100.0
   M . Temperature := 99.9
```

```
    else
       tag M, false
       M.Explanation := "the pipe has burst."
    end if
end GetPumpData
```

8.3.2   Combining Unions and Records

We can combine unions with other types. Arrays and records may contain unions. A union may contain arrays or records. When an array is part of a union, its size must be known at compile-time.

Example 8.7   Inserting a Union into a Record

Some teachers allow their students to do projects instead of tests. We describe how to modify the program of Example 8.5 to accommodate both projects and tests. We show only the code that needs to be changed.

The first step is to declare a type for storing the results of tests or projects. We store marks for tests in an array, as before. We assume that there are two projects, named *First* and *Second*.

```
    type OptType : enum (Tests, Projects)
    type ScoreType :
       union Option : OptType  of
          label OptType.Tests :
             Marks : array TestIndex of real
          label OptType.Projects :
             First, Second : real
       end union
```

The variable *Score* of type *ScoreType* becomes part of the student record:

```
    type StudentRec :
       record
          Name : string (NameLen)
          ID : string (IDLen)
          Score : ScoreType
          Total : real
       end record
```

We must determine whether a student has chosen to do a project or test. We revise the procedure *GetName* on page 232 so that it obtains this information as well as the student's name and ID from the user.

```
procedure GetName (var Student : StudentRec)
  put "Name:   " ..
  get Student.Name
  put "ID: " ..
  get Student.ID
  put "Project?   " ..
  var Reply : string
  get Reply
  if Reply (1) = "Y" or Reply (1) = "y" then
    tag Student.Score, OptType.Projects
  else
    tag Student.Score, OptType.Tests
    for Test : TestIndex
      Student.Score.Marks (Test) := 0.0
    end for
  end if
end GetName
```

Procedure *GetMark* on page 233 requires only a small change; the variable *Student.Marks (Test)* becomes *Student.Score.Marks (Test)*:

```
procedure GetMark (var Student : StudentRec, Test : TestIndex)
  put ShowName (Student), ":   " ..
  get Student.Score.Marks (Test)
end GetMark
```

The action of the revised procedure *Report* depends on whether the student has chosen to do tests or projects.

```
procedure Report (Student : StudentRec, NumTests : TestIndex)
  put ShowName (Student), " ", ShowID (Student) ..
  put Student.Total : 6 : 1 ..
  case Student.Score.Option of
    label OptType.Tests :
      for Test : 1 .. NumTests
        put Student.Score.Marks (Test) : 6 : 1 ..
      end for
    label OptType.Projects :
      put Student.Score.First : 6 : 1, Student.Score.Second : 6 : 1 ..
  end case
  put ""
end Report
```

The revised main section of the program asks for test results first, ignoring students doing projects.

```
for Test : 1 .. NumTests
  put skip, "Please enter results for test ", Test
  for StNum : 1 .. NumStudents
    case Class (StNum). Score. Option of
      label OptType. Tests :
        GetMark (Class (StNum), Test)
      label OptType. Projects :
    end case
  end for
end for
```

The user enters marks for projects after entering all test results. Compare the use of if here with case in the part above.

```
put skip, "Please enter marks for projects."
for StNum : 1 .. NumStudents
  if Class (StNum). Score. Option = OptType. Projects then
    put Class (StNum). Name
    put "Project 1:   " ..
    get Class (StNum). Score. First
    put "Project 2:   " ..
    get Class (StNum). Score. Second
  end if
end for
```

The last step is to change the code that computes total marks. A case statement is appropriate for this because both alternatives require some action.

```
for StNum : 1 .. NumStudents
  Class (StNum). Total := 0.0
  case Class (StNum). Score. Option of
    label OptType. Tests :
      for Test : 1 .. NumTests
        Class (StNum). Total += Class (StNum). Score. Marks (Test)
      end for
    label OptType. Projects :
      Class (StNum). Total := Class (StNum). Score. First+
        Class (StNum). Score. Second
  end case
end for
```

8.3.3   Rules for Unions

A union must not contain two fields with the same name, even if they belong to different variants. Turing reports an error if the program attempts to access an invalid field. Two union types with separate declarations are not equivalent, even if they have identical structure. As with records, union types are equivalent if one is simply a renaming of the other.

8.4   The bind Statement

The use of arrays, records, and unions in combination can lead to cumbersome names. In this chapter, we have seen how nested data structures give rise to names such as *Class (StNum). Score. Option*. With more deeply nested data structures, even longer names may be necessary.

Cumbersome names are annoying to write, hard to read, and slow to compute. The bind statement provides a convenient and safe way of abbreviating a name. In the statement

> bind ☐ to ☐

the first box stands for a simple variable name that has not been used in the current scope, and the second box stands for a variable reference. The reference is usually, but not necessarily, a compound reference.

If the variable *Descriptors (Desc). Row* is used several times in a scope, we could declare the abbreviation *ThisDesc* for it by adding the statement

> bind *ThisDesc* to *Descriptors (Desc). Row*

The new statement is a declaration of *ThisDesc*. Within its scope, we can write *ThisDesc* rather than *Descriptors (Desc). Row*. We can access *ThisDesc* as often as we need, but we cannot alter its value: it is effectively a constant. Alternatively, we could have written

> bind var *ThisDesc* to *Descriptors (Desc). Row*

After this statement, we could both access and alter *ThisDesc*. Assigning to it would have the same effect as assigning to *Descriptors (Desc). Row*. In other words, *ThisDesc* becomes a synonym for *Descriptors (Desc). Row*.

A name declared in a bind statement is similar to a formal parameter declaration in a subprogram. Without var, the new object behaves like a constant. With var, it behaves like a synonym for the corresponding argument or, in the case of the bind statement, the variable reference to which it is bound.

8.5 Summary

Numbers in parentheses refer to sections where material appears.

▶ For any subrange or enumeration T with 31 or fewer values, we can declare a set type whose values are sets of values of T (8.1.1).

▶ If T is a set type, $T\,()$ is the set that contains no values of T, and $T\,(\text{all})$ is the set that contains all values of T (8.1.1).

▶ The operator "in" tests for set membership (8.1.2). The other set operators are "+", "*", "−", "=", "≠", "<", "≤", ">", and "≥". They are defined in Figure 8.1 on page 219.

▶ Set types are equivalent if they have the same base type (8.1).

▶ A record is a data structure that has a small number of named fields that are usually not all of the same type (8.2).

▶ If R is a value of a record type with a field F, then $R.F$ selects the component F of the record R (8.2.1).

▶ Records may have strings and arrays as components (8.2.1). If a record has a field that is an array, the upper bound of the array must be a compile-time constant.

▶ Two record types are equivalent only if one names the other or both name the same type (8.2.2).

▶ A union has a tag, which must be a subrange or an enumeration, and a set of fields (8.3.1). The tag value determines which fields are active.

▶ The tag of a union variable can be changed only by a **tag** statement (8.3.1). After a **tag** statement has been executed, all of the fields of the union are undefined.

▶ Two union types are equivalent only if one names the other or both name the same type (8.3.3).

▶ A bind statement introduces a local name for a variable reference (8.4). If the name declared in the bind statement is preceded by the keyword **var**, the name acts as a synonym for the variable reference. Otherwise, it behaves as an initialized constant.

▶ A bind statement must be nested in a control structure or procedure (8.4).

8.6   Exercises

8.1   Assume that Turing has processed the following declarations:

> type *Numbers* : set of 0 .. 10
> var $A := Numbers\,(1, 2, 4, 6, 8)$
> var $B := Numbers\,(0, 1, 2, 3, 4)$

Decide whether each of the following expressions is legal. If it is, give its value.

(a) 2 in A

(b) $A + B$

(c) $A - B$

(d) $A * B$

(e) A/B

(f) 4 in A and $A \leq B$

(g) $2 + 4$ in $A + B$

(h) $2 * 4$ in $A * B$

8.2   Suppose that the type *SmallSet* is defined as in Section 8.1; its values are therefore subsets of $\{\,0, 1, 2, \ldots, 20\,\}$.

(a) Write a procedure that displays a value of *SmallSet* in a readable notation.

(b) Write a procedure that constructs all values of *SmallSet* and displays them.

(c) Write a procedure that generates a random value of *SmallSet* that contains K elements for a given value of K between 0 and 20.

(d) Write a function that computes the symmetric difference of two values of *SmallSet*. The symmetric difference of two sets A and B contains those elements that belong either to A or to B but not to both.

8.3   Write declarations for a constant array of sets that contains all the information that appears in Figure 8.2 on page 221.

8.4   Suppose that we write a number of invitations and then address corresponding envelopes. Hurrying to catch the mail, we stuff the invitations into envelopes at random.

(a) What are the chances that every invitation will go into the correct envelope?

(b) More generally, if there are N invitations and envelopes, what are the chances that M of them will be correct?

(c) Write a program that simulates random stuffing and derives a probability distribution.

8.5   For each of the entities listed below, declare a suitable record type, a procedure that reads values from the keyboard and stores them in a record, and a procedure that displays a record in a readable format.

(a) a person

(b) a vehicle

(c) an invoice

(d) a building

8.6   Write an inventory program for a collection of objects you find interesting, such as compact disks, video tapes, stamps, coins, recipes, or photographs.

8.7   Organize the code segments of Example 8.5 so that they respect the "declare before use" rule. Check that Turing compiles the program without errors.

Chapter 9

Collections

Two elements of data organization are central to program design. The first element is the design of individual components. The second element, which dominates in all but the simplest programs, is the management of many components of a particular type. A text processor must store many words, and a spreadsheet must store the contents of many cells. Although arrays can be used to store many components, an important restriction governs their use. The size of an array is fixed at the time of declaration. Arrays cannot grow and shrink to match changing requirements as the program runs.

Collections are similar to arrays but one difference is crucial. The size of a collection is not determined at the time of declaration. Collections can grow and shrink as the program runs. When a new component is needed, the program allocates memory for it. When the component is no longer needed, the program can release the memory it has been using.

The advantage of collections over arrays is particularly significant for programs that use several data structures. If the size of the data structures is fixed when the program starts, an overflow in any one of the structures causes the program to fail. If the data structures grow and shrink in accordance with the needs of the program, the program fails only if the entire memory is filled.

9.1   From Arrays to Collections

This section serves two purposes. It introduces collections and it demonstrates the similarities between arrays and collections. We outline the development of two simple programs that store strings. One program stores the strings in an array, and the other stores them in a collection.

Example 9.1   Storing Strings in an Array

The following program declares an array, A, large enough to hold five strings, and it puts one string into the array.

```
type Index : 1 .. 5
var A : array Index of string (50)
var I := 3
A (I) := "Not to put too fine a point upon it."
```

After Turing has executed these statements, the component $A(3)$ of the array A will contain the string in the final assignment. The variable I is called an *index*.

Example 9.2   Storing Strings in a Collection

The following program performs the same task as the program of Example 9.1. It declares a collection, C, to store strings, and it puts one string into the collection.

```
var C : collection of string (50)
var P : pointer to C
new C, P
C (P) := "Not to put too fine a point upon it."
```

After Turing has executed these statements, the component $C(P)$ of the collection C will contain a string. The variable P is called a *pointer*.

The pointer variable P in Example 9.2 plays a role that is similar to the role of the index variable I in the array of Example 9.1. Just as I selects a component of the array A, so P selects a component of the collection C. The difference between the array and the collection is that, whereas I has a limited range of values (1, 2, 3, 4, and 5), the number of possible values of P is limited only by the amount of memory available. In other words, the program can continue to execute **new** statements until it has used up all the available memory.

9.1.1   Pointers

Operations on pointers are conventionally represented by diagrams. The diagram in Figure 9.1 represents the situation after the statement

    var P : pointer to C

has been executed. The diagram consists of a small box labeled with the name of the pointer, P. The box is empty, indicating that P is undefined.

Figure 9.1   Declaring a Pointer Variable

The new statement allocates memory for a new component of the collection. After the statement

    new C, P

has been executed, P contains a pointer to a string, but the string itself is still undefined. Figure 9.2 shows the undefined string as an empty box.

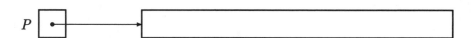

Figure 9.2   Allocating Memory for the String

The name of the new component in the collection is $C\,(P)$. It is a variable, and we can assign to it. Figure 9.3 shows the situation after the statement

    $C\,(P) :=$ "Not to put too fine a point upon it."

has been executed. The component $C\,(P)$ now has a value.

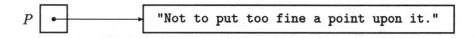

Figure 9.3   Storing a String in a Collection

Copying a Pointer

It is significant that the declaration of a pointer and the allocation of memory are separate operations. There are many situations in which we declare a pointer but do not allocate memory; instead, we use the pointer to point to a component of the collection that was created previously.

Example 9.3   Two Pointers to the Same Item

Suppose that we declare a pointer variable, Q, and assign the value of P to it:

> var Q : pointer to C
> $Q := P$

The result is that P and Q both point to the same component of the collection, as shown in Figure 9.4. The operation performed by the statement $Q := P$ is called *copying a pointer*.

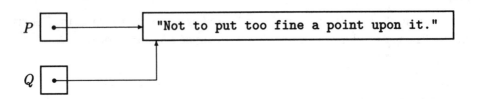

Figure 9.4   Two Pointers to the Same Component

The situation shown in Figure 9.4 has an exact analogy with arrays. In an array, if $I = J$, then $A(I)$ and $A(J)$ denote the same array component. The assignment

> var $J := I$

executed in the context of the array operations of Example 9.1, creates a situation in which $I = J = 3$. Consequently, $A(I)$ and $A(J)$ denote the same string.

Copying a Component

Assignments such as $Q := P$ and $J := I$ change the values of pointers and indexes but do not copy the components of the respective data structures. Although assignments of this kind are useful, it is sometimes necessary to copy the components of a collection, and for this purpose we need a different kind of assignment.

Example 9.4 Copying a Component of a Collection

We declare a third pointer, R, and make it point to a new copy of the string. In the assignment statement, we use the components themselves, $C(R)$ and $C(P)$, rather than the pointers, R and P:

```
var R : pointer to C
new C, R
C (R) := C (P)
```

Figure 9.5 shows the cumulative effect of the operations we have performed on the collection C. There are three pointers, P, Q, and R, and two strings, $C(P)$ and $C(R)$. The pointers P and Q refer to the same string.

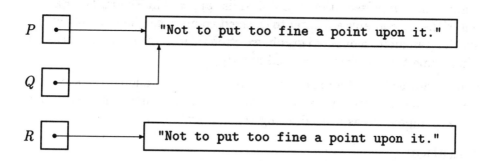

Figure 9.5 **Copying Pointers and Copying Components**

Copying components of a collection is analogous to copying components of an array. The second assignment in the sequence

```
var J := 4
A (J) := A (I)
```

copies the contents of the array component $A(I)$ into the component $A(J)$. To recapitulate, the pointer assignment $Q := P$ is analogous to the index assignment $J := I$ and the collection component assignment $C(R) := C(P)$ is analogous to the array component assignment $A(J) := A(I)$.

The for statement provides a convenient way of processing each component of an array in turn. For example, the following statement makes each component of the array A an empty string.

```
for I : 1 .. 5
    A (I) := ""
end for
```

There is no analogous control structure for collections. In order to process the components of a collection as a unit, we must use pointers to link them together. The result is a *dynamic data structure*.

9.2 Linked Lists

Arrays and records are called *static data structures* because their sizes are determined by their declarations. If the size of a data structure depends on the execution of new statements, the data structure is called *dynamic*. In this section, we introduce the simplest form of dynamic data structure, the linked list. In Section 9.4, we describe a more complex dynamic data structure, the binary tree.

A diagrammatic representation of a linked list appears in Figure 9.6. Each component of the list contains a pointer to the next component. Since a data structure of this kind resembles a directed graph, we often refer to the components as *nodes*. Another name that is sometimes used is *cells*.

The important feature of a linked list is that it can grow and shrink according to the needs of the program. Initially, the list contains no components. The program generates components as needed, using the new statement.

Declaration

Each component of the linked list in Figure 9.6 is a record containing a pointer and an integer. We declare the collection of these records as follows.

```
var Nodes : collection of
  record
    Next : pointer to Nodes
    Value : int
  end record
```

The records appear in Figure 9.6 as boxes with two parts. The top part corresponds to the field *Next* and contains an arrow representing the pointer value *Next*. The arrow appears to point to the field *Next* of each node, but this is just an artifact of the diagram. We should think of each arrow as pointing to the *entire*

Root

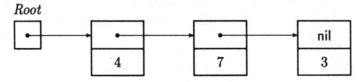

Figure 9.6   A Linked List

node, not to just one field. The bottom part corresponds to the field *Value* and contains a numeral representing the integer value *Value*. The rightmost box contains the special value nil (*Nodes*) in its pointer field, indicating that there are no more components in the list. A pointer with the value nil is called a *null pointer*.

Construction

We construct a dynamic data structure by creating one component at a time. As each component is created, it is linked to the existing structure.

The procedure *MakeList* reads integers from the keyboard and creates a list node for each one. It links each new node into the list starting at *Root*. The value nil(*Nodes*) corresponds to the field labeled nil in Figure 9.6.

```
procedure MakeList (var Root : pointer to Nodes)
    Root := nil (Nodes)
    loop
        var Num : int
        put "Enter a number:   " ..
        get Num
        exit when Num = 0
        var NewNode : pointer to Nodes
        new Nodes, NewNode
        Nodes (NewNode). Value := Num
        Nodes (NewNode). Next := Root
        Root := NewNode
    end loop
end MakeList
```

The procedure *MakeList* links each new node into the beginning of the list. To obtain the list shown in Figure 9.6, the user would enter 3, 7, 4, and 0. Figure 9.7 shows the data structure after the user has entered the numbers 3 and 7.

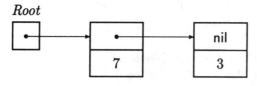

Figure 9.7   The First Two Components

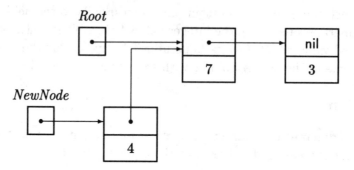

Figure 9.8   Adding a New Component to a Linked List

Suppose now that the user enters the next number, 4. The procedure *MakeList* declares the pointer, *NewNode*, and allocates memory for it. The next statement stores the number, 4, in the new node. The statement after that,

$$Nodes\,(NewNode).\,Next := Root$$

sets the *Next* field of the new node to point to the first component of the list, as shown in Figure 9.8. Finally, the statement

$$Root := NewNode$$

completes the insertion by changing the root pointer to point to the new node, giving the linked list we saw in Figure 9.6 on page 248.

Display

It is useful to have a way of displaying a data structure on the screen. In fact, it is good practice to write display procedures for all data structures, even if the procedures will not be used in the finished program.

The procedure *ShowList* displays a list. Its parameter is a pointer to a list. It uses another pointer, *ThisNode*, to reference and display each component of the list in turn.

```
procedure ShowList (Root : pointer to Nodes)
   var ThisNode := Root
   loop
      exit when  ThisNode = nil (Nodes)
      put Nodes (ThisNode). Value : 4
      ThisNode := Nodes (ThisNode). Next
   end loop
end ShowList
```

The following program uses the procedures *MakeList* and *ShowList* to read numbers from the keyboard, build a list containing the numbers, and display the list.

```
var Root : pointer to Nodes
MakeList (Root)
ShowList (Root)
```

The following interaction with this program constructs the list shown in Figure 9.6.

```
Enter a number:    3
Enter a number:    7
Enter a number:    4
Enter a number:    0
   4 7 3
```

Traversal

When a loop or procedure processes each component of a data structure in turn, we say that the program *traverses* the data structure. The loop statement in procedure *ShowList* traverses the linked list. The following loop statement illustrates a general method for list traversal. The box stands for code that processes the component *Nodes (ThisNode)*.

```
var ThisNode := Root
loop
   exit when ThisNode = nil (Nodes)
   [        ]
   ThisNode := Nodes (ThisNode).Next
end loop
```

A linked list is one of the simplest data structures we can build using pointers. In advanced applications, we can use pointers to create any structure that can be represented using nodes joined by links. The program described in Section 9.5 shows how pointers can be used to build complex data structures that represent algebraic expressions.

9.3   The new and free Statements

When Turing runs a program, it divides the memory into three regions: the *code*, the *stack*, and the *heap*. The code region is used to store the program itself. The stack region is used to store global and local variables. The heap region, which concerns us in this section, is used to store components of collections.

The new statement allocates memory for a component of a collection. The effect of the statement

>   new C, P

is to assign a value to the pointer variable P. After the statement has been executed, P should point to an area of the heap that is not currently being used for something else and is large enough to hold a component of the collection C.

It will sometimes happen that there is not enough memory left in the heap for a new component. In this case, the new statement assigns the special value nil (C) to the pointer P. Because it is possible for the new statement to fail, a well-written program that uses collections should contain statements that check the value of every pointer assigned by a new statement.

The free statement de-allocates memory that was allocated by a new statement. The general form of the free statement is

>   free C, P

in which C is the name of a collection and P is a variable whose type is a pointer to the collection C.

After the free statement has been executed, P is undefined and cannot be used in an expression. The only thing we can do with P after the free statement has been executed is to assign it to another node, using either a new statement or an assignment.

Dangling Pointers

We must use the free statement with care. Incorrect free statements can wreak havoc in the heap region and, what is worse, Turing cannot always detect them. The most serious problem is the dangling pointer — a pointer that references a component that has been de-allocated.

Example 9.5   Creating a Dangling Pointer

The following program creates a situation in which two pointers refer to the same component of a collection. It then invokes free on one of the pointers.

```
var Nodes : collection of int
var P, Q : pointer to Nodes

new Nodes, P
Nodes (P) := 5
Q := P
free Nodes, P
put Nodes (Q)
```

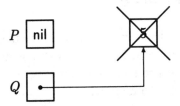

Figure 9.9   A Dangling Pointer

After the assignment $Q := P$, the pointers P and Q both point to a node that contains 5. Figure 9.9 shows the situation after the **free** statement has been executed.

The node containing 5 has been deleted, as shown by the cross over it. The memory occupied by this node is now part of the free space on the heap. The pointer Q, however, still refers to the node. A pointer that refers to a node that has been de-allocated is called a *dangling pointer*; it is an arrow whose target no longer exists. When the program reaches the statement put *Nodes* (Q), it stops with an error message saying that *Nodes* (Q) is not a valid pointer.

Since the program in Example 9.5 is very short, it is not difficult to determine the source of the error. If a program is small, we can usually recognize situations such as that of Example 9.5 and avoid operations that free a node to which there are other pointers. If the program is large, the statement that causes the problem by freeing a component may be far away from the statement that uses the de-allocated component and detects the error.

In general, it is not easy to determine when a node can be safely de-allocated. We may decide not to use **free** at all, in the hope that the user will never run the program for long enough to run out of memory. The alternative is to provide some kind of disciplined memory management.

9.4   Collections and Recursion

Some problems can be analyzed in a way that reveals subproblems that are similar to the original problem but smaller. Consider the problem of displaying a list of four nodes. The following statement is a partial solution of the problem: Display the first node and then display a list of three nodes. In general, we can split the problem of displaying a list of N nodes into two parts; display one node and then display a list of $N - 1$ nodes.

9.4.1   Recursive Traversal

Expressing the problem in this way suggests a recursive solution, as we saw in Section 5.4. If the recursive solution is to work correctly, we need a trivial case in which recursion is not required. The trivial case for linked lists is the empty list, for which there are no nodes to display.

Example 9.6   Recursive List Traversal

The following procedure accomplishes the same task as procedure *ShowList* but it uses a recursive call instead of a loop statement.

```
procedure RecShow (Root : pointer to Nodes)
   if Root not= nil (Nodes) then
      put Nodes (Root). Value : 4
      RecShow (Nodes (Root). Next)
   end if
end RecShow
```

A recursive procedure that operates on lists must consider two cases. Its argument is a pointer to a list node. If the argument is nil, the list is empty, and the procedure performs a trivial task or may even do nothing. If the argument is not nil, it points to a node that has two fields, *Value* and *Next*. The procedure processes *Value* and passes *Next* as an argument in the recursive call. The general pattern is

```
procedure Rec (P : pointer to Nodes
   if P = nil (Nodes) then
      [        ]
   else
      [        ]
      Rec (Nodes (P). Next
   end if
end Rec
```

The first box in this pattern stands for code that will process the empty list. There will often be nothing to do in this case, as in procedure *RecShow* above. The second box stands for code that will process each node in the list, accessing *Nodes (P). Value*.

A procedure that recursively processes a list usually contains one recursive call because a list node contains one pointer. If a node contained two pointers, we would expect the procedure to contain two recursive calls. We consider next a data structure that fulfills this expectation.

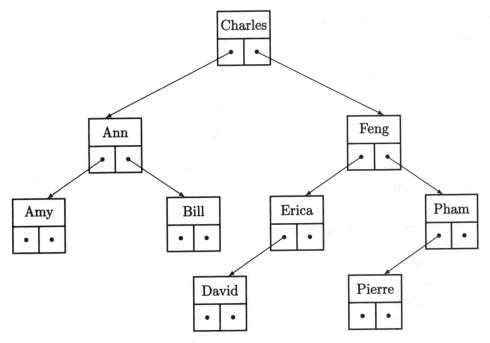

Figure 9.10 A Binary Search Tree

9.4.2 Binary Search Trees

A binary search tree stores information in such a way that components can be retrieved quickly. For the binary search tree shown in Figure 9.10, each component is a person's name. In a practical application, the nodes might contain additional information, such as the person's full name, address, and telephone number.

Each node of a binary search tree contains a *key*, additional information, and two pointers. Each pointer either points to a subtree or is nil. In Figure 9.10, the key is a person's name and there is no additional information. The nodes labeled Ann, Charles, and Feng each have two subtrees. Nodes Erica and Pham have a left subtree but no right subtree. The other nodes each have two empty subtrees. The node labeled Charles is called the *root* of the binary search tree.

In Figure 9.10, note that all the names in the left subtree of the node labeled Charles — that is, Amy, Ann, and Bill — come before Charles in alphabetical order. Similarly, all the names in the right subtree of the node labeled Charles come after Charles in alphabetical order. Moreover, this property is true for every node of the binary search tree. This arrangement enables us to write simple, efficient procedures that find names in the tree and add names to the tree.

Every node of a binary search tree must contain a value from an ordered set. This value is called the *key* of the node. We can use people's names as keys because the set of names is ordered alphabetically. We could also use numbers as keys because numbers are ordered by the relation "less than".

Example 9.7   Storing Information in a Binary Search Tree

We develop a program that builds and uses a binary search tree such as the one shown in Figure 9.10. We begin by declaring data types. The keys are strings of up to twenty characters. The tree itself is a collection of nodes; each node is a record containing a key and pointers to two subtrees named *Left* and *Right*.

```
const MaxNameLen := 20
type NameType : string (MaxNameLen)
var TreeNodes : collection of
   record
      Name : NameType
      Left, Right : pointer to TreeNodes
   end record
```

The following procedure, *Insert*, attempts to store a new name in the tree.

```
procedure Insert (Name : NameType, var Tree : pointer to TreeNodes)
   if Tree = nil (TreeNodes) then
      new TreeNodes, Tree
      TreeNodes (Tree).Name := Name
      TreeNodes (Tree).Left := nil (TreeNodes)
      TreeNodes (Tree).Right := nil (TreeNodes)
   elsif Name < TreeNodes (Tree).Name then
      Insert (Name, TreeNodes (Tree).Left)
   elsif Name > TreeNodes (Tree).Name then
      Insert (Name, TreeNodes (Tree).Right)
   else % The name is already in the tree.
   end if
end Insert
```

The first possibility that we consider is that the tree might be empty: that is, the condition *Tree* = *nil* (*TreeNodes*) is true. In this case, we create a new node, store the new name in it, and make its subtrees empty.

If the tree is not empty, it must have at least one node. The name at the root node is *TreeNodes* (*Tree*).*Name*. There are three possibilities to consider: the name we are inserting may be less than, equal to, or greater than the name in the node. If the new name is less than the name in the node, we must insert it in the left subtree because this will maintain the binary search tree property. We do this by calling *Insert* recursively. Similarly, if the new name is greater than the name in the node, we insert it in the right subtree. The remaining case is that the two names are equal. In this case, the procedure *Insert* does nothing. In another application, some action might be required, such as reporting the error "Duplicate key" or modifying the entry in some way.

In the assignment *TreeNodes* (*Tree*). *Name* := *Name* in the procedure *Insert*, the first occurrence of *Name* refers to a field in a node and the second occurrence refers to the first parameter of the procedure. There is no ambiguity because the left side of the assignment is a selector. Although some programmers prefer to use different identifiers in situations such as this, there is little point in introducing more identifiers than necessary.

The procedure *Show* displays the keys of a binary search tree on the screen. It is organized in a similar way to procedure *Insert*, but it is simpler. There is nothing to do if the argument is the null pointer. If the argument is not null, *Show* calls itself recursively to display the left subtree, uses a put statement to display the name in the node, and calls itself again to display the right subtree.

```
procedure Show (Tree : pointer to TreeNodes)
    if Tree ≠ nil (TreeNodes) then
        Show (TreeNodes (Tree). Left)
        put TreeNodes (Tree). Name
        Show (TreeNodes (Tree). Right)
    end if
end Show
```

The following program uses the procedures *Show* and *Insert* in a simple application. It maintains a single tree, called *Root*. It asks the user to enter names and uses *Insert* to store them in the tree. When the user enters the empty string, it calls *Show* to display the names that have been entered.

```
var Root := nil (TreeNodes)
loop
    var Name : NameType
    put "Enter name (CR to terminate):  " ..
    get Name : *
    exit when Name = ""
    Insert (Name, Root)
end loop
put "You entered the following names:  "
Show (Root)
```

9.5 Designing a Symbolic Calculator

In a linked list, every node has a single pointer. In a binary search tree, every node has two pointers. In this section, we introduce a pointer structure with several different kinds of node. A node may contain zero, one, or two pointers, as well as other data. We use these nodes to store information in an interactive calculator that stores expressions in symbolic form.

We represent an algebraic expression such as $A+B$ using three nodes: one each for "A", "$+$", and "B". The node for "$+$" contains pointers to the nodes for "A" and "B". It is easier to manipulate expressions if they are represented in this way than if they are represented as strings.

The calculator illustrates several important aspects of the use of collections as well as some general principles of programming. The data structure that it uses, a graph with records as nodes and pointers as arcs, is the principal data structure of many complex programs. Data structures of this kind provide the flexibility and generality that we need for complex applications. Finding an appropriate data structure is a key step in the construction of programs of this kind; when that is done, the code follows easily.

In the following dialogue, lines beginning with a colon ("$:$") are the user's input and other lines are the program's response. The line numbers on the left are for reference only; they do not appear on the screen.

```
1   : 0.5 * (27 + 46)
2   36.5
3   : a = (b − 1)/(b + 1)
4   : b = 5
5   : a
6   0.666667
7   : b =
8   : a
9   ((b-1)/(b+1))
```

At line 1, the user entered a numeric expression. At line 2, the program responds with the value of the expression. At line 3, the user gave the variable a the symbolic value $(b-1)/(b+1)$. Similarly, line 4 gives the variable b the numeric value 5. At line 5, the user asks for the value of a, and the program responds at line 6 by displaying 0.666667, the value of $(5-1)/(5+1)$.

Line 7 is valid input: it has the effect of undefining b. Since b now has no value, the response to line 8, in which the user again asks for the value of a, is the symbolic value of a, as defined at line 3.

9.5.1 Data Structure

The symbolic calculator is quite a large program, and we construct it piece by piece. The first step is to define a data structure to represent expressions. This is fundamental: if we choose an inappropriate data structure, it will be very difficult to complete the program.

Next, we will need procedures that display, evaluate, and build expressions. The last of these is the most complicated because it must accept an expression in the form of a string and convert it to the corresponding data structure. The code that performs this conversion is called the *parser*.

The data structure we use to represent expressions is a collection of nodes. Each node contains a variable name, a number, or an operator. Most nodes contain pointers to other nodes. The data structure that represents $a = (b-1)/(b+1)$ and $b = 5$ is shown in Figure 9.11.

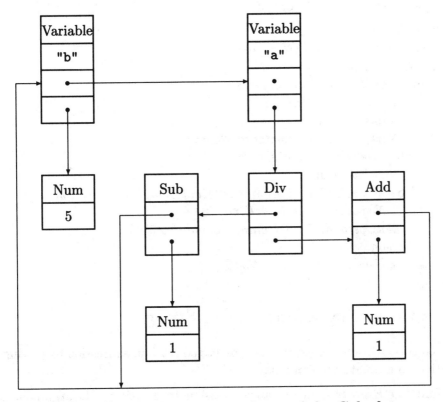

Figure 9.11   Representing a State of the Calculator

We need an enumerated type for the different kinds of node. There will be a value for variables, such as *a* and *b*; a value for numbers, such as 1 and 5; and values for the operators. Another value is required for definitions, such as $b = 5$.

The definition of *NodeKind* below includes other values — *LeftPar*, *RightPar*, *EndMarker*, and *Illegal* — whose purpose we explain later.

> **type** *NodeKind* : **enum** (*Variable, Number, Definition, Add, Sub, Mul, Div,*
>   *LeftPar, RightPar, EndMarker, Illegal*)

The nodes themselves should belong to a collection, since the program will allocate them dynamically. Each component of the collection is a value of a union type. The discriminating tag of the union is *NodeKind*. There are no nodes corresponding to the values *LeftPar, RightPar, EndMarker, Illegal* of *NodeKind*.

A *Variable* node contains the name and value of the variable. It also contains a field, *Next*, which we use to link all the variable nodes together. A *Number* node contains the value of the number. An operator node contains pointers to the left and right operands of the operator.

> **const** *NameLength* := 20
> **type** *NameType* : **string** (*NameLength*)
> **var** *Nodes* : **collection of**
>   **union** *Kind* : *NodeKind* **of**
>   **label** *NodeKind.Variable* :
>   *Name* : *NameType*
>   *Next, NameVal* : **pointer to** *Nodes*
>   **label** *NodeKind.Number* :
>   *NumVal* : **real**
>   **label** *NodeKind.Definition, NodeKind.Add, NodeKind.Sub,*
>   *NodeKind.Mul, NodeKind.Div* :
>   *LeftOperand, RightOperand* : **pointer to** *Nodes*
>   **end union**
> **type** *NodePointer* : **pointer to** *Nodes*

9.5.2   Converting Expressions to Strings

We need two functions for expressions, one to convert an expression to a string and the other to evaluate an expression.

The function *ExprStr* converts an expression to a string. Its argument must be a pointer to a node. If the node is a variable or name, *ExprStr* returns the corresponding string. If the node is an operator, *ExprStr* constructs a string from the left operand, the operator symbol, and the right operand. It places parentheses around the result to avoid ambiguity. An improved version would include parentheses only if they were necessary.

In the code that follows, the function *ExprStr* uses the constant *NodeChars* to convert values of type *NodeKind* to strings.

```
const NodeChars :
    array NodeKind.Definition .. NodeKind.EndMarker of string(1) :=
        init ("=", "+", "-", "*", "/", "(", ")", "$")
```

The argument of *ExprStr* should never be nil and *ExprStr* should never be required to convert a definition node. The precondition expresses these restrictions.

```
function ExprStr (Expr : NodePointer) : string
    pre Expr ≠ nil (Nodes) and Nodes (Expr).Kind ≠ NodeKind.Definition
    case Nodes (Expr).Kind of
        label NodeKind.Variable :
            result Nodes (Expr).Name
        label NodeKind.Number :
            result realstr (Nodes (Expr).NumVal, 1)
        label NodeKind.Add, NodeKind.Sub, NodeKind.Mul, NodeKind.Div :
            result "(" +
                ExprStr (Nodes (Expr).LeftOperand) +
                NodeChars (Nodes (Expr).Kind) +
                ExprStr (Nodes (Expr).RightOperand) +
            ")"
    end case
end ExprStr
```

Evaluating Expressions

The next function, *Evaluate*, attempts to evaluate an expression. It expects a pointer to a node as argument and returns a pointer as its result. Like *ExprStr*, *Evaluate* does not expect a null pointer or a definition as its argument.

The structure of *Evaluate* is a case statement. The action depends on the kind of node passed to it. We show first the structure of the function and then the actions for each case.

```
function Evaluate (Expr : NodePointer) : NodePointer
  pre Expr ≠ nil (Nodes) and Nodes (Expr). Kind ≠ NodeKind. Definition
  case Nodes (Expr). Kind of
    % Cases are described below.
  end case
end Evaluate
```

The node corresponding to a variable may not provide a value for the variable. In such a case, *NameVal* = nil, and *Evaluate* returns the original expression unchanged. If the variable has been defined, the definition is evaluated and the result returned.

```
label NodeKind. Variable :
  if Nodes (Expr). NameVal = nil (Nodes) then
    result Expr
  else
    result Evaluate (Nodes (Expr). NameVal)
  end if
```

If the node contains a number, *Evaluate* returns the expression unchanged. We might expect *Evaluate* to return the number itself, but it cannot do so because the return type of *Evaluate* is *NodePointer* rather than real:

```
label NodeKind. Number :
  result Expr
```

The last possibility is that the node contains an operator. The first step is to evaluate the left and right operands. If both operands turn out to be numbers, we can perform the arithmetic operation, obtaining a new number. If the operation is divide, and the right operand is zero, *Evaluate* reports an error and returns zero.

If one or both operands are not numbers, *Evaluate* constructs a new node with the same operator symbol and pointers to the evaluated operands. This ensures that parts of the expression will be evaluated even if the entire expression cannot be evaluated.

```
label NodeKind. Add, NodeKind. Sub, NodeKind. Mul, NodeKind. Div :
  const Left := Evaluate (Nodes (Expr). LeftOperand)
  const Right := Evaluate (Nodes (Expr). RightOperand)
  var NewExpr : NodePointer
  new Nodes, NewExpr
  if Nodes (Left). Kind = NodeKind. Number  and
      Nodes (Right). Kind = NodeKind. Number then
    tag Nodes (NewExpr), NodeKind. Number
```

```
      case Nodes (Expr). Kind of
        label NodeKind. Add :
          Nodes (NewExpr). NumVal :=
            Nodes (Left). NumVal + Nodes (Right). NumVal
        label NodeKind. Sub :
          Nodes (NewExpr). NumVal :=
            Nodes (Left). NumVal − Nodes (Right). NumVal
        label NodeKind. Mul :
          Nodes (NewExpr). NumVal :=
            Nodes (Left). NumVal * Nodes (Right). NumVal
        label NodeKind. Div :
          if Nodes (Right). NumVal = 0 then
            put "Division by zero!"
            Nodes (NewExpr). NumVal := 0
          else
            Nodes (NewExpr). NumVal :=
              Nodes (Left). NumVal / Nodes (Right). NumVal
          end if
      end case
    else
      tag Nodes (NewExpr), Nodes (Expr). Kind
      Nodes (NewExpr). LeftOperand := Left
      Nodes (NewExpr). RightOperand := Right
    end if
    result NewExpr
```

9.5.3   Variable Names

The calculator must keep track of all the variable names entered by the user. It does this by linking them together in a list, using the *Next* field of the node as the link. In Figure 9.11, this link is the third field of a variable node. The third field of the node for the variable b points to the node for the variable a. The third field of the node for the variable a is nil, indicating that there are no more variables.

To maintain this list, we need a single variable, *NameList*, which is a pointer to the first name on the list. The name list is initially empty.

```
    var NameList := nil (Nodes)
```

The procedure *ShowVariables* displays the value of each variable in the list. If a variable has no value, that is, its value field is nil, *ShowVariables* does not display it. We use a loop statement to visit each node of the list, starting at *NameList* and stopping at nil. If the name list is empty, *NameList* will be nil, and the loop will do nothing.

```
procedure ShowVariables
   var S := NameList
   loop
      exit when S = nil (Nodes)
      if Nodes (S). NameVal ≠ nil (Nodes) then
         put Nodes (S). Name, " = ", ExprStr (Nodes (S). NameVal)
      end if
      S := Nodes (S). Next
   end loop
end ShowVariables
```

When the user enters a definition such as $b = 5$, there are two possibilities to consider. The name defined, b in the example, may already be in the list of names, or it may not.

Finding Names

The procedure *LookUpName* visits each node of the name list looking for a node with a variable name that matches its argument. If it finds a matching node, it returns the corresponding pointer. Otherwise, it creates a new node and initializes it. The new node is linked into the beginning of the list. Consequently, *ShowVariables* will list the most recently declared variable first. This is why, in Figure 9.11, the node for the variable b contains a pointer to the node for the variable a, rather than the other way around.

```
procedure LookUpName (Name : NameType, var Entry : NodePointer)
   Entry := NameList
   loop
      if Entry = nil (Nodes) then
         exit
      elsif Nodes (Entry). Name = Name then
         return
      else
         Entry := Nodes (Entry). Next
      end if
   end loop
```

> new *Nodes*, *Entry*
> tag *Nodes* (*Entry*), *NodeKind* . *Variable*
> *Nodes* (*Entry*) . *Name* := *Name*
> *Nodes* (*Entry*) . *NameVal* := nil (*Nodes*)
> *Nodes* (*Entry*) . *Next* := *NameList*
> *NameList* := *Entry*
> end *LookUpName*

The loop statement in procedure *LookUpName* contains both exit and return statements. The exit statement transfers control to the statements following the loop, which create the new node and link it into the name list. The return statement jumps out of both the loop and the procedure, leaving the name list unchanged. If the loop statement reaches the end of the list without matching the name, *LookUpName* creates a new node containing the name and inserts it at the front of the name list.

9.5.4 Parsing the Input

The last component of the calculator is the parser, which converts the user's input strings into node structures representing the corresponding expressions. We use constant strings to define the characters that are acceptable as input:

> const *Letters* := `"abcdefghijklmnopqrstuvwxyz"`
> const *Digits* := `"0123456789"`
> const *Symbols* := `"+-*/=()$"`

We need several variables to represent the state of the parser. The string *Buffer* holds the string entered by the user. The parser considers the input to be a sequence of *tokens*. A token is a variable name, a number, an operator, or a parenthesis. Blanks are not part of a token. Figure 9.12 shows a typical state of the parser, just after it has read the variable name x2 from the buffer. The integer *BufPos* indexes the character immediately following the token. The value of the current token is the string `"x2"`, indicated with an underscore in Figure 9.12. It is stored in the string *TokenValue*. The parser also records the kind of the token it has read in the variable *TokenKind*. The remaining parser variable is the Boolean *ErrorFlag*, which the parser sets to true if it cannot understand the input string.

> var *Buffer* : string
> var *BufPos* : int
> var *TokenValue* : string
> var *TokenKind* : *NodeKind*
> var *ErrorFlag* : boolean

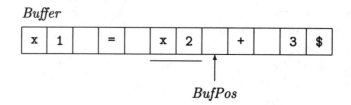

Figure 9.12   Scanning the Input

When the parser encounters an error, it displays a line containing the character
"^", pointing approximately to the place where it got stuck, followed by an error
message.

```
procedure Error(Message : string)
    if not ErrorFlag then
        put repeat(" ", BufPos + 1), "^", skip, Message
        ErrorFlag := true
    end if
end Error
```

Finding a Token

The task of *NextToken* is to adjust the values of *BufPos*, *TokenValue*, and
TokenKind so that they correctly describe the next token in *Buffer*. The first
action of *NextToken* is to skip over blanks and to store the first nonblank character
that it finds in the string *TokenValue*.

The next step is to determine the kind of token. This is easy because the first
character determines the kind: a letter indicates a variable name, a digit indicates
a number, and any other character is either an operator or an illegal symbol.

A problem for *NextToken* is determining when it has reached the end of the input
string. We solve this problem by putting a terminating character at the end of the
string. We assume in *NextToken* that the last character in the buffer is "$".

```
procedure NextToken
    loop
        exit when Buffer(BufPos) ≠ " "
        BufPos += 1
    end loop
    TokenValue := Buffer(BufPos)
```

At this point, we have found a nonblank character and stored it in *TokenValue*.
The next action depends on the value of this character. If it is a letter, we

construct a variable name in *Token Value*. A variable name consists of a letter followed by letters and digits.

```
if index (Letters, Buffer (BufPos)) > 0 then
   loop
      BufPos += 1
      exit when index (Letters + Digits, Buffer (BufPos)) = 0
      if length (Token Value) < NameLength then
         Token Value += Buffer (BufPos)
      end if
   end loop
   TokenKind := NodeKind . Variable
```

If the character is a digit, we read a number. The code given below accepts a decimal point but does not recognize exponential notation. The program can understand "3.14159" but not "5.6e19".

```
elsif index (Digits, Buffer (BufPos)) > 0 then
   loop
      BufPos += 1
      exit when index (Digits, Buffer (BufPos)) = 0
      Token Value += Buffer (BufPos)
   end loop
   if Buffer (BufPos) = "." then
      Token Value += Buffer (BufPos)
      loop
         BufPos += 1
         exit when index (Digits, Buffer (BufPos)) = 0
         Token Value += Buffer (BufPos)
      end loop
   end if
   TokenKind := NodeKind . Number
```

If the character was not a letter or a digit, it should be one of the valid symbols. The loop statement finds the matching value of the enumeration *NodeKind*.

```
elsif index (Symbols, Buffer (BufPos)) > 0 then
   TokenKind := NodeKind . Definition
   loop
      exit when NodeChars (TokenKind) = Buffer (BufPos)
      TokenKind := succ (TokenKind)
   end loop
   BufPos += 1
```

If the character has not been matched at this point, it cannot be legal. We report an error and set *TokenKind* to *Illegal*. Leaving *TokenKind* unchanged might cause the program to parse the input incorrectly or even to fail.

```
else
    Error ("Illegal symbol")
    TokenKind := NodeKind.Illegal
end if
end NextToken
```

Initializing the Parser

The procedure *InitializeParser* sets each parser variable to a value consistent with the rules described above. In particular, it appends "$" to the buffer and sets *BufPos* to the first character position. If *Buffer* was previously empty, it will now consist of the string "$", and *NextToken* will return with *TokenKind* set to *EndMarker*.

```
procedure InitializeParser
    Buffer += "$"
    BufPos := 1
    ErrorFlag := false
    NextToken
end InitializeParser
```

Before we move on to the real work of the parser, we need one more utility procedure. It is called *MakeNode*, and it constructs a new operator node from an operator and two operands.

```
function MakeNode (Op : NodeKind, Left, Right : NodePointer)
        : NodePointer
    var Expr : NodePointer
    new Nodes, Expr
    tag Nodes (Expr), Op
    Nodes (Expr).LeftOperand := Left
    Nodes (Expr).RightOperand := Right
    result Expr
end MakeNode
```

A Grammar for the Calculator

We use a simple grammar to describe the input accepted by the parser. In the following grammar, [...] denotes an optional item and {...} denotes an item that may occur zero or more times. The rule for *expression*, for example, says that an *expression* consists of a *term*, followed by zero or more instances of a sign ("+" or "-") and a *term*.

$$\begin{aligned}
\text{definition} \quad &\longrightarrow \quad \text{expression} \ [\ "=" \ [\ \text{expression} \ ] \ ] \\
\text{expression} \quad &\longrightarrow \quad \text{term} \ \{ \ (\ "+" \ | \ "-" \ ) \ \text{term} \ \} \\
\text{term} \quad &\longrightarrow \quad \text{factor} \ \{ \ (\ "*" \ | \ "/" \ ) \ \text{factor} \ \} \\
\text{factor} \quad &\longrightarrow \quad \text{variable} \ | \ \text{number} \ | \ "(" \ \text{expression} \ ")"
\end{aligned}$$

The rule for a definition allows three possibilities. If the input consists of a single expression not followed by "=", the calculator attempts to evaluate the expression and returns the result. If "=" is present, the first expression must be a simple variable. A definition of the form "$x =$" is allowed and removes any value that x previously possessed. A definition of the form "$x = E$", in which E stands for an expression, assigns the expression to x.

The parser consists of four procedures, one corresponding to each grammar rule. The structure of the procedure matches the structure of the rule, with case statements simulating "|", if statements simulating "[...]", and loop statements simulating "{...}", respectively. This kind of parser is called a *recursive descent* parser.

The grammar is recursive because an expression may be part of a factor, but a factor is itself part of an expression. The recursion is reflected in the procedures: *ParseExpr* calls *ParseTerm*, *ParseTerm* calls *ParseFactor*, and *ParseFactor* calls *ParseExpr*. We must therefore provide **forward** declarations and import lists for these procedures.

```
type SymbolSet : set of NodeKind
const AddOpSyms := SymbolSet (NodeKind.Add, NodeKind.Sub)
const MulOpSyms := SymbolSet (NodeKind.Mul, NodeKind.Div)

forward procedure ParseExpr (var Expr : NodePointer)
import forward ParseTerm, NextToken, MakeNode, var Nodes, NodePointer,
    TokenKind, AddOpSyms

forward procedure ParseTerm (var Term : NodePointer)
import forward ParseFactor, NextToken, MakeNode, var Nodes, NodePointer,
    TokenKind, MulOpSyms

forward procedure ParseFactor (var Factor : NodePointer)
import NextToken, ParseExpr, var Nodes, NodeKind,
    TokenKind, TokenValue, LookUpName, Error
```

Each parsing procedure follows a strict convention. On entry to the procedure, the variables *TokenValue* and *TokenKind* correspond to the first token of the pattern the procedure is supposed to match. On exit, the procedure has read all of the tokens that it needs to match the pattern, and the variables *Token Value* and *TokenKind* correspond to the next token in the input.

The action of *ParseExpr* closely follows the syntax. Since an expression must begin with a term, *ParseExpr* starts by calling *Parse Term*. There may be further terms, separated by signs; if there are, *ParseExpr* reads them in a loop.

```
body procedure ParseExpr
    Parse Term (Expr)
    loop
        exit when TokenKind not in AddOpSyms
        const Op := TokenKind
        Next Token
        var Term : NodePointer
        Parse Term (Term)
        Expr := MakeNode (Op, Expr, Term)
    end loop
end ParseExpr
```

The procedure *Parse Term* has the same organization as *ParseExpr*, but it parses factors separated by multiplication and division operators.

```
body procedure Parse Term
    ParseFactor (Term)
    loop
        exit when TokenKind not in MulOpSyms
        const Op := TokenKind
        Next Token
        var Factor : NodePointer
        ParseFactor (Factor)
        Term := MakeNode (Op, Term, Factor)
    end loop
end Parse Term
```

A factor can be recognized by its first token. We use a **case** statement to determine the kind of factor in the input. If the token is not one that could legally be a factor, there must be a syntax error in the input.

```
body procedure ParseFactor
    case TokenKind of
        label NodeKind . Variable :
            LookUpName (Token Value, Factor)
            Next Token
```

```
    label NodeKind.Number :
      new Nodes, Factor
      tag Nodes (Factor), NodeKind.Number
      Nodes (Factor).NumVal := strreal (TokenValue)
      NextToken
    label NodeKind.LeftPar :
      NextToken
      ParseExpr (Factor)
      if TokenKind = NodeKind.RightPar then
        NextToken
      else
        Error ("Missing )")
      end if
    label :
      Error ("Factor expected here")
      new Nodes, Factor
      tag Nodes (Factor), NodeKind.Illegal
  end case
end ParseFactor
```

There are several kinds of definition, depending on whether there is an "=" symbol and, if there is, whether it is followed by an expression. The procedure *ParseDefinition* detects two errors: a left-hand side that is not a variable, and a symbol that is not the end marker at the end of an expression. The second kind of error usually occurs because the user has made a syntax error.

```
procedure ParseDefinition (var Def : NodePointer)
  ParseExpr (Def)
  if TokenKind = NodeKind.Definition then
    if Nodes (Def).Kind = NodeKind.Variable then
      NextToken
      var RightDef : NodePointer
      if TokenKind = NodeKind.EndMarker then
        RightDef := nil (Nodes)
      else
        ParseExpr (RightDef)
      end if
      Def := MakeNode (NodeKind.Definition, Def, RightDef)
    else
      Error ("Left side of definition must be a variable")
    end if
```

```
      end if
      if TokenKind ≠ NodeKind.EndMarker then
         Error ("Unexpected symbol")
      end if
   end ParseDefinition
```

The program provides help if the user requests it. The procedure *DisplayHelp* below is a start. It could easily be improved.

```
   procedure DisplayHelp
      put "Letter commands:"
      put " H help"
      put " Q quit"
      put " V variable values"
      put "Command syntax"
      put " definition --> expression [ '=' [ expression ] ]"
      put " expression --> term { ( '+' | '-' ) term }"
      put " term --> factor { ( '*' | '/' ) factor }"
      put " factor --> identifier | number | '(' expression ')'"
      put " identifier --> letter { letter | digit }"
      put " number --> digit { digit } [ '.'  { digit } ]"
   end DisplayHelp
```

9.5.5   The Main Program

All that remains to be coded is the main program. The basic structure is a loop that reads a line of input and responds appropriately. Most of the work is done by *ParseDefinition* and *ExprStr*. We include the auxiliary commands: "H", to provide help to the user; "Q", to leave the program gracefully; and "V", to display the values of variables.

```
   loop
      put ":    " ..
      get Buffer : *
      if length (Buffer) ≥ 1 then
         if Buffer (1) = "H" then
            DisplayHelp
         elsif Buffer (1) = "Q" then
            exit
         elsif Buffer (1) = "V" then
            ShowVariables
```

```
        else
            InitializeParser
            var Expr : NodePointer
            ParseDefinition (Expr)
            if not ErrorFlag then
                if Nodes (Expr).Kind = NodeKind.Definition then
                    bind Left to Nodes (Expr).LeftOperand
                    Nodes (Left).NameVal := Nodes (Expr).RightOperand
                else
                    put ExprStr (Evaluate (Expr))
                end if
            end if
        end if
    end if
end loop
```

As the calculator runs, it continues to allocate nodes and uses up memory in the heap. Eventually, there will be no memory left, and the program will fail. A node becomes useless when it can no longer be accessed by the program, but since expressions may be shared between variables, it is difficult to detect the precise point at which this happens. If we intended to use the calculator extensively, we would have to modify the program to recycle inaccessible nodes. The procedure that does this is usually called a *garbage collector*.

The techniques used by the symbolic calculator to read the input strings are typical of many programs. The input is processed by a *scanner* and a *parser*. The scanner recognizes individual components, or *tokens*, in the input. The parser assembles the tokens into linked data structures according to grammatical rules. There is one *parsing procedure* for each rule of the grammar. The technique is called *parsing by recursive descent* and it is widely used in simple compilers and translators.

9.6   Summary

Numbers in parentheses refer to sections where material appears.

▶ Collections are similar to arrays except that components of collections are indexed by pointers rather than by subscripts (9.1).

▶ A collection cannot be declared inside a subprogram, a data structure, or a statement (9.1).

▶ Corresponding to every collection, C, there is a type **pointer to** C (9.1). Values of this type are indexes for the collection.

▶ The number of components of a collection is not fixed when the collection is declared (9.1.1). Components can be allocated, using the **new** statement, until there is no more memory.

▶ For every collection, C, there is a value, nil (C), which is a pointer that does not point to any component of the collection (9.2). This pointer, which is often called a *null pointer*, is used to terminate lists and other linked structures.

▶ Components of a collection are usually, but not necessarily, records or unions whose fields include pointers to the collection (9.2).

▶ Components of a collection are allocated by the **new** statement and deallocated, or released, by the **free** statement (9.3). If there is not enough memory to satisfy an allocation request, the **new** statement sets its pointer argument to nil.

▶ There is a natural relationship between data structures containing pointers and recursive subprograms (9.4). In fact, the data structures we can build with pointers are often called *recursive data structures*. The null pointer provides the "trivial" case required for a recursive solution.

9.7   Exercises

9.1   Draw a picture of the data structure built by the following statements. Assume that *Nodes* has been declared as in Section 9.2.

> var *P*, *Q* : pointer to *Nodes*
> new *Nodes*, *P*
> new *Nodes*, *Q*
> *Nodes* (*P*). *Value* := 1
> *Nodes* (*P*). *Next* := *Q*
> *Nodes* (*Q*). *Value* := 2
> *Nodes* (*Q*). *Next* := *P*

9.2   The following procedure uses the declarations for a linked list given in Section 9.2. Explain what it does.

> procedure *Walk* (*Root* : pointer to *Nodes*)
>   if *Root* ≠ nil (*Nodes*) then
>   *Walk* (*Nodes* (*Root*). *Next*)
>   put *Nodes* (*Root*). *Value* : 4
>   end if
> end *Walk*

9.3   Write a procedure that displays a list of numbers with appropriate punctuation symbols. The list should be enclosed in parentheses, and the items should be separated by commas. For example, the procedure would display the list of Figure 9.6 as

> (4, 7, 3)

9.4   The following questions are about the binary search tree program discussed in Example 9.7.

> (a) Explain what happens when the procedure *Insert* in Example 9.7 is used to insert the name "Benjamin" into the tree of Figure 9.10.
>
> (b) In what sequence does the procedure *Show* display the names in the tree?
>
> (c) Provide procedure *Insert* with an additional Boolean parameter called *Duplicate* that is set to true if the user attempts to insert the same name twice. The program should display an error message if the corresponding argument becomes true.

(d) Explain in detail how *Insert* works when it inserts a new name into a nonempty tree. When does the argument that represents the tree change value?

(e) Write a recursive Boolean function *LookUp* that takes a name and a tree as arguments and returns true if the name is in the tree and false otherwise.

(f) Rewrite the function *LookUp* of the previous part *without* using recursion.

9.5　Here is an extract of a conversation between a user and the calculator program:

```
: a = 4 + 5 + b
: a
(9+b)
: a = 4 + b + 5
: a
((4+b)+5)
```

Explain why the calculator evaluated $4 + 5 \longrightarrow 9$ the first time but not the second time. How could this failure be corrected?

9.6　When the function *Evaluate* in the calculator program receives a pointer to a structure such as $a+b$, it returns a different pointer, although no evaluation has taken place. Explain this and show how it can be corrected.

9.7　The symbolic calculator described in Section 9.5 can be improved in several ways. Here are some suggestions.

(a) Rewrite *ExprStr* so that it includes parentheses in the result string only when they are necessary.

(b) Modify the procedure *NextToken* so that it can handle real numbers written with exponential notation, such as 3.4e-7.

(c) The calculator does not accept an expression with a leading minus sign, such as -24. Modify *ParseExpression* so that it allows leading signs.

(d) Add an exponentiation operator. Because of the way *NextToken* is written, it is easiest to use a single character, such as "^". Modify the function *Evaluate* to compute exponents, with appropriate checks for the signs of operands.

(e) The function *Evaluate* can perform some simplifications even if the operands are not numeric. For example, a-a is always 0, and 1*y is always y. Add a few simplifications to *Evaluate*.

(f) As presented here, the symbolic calculator does not attempt to use the screen in an attractive way. Modify it so that symbol values are stored at the top of the screen and dialogues are displayed at the bottom of the screen. Include a screen position as part of the information about a name. You may have to limit the number of names permitted.

9.8 The calculator program can be modified so that it recycles nodes it no longer needs. The following notes outline one way of doing this.

(a) Add two extra fields to all nodes. Since the new field belongs to all kinds of node, the declaration of *Nodes* will be a record containing a union. One new field is called *InUse* and has type boolean. The other is called *Next* and contains a pointer.

(b) Declare a variable called *AllNodes* of type pointer to *Nodes* with initial value nil. *AllNodes* points to a linked list that contains all nodes known to the program.

(c) All nodes are allocated by a procedure called the *allocator*. Every time a node is allocated, the allocator adds it to the list *AllNodes* and sets its *InUse* flag to true.

(d) After executing a new statement, the allocator checks the value of the new pointer. If the new pointer is nil, there is no more free memory. In this case, the allocator looks in the list *AllNodes*. If *AllNodes* contains a node with *InUse* set to false, it changes the value of *InUse* to true and returns a pointer to the node. If *AllNodes* does not contain any nodes not in use, the allocator calls the garbage collector.

(e) The garbage collector first sets the *InUse* flag of all nodes to false. It then finds all accessible nodes by visiting each node of the variable list and, for each variable, scanning its value. Each accessible node is marked by setting its *InUse* field to true. If garbage collection was successful, there will now be a node with *InUse* set to false that the allocator can use to satisfy the request.

Chapter 10

Organizing Large Programs

The programs we have seen so far consist of declarations and statements. The declarations introduce new types, constants, variables, functions, and procedures. The statements that are not part of functions or procedures constitute the main program. This simple structure is adequate for small programs, but as our programs get larger, we need more effective ways of organizing them. Just as books are divided into chapters and sections, so programs should be divided into separate components.

Turing provides two mechanisms that help us to organize large programs. The first mechanism is the *module*. Modules provide for *logical* management of programs by allowing us to divide programs into meaningful sections. The second mechanism is the include directive, which provides for *physical* management of programs. It allows us to create programs for which the code is stored in several different files. A particular file may be used by many different programs.

Although the techniques described in this chapter can be applied to programs of any size, they are intended primarily for large programs. Whether we should call a program "large" depends on various factors, such as the complexity of its algorithms and the style in which it is written. As a rough guide, if a program contains a thousand or more lines of code, we should structure it using modules and include directives.

10.1   Modules

A program typically consists of a number of components that play distinct roles. One component might deal with reading input data, another with intermediate processing, a third with reporting results. In a small program, each function or procedure is a component. In a large program, a single component may have its own constants, types, variables, procedures, and functions.

Although we can organize a large program as a sequence of variables, functions, and procedures, there are a number of drawbacks with this approach. The structure of the program is determined only by the order in which the various components are written. We can include comments that clarify the structure, but since the compiler ignores comments, this does not help much. Without additional mechanisms, we have no way of ensuring that code in one part of the program does not accidentally interfere with the data of another part.

We have seen how subprograms give structure to programs that contain tens or hundreds of lines. Modules perform a similar task for programs that contain many hundreds or even thousands of lines. A module contains declarations of constants, types, variables, and subprograms. Most of the names declared in a module are hidden from the rest of the program in the same way that the local variables of a procedure are hidden from callers of the procedure. Some of the names declared within a module are intended to be used by clients of the module; these names are explicitly *exported* by the module. A name that is not explicitly exported by the module is invisible to the rest of the program. We say that the module *encapsulates* entities described by these names.

Most modules fall into one of two classes, depending on whether they encapsulate a single data structure or introduce a new data type with associated operations. Section 10.1.1 discusses modules that encapsulate a data structure, and Section 10.1.4 discusses modules that introduce new types.

10.1.1   Encapsulating a Data Structure

A module with variable declarations encapsulates a data structure that the user accesses by calling procedures and functions declared within the module. The module typically contains declarations of constants, types, variables, and subprograms. The only names that are visible outside the module are the names of the subprograms needed to manipulate the data structure.

Example 10.1   A Symbol Table Module

Language processing programs such as compilers often contain a *symbol table*. The symbol table maintains a set of associations between names and attributes of the names. A telephone directory is a real-world example of a symbol table. The names in a telephone directory are names of people and businesses. The attributes are the address and telephone number corresponding to the name.

In this example, we define a symbol table in which each name is a string and the associated attribute is an integer value. First, we introduce the complete code for the module.

The module is introduced by the keyword **module** and the name of the module:

 module *Syms*

The name of this module is *Syms*. It might seem better to use a longer name, such as *SymbolTable*, but as we will see, the module name appears frequently outside the module and a short name is more convenient than a long name.

The first thing that appears in the module is an *export list*:

 export *KeyType, Initialize, Insert, LookUp, Delete, Show*

The export list contains the name of each entity in the module that can be used outside the module. The export list for *Syms* consists of a type, *KeyType*, and five procedures: *Initialize, Insert, LookUp, Delete*, and *Show*.

The symbol table itself is represented by an array, *Table*, of entry records:

```
const MaxKeyLength := 20
const MaxEntries := 100
type KeyType : string (MaxKeyLength)
type EntryRecord :
  record
    Key : KeyType
    Value : int
  end record
var Table : array 1 .. MaxEntries + 1 of EntryRecord
var NumEntries : 0 .. MaxEntries
```

Each entry record consists of a key, *Key*, which is a string of up to 20 characters, and a value, *Value*, which is an integer. The table can hold up to 100 entries, but the array is declared with components $1, 2, \ldots, 101$. The extra entry, *Table* (101), is used by *LookUp* and *Delete*. The variable *NumEntries* records the number of entry records actually in the table.

The procedure *Initialize* creates a new table with no entries in it:

```
    procedure Initialize
      NumEntries := 0
    end Initialize
```

It is not necessary to initialize the components of the array *Table*. The other procedures of the module ensure that $Table[i]$ is accessed only if $1 \leq i \leq NumEntries$.

The remaining three procedures of the module may succeed or fail. The task of the procedure *Insert* is to insert a new entry into the table. It will fail if there are already *MaxEntries* entries in the table and we attempt to insert another one.

```
    procedure Insert (Key : KeyType, Value : int, var Success : boolean)
      if NumEntries ≥ MaxEntries then
        Success := false
      else
        NumEntries += 1
        Table (NumEntries).Key := Key
        Table (NumEntries).Value := Value
        Success := true
      end if
    end Insert
```

There are various ways of dealing with failure. The solution we adopt here is that the procedure has a Boolean variable parameter, *Success*, which is set to true if the procedure completes its task successfully. The user of the module is responsible for checking the value of *Success* to see if the operation was successful.

The user provides *Insert* with a key and a value. If there is space in the table for a new entry, *Insert* stores the new entry, increments *NumEntries*, and reports success. If there is no more room, it reports failure. Notice that *Insert* does not check to see if there is already an entry with the given key; it is the user's responsibility to avoid entering the same key twice.

The procedure *LookUp* searches the table for an entry that has the parameter *Key* in its key field. If there is such an entry, *LookUp* sets the parameter *Value* to the value of the field and the parameter *Success* to true. If there is no such entry, the parameter *Success* becomes false.

```
    procedure LookUp (Key : KeyType, var Value : int, var Success : boolean)
      Table (NumEntries + 1).Key := Key
      var Ent := 1
      loop
        exit when Table (Ent).Key = Key
        Ent += 1
      end loop
```

```
    if Ent ≤ NumEntries then
        Value := Table (Ent). Value
        Success := true
    else
        Success := false
    end if
end LookUp
```

The loop statement in procedure *LookUp* examines each entry of the table in turn. The loop terminates when the entry that is examined has a key field that matches the parameter *Key*. To ensure that the match will eventually occur, the first statement of the procedure stores *Key* at the next free position in the table. If the table is full, with 100 entries in this example, *Key* will be stored at *Table* (101), which is why we need the extra component of *Table*.

When the loop terminates, we examine the subscript *Ent*. If it is greater than *NumEntries*, we matched the key and the search failed. Otherwise, we have found a valid entry, and we return its value.

The algorithm that *LookUp* uses is called *linear search*. A linear search algorithm examines components of a data structure until a specified condition is satisfied. In this case, the condition is that the keys match. On average, a linear search algorithm examines half the components of the data structure. In the worst case, it examines every component. The special entry that we place at the end of the table is called a *sentinel*. The sentinel simplifies the loop by ensuring that a match will always occur.

The procedure *Delete* looks for an entry that has the parameter *Key* as the value of its key field. If there is such an entry, *Delete* removes it from the table and sets the parameter *Success* to true. If there is no matching entry in the table, *Delete* sets *Success* to false and does not change the table.

```
procedure Delete (Key : KeyType, var Success : boolean)
    Table (NumEntries + 1). Key := Key
    var Ent := 1
    loop
        exit when Table (Ent). Key = Key
        Ent += 1
    end loop
    if Ent ≤ NumEntries then
        Table (Ent) := Table (NumEntries)
        NumEntries -= 1
        Success := true
```

```
      else
         Success := false
      end if
   end Delete
```

The procedure *Delete* has a similar structure to *LookUp*. The first step is to find the entry to be deleted. If such an entry exists, *Delete* does not actually delete it because this would leave a gap in the middle of the table. Instead, *Delete* overwrites the entry with the last entry in the table and decrements *NumEntries*. This has the effect of deleting the matching entry.

The procedure *Show* displays the subscript, key, and value of each entry in the table. If there are no entries in the table, *Show* displays a message instead.

```
   procedure Show
      if NumEntries = 0 then
         put "The table is empty."
      else
         for Ent : 1 .. NumEntries
            put Ent : 4, " ", Table (Ent).Key : 20, " ", Table (Ent).Value : 6
         end for
      end if
   end Show
```

Like other Turing constructs, the module declaration finishes with an **end** statement that contains the name of the module:

```
   end Syms
```

Here is the structure of the complete module *Syms*. The dots stand for the declarations introduced during the discussion above.

```
   module Syms
   export ....
   const ....
   type ....
   var ....
   procedure Initialize ....
   procedure Insert ....
   procedure LookUp ....
   procedure Delete ....
   procedure Show ....
   end Syms
```

10.1.2   Using a Module in a Program

Modules add a new level of structure to programs. At the first level, a program is a sequence of statements. At the second level, a program is a collection of named procedures, each consisting of variables and statements. At the third level, a program is a collection of named modules, each consisting of variables and procedures.

Example 10.2   Using a Module

The following program provides a simple test of the symbol table module. It initializes the table once and then allows the user to perform various operations. For each operation, the program displays the result, if there is one, or the value of the *Success* indicator otherwise.

```
var Key : Syms.KeyType
var Value : int
var Success : boolean

Syms.Initialize
loop
   put skip,"Enter a table operation (i,l,d,s,x):   "..
   var Op : string (1)
   getch (Op)
   if Op = "i" then
      put skip,"Enter key:   "..
      get Key
      put "Enter value:   "..
      get Value
      Syms.Insert (Key, Value, Success)
   elsif Op = "l" then
      put skip,"Enter key:   "..
      get Key
      Syms.LookUp (Key, Value, Success)
      if Success then
         put "Value = ", Value
      else
         put "Failed"
      end if
   elsif Op = "d" then
      put skip,"Enter key:   "..
      get Key
```

```
          Syms.Delete (Key, Success)
          if Success then
            put "Done"
          else
            put "Failed"
          end if
        elsif Op = "s" then
          put ""
          Syms.Show
        elsif Op = "x" then
          exit
        else
          put "That's not an operation - try again!"
        end if
      end loop
```

Within the test code, the only entities of the module that are visible are those named in the export list. Even these cannot be referred to directly but must be *qualified* by the module name. In the first line of the test program, for example, we declare *Key* to have the type *Syms.KeyType*. If we omit *Syms*, Turing would complain that *KeyType* was not defined. The procedure names must also be qualified, which is why we write, for example, *Syms.Initialize*.

10.1.3   Reusing Modules

We can construct modules as we need them for a particular program. Programs built in this way are easier to debug and maintain than programs that do not use modules. But we achieve the greatest benefit from modules when we are able to use one module in several different programs. This will happen only if we design the module for reuse.

There are several ways of making the module *Syms* reusable. We consider one of them here. The first point to notice is that modules can import names as well as export them. Since we have incorporated the type *KeyType* and the value *NumEntries* into the module, a user of the module cannot change them. It might be more appropriate for the type *KeyType* and the value of *MaxEntries* to be defined by the user of the module rather than by the module itself. We can do this by rewriting the code of Example 10.1.

First, we move the relevant declarations outside the module:

> const *MaxKeyLength* := 20
> const *MaxEntries* := 100
> type *KeyType* : string (*MaxKeyLength*)

Second, we add an import list to the module. Without the import list, the names *KeyType* and *MaxEntries* would not be visible *inside* the module. Here are the first three lines of the revised module. The rest of the module code is unchanged.

> module *Syms*
> import *KeyType, MaxEntries*
> export *Initialize, Insert, LookUp, Delete, Show*

In the code that we wrote for testing the module, the type *Syms.KeyType* is no longer valid. If we use it, Turing will complain that *KeyType* is not exported by module *Syms*. The type is visible outside the module because we have moved its declaration outside the module. Consequently, we must include the declaration

> var *Key* : *KeyType*

10.1.4 Implementing a Data Type

The module *Syms* described in Example 10.1 declares a data structure and procedures that allow us to access it. A limitation of module *Syms* is that it provides only one table. We are not obliged to declare a data structure in a module, however. An alternative approach is to write a module that defines a data *type* and subprograms that perform operations on instances of the type. In a program that contains the module, we can declare as many instances of the type as we need.

Modules that define and implement new data types enhance the expressive power of a programming language. They enable us to customize the language to our particular requirements and to write concise and readable solutions to complex problems.

Example 10.3   A Data Type for Rational Numbers

Suppose we want to perform operations with fractions or, more technically, rational numbers. We define a rational number to be a pair of integers, (N, D), which behave for purposes of computation like the fraction N/D. We want to add, subtract, multiply, and divide rational numbers, and we want also to display them, either as fractions, such as $2/3$, or as real numbers, such as 0.666667. Rational numbers should be in lowest terms, so that $4/6$ is automatically converted to $2/3$, and there should be a warning of some kind if we accidentally create an invalid rational number such as $3/0$.

We construct a module, *Rat*, that defines a data type for rational numbers and provides the necessary operations for rational numbers. The module begins as follows:

> module *Rat*
> > export opaque *Rational*, *RationalError*, *ResetError*, *RatString*, *RatReal*,
> > *Make*, *Add*, *Sub*, *Mul*, *Div*, *Num*, *Den*

The entry opaque *Rational* in the export list indicates that the name *Rational* may be used outside the module. *Rational* is the name of the type of rational numbers, declared as follows:

> type *Rational* :
> > record
> > > *Num*, *Den* : int
> >
> > end record

If the export list had contained the name *Rational* without opaque, users of the module would be able to use the type *Rational* as if its declaration had appeared in the program. In such a case, they could access and even change the fields *Num* and *Den* of a rational number. By writing opaque in the export list, we hide the declaration of *Rational* and make the fields *Num* and *Den* inaccessible to the user. Users of the module *Rat* can declare variables of type *Rational* in the usual way, but they cannot do anything with the variables except pass them as arguments to the procedures and functions exported by *Rat*. Technically, we say that the *name* of the type *Rational* is visible, but its *representation* is hidden.

The function *GCD*, which computes the greatest common divisor of two positive integers, is used within the module but is not exported from it. We call it a *private function* of the module.

> function *GCD* (*M*, *N* : int) : int
> > pre $M > 0$ and $N > 0$
> > var *Mc* := *M*
> > var *Nc* := *N*
> > loop
> > > const T := *Mc* mod *Nc*
> > > exit when $T = 0$
> > > *Mc* := *Nc*
> > > *Nc* := *T*
> >
> > end loop
> > result *Nc*
>
> end *GCD*

We use a Boolean variable to record errors. It is called *Error* and it is initialized to false:

> var *Error* := false

When a procedure in the module detects an error, it sets *Error* to true. After invoking an operation that might fail, the calling program should check the value of *Error*. The module cannot export *Error*, but the function *RationalError* returns its value:

> function *RationalError* : boolean
>> result *Error*
>
> end *RationalError*

The procedure *ResetError* allows the calling program to set the value of *Error* back to false:

> procedure *ResetError*
>> *Error* := false
>
> end *ResetError*

The next two functions perform conversions from the type *Rational* to other types. *RatString* converts a rational number to a string such as "2/3".

> function *RatString* (*R* : *Rational*) : string
>> if *R*.*Den* = 1 then
>>> result *intstr* (*R*.*Num*)
>>
>> else
>>> result *intstr* (*R*.*Num*) + "/" + *intstr* (*R*.*Den*)
>>
>> end if
>
> end *RatString*

The function *RatReal* converts a rational number to a real value, such as 0.6667. If the denominator of the rational number is 1, the number represents an integer and is converted accordingly.

> function *RatReal* (*R* : *Rational*) : real
>> pre *R*.*Den* $\neq$ 0
>> result *R*.*Num*/*R*.*Den*
>
> end *RatReal*

The function *RatReal* has the precondition $R.Den \neq 0$. It would be incorrect for *RatReal* to set *Error* to true if the denominator of *R* is zero. If $R.Den = 0$, an error must have occurred before *RatReal* was called. The program should have detected this error but it has not. The precondition has failed not because the user has made a mistake but because there is a logical error in the program.

The function *Num* returns the numerator of a rational number and the function *Den* returns the denominator:

    function *Num* (*R* : *Rational*) : int
        result *R*.*Num*
    end *Num*

    function *Den* (*R* : *Rational*) : int
        result *R*.*Den*
    end *Den*

It might seem pointless to hide the representation of *Rational* and then provide functions that access its components, but there are two reasons for doing so. First, the functions *Num* and *Den* allow users to obtain the values of the numerator and denominator of a rational number but not to alter them. Second, the interface of a module should not commit the implementer of the module to a particular representation. For rational numbers, there is only one obvious representation, but for a more complicated data type there might be several possible representations. The feature of modules that provides expressive power is the ability to hide the data structure and to reveal only the procedures and functions that manipulate it.

The function *Make* is the heart of module *Rat*. Given two integers, it constructs a rational number in normal form.

    function *Make* (*Num*, *Den* : int) : *Rational*
        var *T* : *Rational*
        if *Den* = 0 then
            Error := true
            T.*Num* := 0
            T.*Den* := 0
        elsif *Num* = 0 then
            T.*Num* := 0
            T.*Den* := *sign* (*Den*)
        else
            const *Neg* := *sign* (*Num*) * *sign* (*Den*) < 0
            const *N* := *abs* (*Num*)
            const *D* := *abs* (*Den*)
            const *G* := *GCD* (*N*, *D*)
            if *Neg* then
                T.*Num* := −*N* div *G*
            else
                T.*Num* := *N* div *G*
            end if

$$T.Den := D \text{ div } G$$
     end if
    result T
end $Make$

If the denominator is 0, the function $Make$ forms 0/0 and sets $Error$ to true, indicating that something has gone wrong. If the numerator is 0, it sets the denominator to 1. This ensures that there is a unique form for the rational number zero, namely 0/1. In all other cases, $Make$ divides the numerator and denominator by their greatest common divisor to ensure that there are no common factors. It also ensures that the denominator of a rational number is always positive: if the number is negative, its numerator is negative.

The next four functions implement the basic arithmetic operations for rational numbers. Each function calls $Make$ to construct the result, thereby ensuring that the result is in normal form and that errors are detected. In fact, if we assume that the arguments are valid rational numbers, the only function that can set the error flag is Div.

    function $Add\,(X, Y : Rational) : Rational$
      result $Make\,(X.Num * Y.Den + X.Den * Y.Num, X.Den * Y.Den)$
    end Add

    function $Sub\,(X, Y : Rational) : Rational$
      result $Make\,(X.Num * Y.Den - X.Den * Y.Num, X.Den * Y.Den)$
    end Sub

    function $Mul\,(X, Y : Rational) : Rational$
      result $Make\,(X.Num * Y.Num, X.Den * Y.Den)$
    end Mul

    function $Div\,(X, Y : Rational) : Rational$
      result $Make\,(X.Num * Y.Den, X.Den * Y.Num)$
    end Div

  end Rat

10.1.5   Testing Modules

Before we use a procedure or function in a program, we should test it. Modules, too, should be tested before use. Testing a module is both more important and more difficult than testing a subprogram because modules declare several interdependent subprograms.

It is usually worthwhile to write a program for the specific purpose of testing each component of a module thoroughly. A program of this kind is often called a *driver*. The driver should test each procedure and function with a variety of arguments. If subprograms depend on one another, the test program should exploit the dependencies fully.

Example 10.4   Testing a Data Type

Here is a simple program we can use to test module *Rat*. The function *Test* tests both conversion functions. The main loop asks the user for two rational numbers and then performs all four operations on them, displaying the results in both rational and real form.

```
function Test (R : Rat.Rational) : string
    result Rat.RatString (R) + realstr (Rat.RatReal (R), 12)
end Test

var A, B : Rat.Rational
var Num, Den : int
loop
   put ""
   put "Enter A as two integers:   " ..
   get Num, Den
   A := Rat.Make (Num, Den)
   put "Enter B as two integers:   " ..
   get Num, Den
   B := Rat.Make (Num, Den)
   put "A + B = ", Test (Rat.Add (A, B))
   put "A - B = ", Test (Rat.Sub (A, B))
   put "A * B = ", Test (Rat.Mul (A, B))
   put "A / B = ", Test (Rat.Div (A, B))
   if Rat.RationalError then
      put "The Rational Module has reported an error!"
      ResetError
   end if
   put skip, "Try again?   " ..
   var Reply : string (1)
   getch (Reply)
   exit when Reply ≠ "y"
end loop
```

Running the test program yields results such as:

```
Enter A as two integers:  2 -3
Enter B as two integers:  5 3
A + B = 1 1
A - B = -7/3 -2.333333
A * B = -10/9 -1.111111
A / B = -2/5 -0.4
```

The test program relies on the programmer to choose arguments for the operations. Most programmers do not have the patience to try many different combinations of arguments. If testing uncovers an error, it is unlikely that all the tests will be repeated after the error has been corrected. For modules that will be used in critical applications, we should write a program that performs a sequence of tests automatically, checking the results as it goes. If we change the module, it is easy to run all the tests again, ensuring that our attempts at correction have not introduced new errors.

10.1.6 Application of a Module

We do not write modules solely in order to test them. The next example illustrates a simple application of the module *Rat*.

Example 10.5 Using a Data Type

The following program reads a positive integer N and calculates the sum

$$1 + \frac{1}{2} + \frac{1}{3} + \cdots + \frac{1}{N}$$

as an exact fraction. If we attempt to compute this sum for values of N larger than about 20, the result will be integer overflow.

```
loop
  var  N : int
  put "Enter N: " ..
  get N
  exit when N ≤ 0
  var Sum := Rat.Make (0, 1)
  for I : 1 .. N
    Sum := Rat.Add (Sum, Rat.Make (1, I))
  end for
  put Rat.RatString (Sum), " ", Rat.RatReal (Sum), skip
end loop
```

Here is an example of a dialogue between the user and the program.

```
Enter N:  1
1 1
Enter N:  10
7381/2520 2.928968
Enter N:  0
```

10.1.7   Initialization and Assertions

A module may contain initialization statements, a precondition, a postcondition, and an invariant. Turing processes module declarations like other declarations, performing any required initialization when it encounters the module declaration in the code. When it initializes a module, Turing processes constant declarations, variable declarations with initializers, and any statements that are not inside subprograms.

If there is a **pre** statement in the module, it must occur between the import/export lists and the first executable statement. It is executed only once, before the module is initialized. If there is a **post** statement in the module, it must be the last statement. It is executed only once, at the end of initialization. If there is an **invariant** statement in the module, it must come before any exported attributes. The invariant is checked at each entry or exit of the module. An "entry" occurs when an exported subprogram is called from outside the module. An "exit" occurs when an exported subprogram returns control to a caller outside the module.

The following module skeleton summarizes these constraints.

```
module ModuleName
    import . . . .      % names imported by the module
    export . . . .      % names exported by the module
    pre . . . .         % a condition that must be true before initialization
    invariant . . . .   % a condition that must be true at every entry and exit
    post . . . .        % a condition that must be true after initialization
end ModuleName
```

The expressions following **invariant** and **post** assert facts about data within the module. Some modules, such as *Rat* in Section 10.1.4, do not contain any data and therefore do not have invariants or postconditions.

Example 10.6   Assertions in Modules

To illustrate the uses of initialization and invariants, we outline the principal features of a module that maintains a set of observations and allows them to be displayed on the screen.

The module exports three procedures, *Display*, *Erase*, and *Update*, and it maintains an array of five observations. Most of the time, an observation may have any integer value. When we display an observation, however, we require its value to be in the range $-10 .. 10$. There is a Boolean variable, *Visible*, that is true if the observations are currently displayed on the screen. This variable is initially false.

```
module Bars
    export Display, Erase, Update
    type ObsIndex : 1 .. 5
    var Observations : array ObsIndex of int
    const MinObsVal := -10
    const MaxObsVal := 10
    var Visible := false
```

The Boolean function *Valid* determines whether the observations can be displayed. It returns true if each observation is within the permitted range.

```
function Valid : boolean
    for N : ObsIndex
        if Observations (N) < MinObsVal
            or Observations (N) > MaxObsVal then
            result false
        end if
    end for
    result true
end Valid
```

The module contains initialization code that sets each observation to zero:

```
for N : ObsIndex
    Observations (N) := 0
end for
```

The invariant comes next because it must appear earlier in the text of the module than any attributes that the module exports:

```
invariant Visible ⇒ Valid
```

The invariant states that if the observations are visible, they must be valid. In other words, an attempt to display the observations when one or more of them is out of range would violate the invariant.

Next, we declare the exported procedures *Display* and *Erase*. We omit the details of how these procedures work, indicating the missing code by boxes. For instance, the only property of the procedures *Display* and *Erase* that is relevant to this example is that they change the value of *Visible*.

```
procedure Display
    Visible := true
    [_____]
end Display

procedure Erase
    Visible := false
    [_____]
end Erase
```

The procedure *Update* adds a value, *Delta*, which may be positive or negative, to an observation. Since observations are allowed to go outside the range $-10 .. 10$, we do not check the final value of *Observations* (N).

```
procedure Update (N : ObsIndex, Delta : int)
    Observations (N) += Delta
end Update
```

Finally, the module has a postcondition that is checked after the module has been initialized. The module invariant is a logical consequence of the postcondition. Consequently, if initialization makes the postcondition **true**, the invariant must also be **true**.

```
    post not Visible and Valid
end Bars
```

The assertions have two purposes. First, they provide dynamic checks that the module is working correctly. Second, they help human readers to understand the module. The second reason is particularly important because modules are often modified by programmers other than their original authors. The assertions express facts that should remain true even after changes are made.

10.1.8   The pervasive Attribute

Although the protection that modules provide is an aid to program organization, there are times when the security measures interfere with good programming practice. Suppose, for example, that we are writing a program that uses many modules, all of which need the value of π. It would be inconvenient to declare the appropriate constant in every module or to import it into every module.

Instead, we use the declaration

> const pervasive $Pi := 3.1415926535$

After this declaration, we can use the name Pi in subsequent modules without importing it.

The symbol **pervasive** is a keyword. The attribute **pervasive** may be used to qualify declarations of constants and types but it may not be used to qualify declarations of variables or subprograms.

The attribute **pervasive** should be used with care. One of the purposes of modules is to *reduce* the scope of names. Since a **pervasive** declaration *increases* the scope of a name, it undoes some of the benefits of modules.

10.2   The include Directive

The include directive tells Turing to read part of the program from a named file. It is called a directive rather than a statement because it is an instruction to the compiler rather than a declaration or a statement.

The include directive is a simple and general device with many applications. We can use it to build a repertoire of program components that are useful in a wide variety of situations. Without include, the components would be replicated many times in different programs.

Example 10.7   Using **include** with a Function Library

For advanced mathematical applications, the functions provided by Turing are not sufficient. We can easily declare additional functions, but we do not want to copy these declarations into every program that uses them. Instead, we create a file called, for example, `math.lib`. We put constants and functions that are likely to be useful for mathematical applications into this file.

```
const Pi := 3.1415926535
const TwoPi := 2 * Pi
const HalfPi := 0.5 * Pi

function tan (A : real) : real
    pre cos (A) ≠ 0
    result sin (A)/cos (A)
end tan
```

```
function arcsin (R : real) A : real
   pre abs (R) ≤ 1
   post −HalfPi ≤ A and A ≤ HalfPi
   if R = 1 then
     result HalfPi
   elsif R = −1 then
     result −HalfPi
   else
     result arctan (R/sqrt (1 − R ** 2))
   end if
end arcsin

function arccos (R : real) A : real
   pre abs (R) ≤ 1
   post 0 ≤ A and A ≤ Pi
   if R = 0 then
     result HalfPi
   elsif R < 0 then
     result arctan (sqrt (1 − R ** 2)/R) + Pi
   else
     result arctan (sqrt (1 − R ** 2)/R)
   end if
end arccos
```

If any function in the mathematical library is called with an invalid argument, its precondition yields false and the program terminates with an error message. This behavior is appropriate because an invalid argument indicates a logical error in the program; it is not a situation from which the program should attempt to recover.

At the beginning of a program that uses these declarations, we write simply

```
include "math.lib"
```

The effect is as if the declarations in **math.lib** had been copied into the program at this point. All the rules of scope and of declaration-before-use apply in the usual way. Here is a complete program that uses the mathematics library:

```
include "math.lib"
put tan (Pi/6)     % Display tan(30) degrees.
```

The argument of include must be a string. Since Turing interprets the string as a file name, it must be correctly constructed for the system on which Turing is running. On the PC, for example, we could write

```
include "c:\turing\math.lib"
```

We might choose to keep a number of libraries in a directory called libs. If libs is a subdirectory of the directory turing, we could write

include "c:\turing\libs\math.lib"

to obtain the mathematical library.

The file named by an include directive may contain include directives. There must not, of course, be a circular dependency. For example, if file A contains the directive include "B", the file B must not contain the directive include "A".

Example 10.8   Nested include Files

This example illustrates the use of include directives within included files. We begin by creating a file called str.t that contains the code

```
var Reply : string
put "Please enter a string:   " ..
get Reply
put "Your string has ", length (Reply), " characters."
```

This program is complete but not useful. We can incorporate the code into a loop by creating another file called loop.t that contains the code

```
loop
   include "str.t"
   var Ch : string (1)
   put "Try again?   " ..
   getch (Ch)
   exit when Ch ≠ "y"
   put ""
end loop
```

The program loop.t is slightly more useful than str.t because it lets us run the test several times. It is still not very informative, however, so we create a third file, called test.t, containing the following code:

```
put "This program checks the lengths of strings."
put ""
include "loop.t"
put skip, skip, "That's all."
```

When Turing compiles test.t, it reads as far as the statement include "loop.t" and then begins to read from loop.t. Reading this file, it encounters the statement include "str.t" and begins to read from str.t. At the end of each included file, Turing continues to read from the file containing the include statement.

This example demonstrates the possibilities offered by include directives. We should ensure that files intended to be included in other programs should contain self-contained entities, such as procedures or modules, rather than arbitrary chunks of code.

Using the include Construct

We can improve the programs of Section 10.1 by using include. For example, we could put the code for the module *Syms* of Example 10.1 into a file called `symtab.t`. A program that used the module *Syms*, such as the program of Example 10.2, would contain the directive

```
include "symtab.t"
```

Similarly, we could put the code for the module *Rat* of Example 10.3 into a file called `rational.t` and write the directive

```
include "rational.t"
```

in the programs of Examples 10.4 and 10.5.

Style

Every piece of code should contain assertions and comments, especially if it appears in a file that will be included in many programs. Preconditions and postconditions in each function or procedure provide useful information to programmers who use the code. Good comments may lead to the reuse of code that would otherwise be abandoned.

10.3   Summary

Numbers in parentheses refer to sections where material appears.

▶   Modules provide a way of dividing a large program into manageable sections (10.1). A general-purpose module may be shared by many programs.

▶   A module declaration may appear inside a module but not inside a subprogram or statement (10.1).

▶   A module may contain declarations of constants, types, variables, subprograms, and modules (10.1.1).

▶   Names declared inside the module but used outside it must be declared in the module's export list (10.1.1).

▶   Some modules encapsulate data structures (10.1.1). The data structure is defined in terms of variables that are local to the module and can be accessed only by the subprograms of the module. By coding the subprograms carefully, the author of the module can ensure that the data structure is always in a consistent state.

▶   Names declared outside the module but used inside it must be mentioned in the module's import list (10.1.3).

▶   Some modules implement a data type (10.1.4). The module defines and exports a type. Users of the module may declare instances of this type and manipulate them by calling subprograms in the module.

▶   If a module exports a type, the attributes of the type are visible outside the module (10.1.4).

▶   If a module exports an **opaque** type, the attributes of the type are not visible outside the module (10.1.4). Users of the module can declare instances of the type and can call subprograms of the module.

▶   A module may include a precondition, a postcondition, and an invariant, but none of these is required (10.1.7).

▶   If the name of a constant or type is declared to be **pervasive**, it is visible throughout the current scope (10.1.8). Variables and subprograms cannot be declared pervasive.

▶   The **include** directive tells Turing to read source code from a named file (10.2).

▶   The name of the file in an **include** directive must respect the conventions of the operating system (10.2).

▶   Modules and **include** directives are often used in conjunction (10.2). Typically, we would store a module declaration in its own file and **include** it in programs that need it.

10.4   Exercises

10.1 Explain the action of *Delete* in module *Syms* when there is only one entry in the table.

10.2 Modify the procedure *Insert* in module *Syms* so that it reports an error if the key to be inserted is already in the table.

10.3 Rewrite the procedures of module *Syms* so that the components of the table are stored in ascending order. The procedures *Insert* and *Delete* must maintain this order. The procedure *LookUp* should use binary search for fast access.

10.4 Rewrite the declarations and procedures of module *Syms* so that entries are stored in a binary search tree rather than in an array. Make the changes in such a way that code using the module does not need to be changed.

10.5 Write a test program for module *Rat* that reads test data from a file called `testrat.dat`. A line of `testrat.dat` contains the numerators and denominators of two rational numbers, followed by the results of applying the four basic operations to these numbers. For example, the line

$$2\ 3\ 1\ 4\ 11\ 12\ 5\ 12\ 1\ 6\ 8\ 3$$

expresses the following facts:

$$\frac{2}{3} + \frac{1}{4} = \frac{11}{12};$$
$$\frac{2}{3} - \frac{1}{4} = \frac{5}{12};$$
$$\frac{2}{3} \times \frac{1}{4} = \frac{1}{6};$$
$$\frac{2}{3} \div \frac{1}{4} = \frac{8}{3}.$$

The test program reads each line of `testrat.dat`, performs the indicated operations using the first four numbers, and checks the results against the last eight numbers.

10.6 Write a module, similar to *Rat* in Example 10.3, for complex numbers.

10.7 Write a module that manages a bank account. The module should store the current balance in the account and provide a function that reports the balance. It should also provide procedures to deposit money into the account and withdraw money from the account. A withdrawal that would make the balance negative should not be accepted.

10.8 Rewrite the calculator of Section 9.5 using modules. Include a module that encapsulates all information about the parser.

10.9 Create a file containing constant declarations for keyboard and screen management. It should contain, for example, keyboard codes and codes for special display characters. Write a program that uses the include directive to obtain the declarations.

10.10 Design useful functions for string processing. Useful operations include padding a string with blanks, centering a string, extracting particular characters from strings, and finding patterns in strings. Construct a file that contains these functions, and write a test program that uses the include directive to access the string operations.

Chapter 11

Additional Features

The features of Turing described in the previous ten chapters are adequate for almost all programs. There are some situations, however, in which additional features are useful. We can divide additional features into two categories. The first category consists of features that are essential in the sense that we cannot write programs to perform certain tasks if we cannot use these features. The second category consists of features that are luxuries in the sense that they provide convenient solutions to problems that would be hard to solve using simpler features.

This chapter provides one example in each category. The first additional feature we describe allows us to read and write binary files. This ability is needed only occasionally and cannot be simulated by other features. The input and output features described in Chapter 6 allow us to read and write text but not arbitrary data; using binary files, we can read and write data of any kind.

The second additional feature allows us to pass subprograms as arguments to other subprograms. This feature is not essential, because we can always find alternative methods that do not make use of it, but it can provide concise and elegant solutions to problems that would otherwise require cumbersome techniques.

11.1   Binary Files

Programs communicate with one another by means of files. A file that is created by one program may be used by another program or even by several other programs. We can use the techniques described in Section 6.3 to read and write files that contain data in the form of text. In this section, we describe techniques for reading and writing data in binary form.

A *binary file* is an exact copy of a region of memory. When a program writes to a binary file, it copies bytes from the memory to the disk without performing any conversion or transformation. Similarly, when a program reads a binary file, it copies bytes from the disk into memory. We can use binary files to store most kinds of data, including sets, arrays, records, and unions. We cannot, however, store pointer values in binary files.

Binary files are normally used to store data that cannot be represented accurately and efficiently in textual form. Text is not a suitable medium for storing real numbers and screen images. Textual representations are potentially inaccurate because conversion errors occur. Suppose that we calculate an accurate value of π, write the value in a text file as 3.14159265359, and use another program to read this value. The two programs will have different values of π because Turing provides fifteen digits of precision but we have stored only twelve in the file. Because of the differences between decimal and binary representation, even if we write all fifteen digits to the file, there is no guarantee that the two values will match exactly.

As well as being inaccurate, textual representations are also inefficient with respect to both time and space. Time is required to convert between the binary and textual representations of numbers. More importantly, a textual representation requires more space than a binary representation; sixteen or more characters are needed to represent a real number that occupies only eight bytes of memory. Consequently, a file containing textual representations of numbers will be more than twice the size of a file that contains binary representations.

11.1.1   Sequential Binary Files

The Turing statements for binary file operations are similar to the statements for text file operations. The major difference is that we use **read** instead of **get** and **write** instead of **put**. These new keywords occur in two places, as arguments in the **open** statement and as statements in their own right.

Example 11.1   Storing Real Numbers in a File

The following program creates an array of random data, writes it to a file, and reads it back into another array. The program then checks that the arrays contain exactly the same data.

The first step is to declare the arrays and to fill the first one with random data:

```
const Size := 100
var  Source, Dest : array 1 .. Size of real
for N : 1 .. Size
   rand (Source (N))
end for
```

The program then opens the file for writing, writes the array to it, and closes the file:

```
const FileName := "randvals.dat"
var  FileNum : int
open : FileNum, FileName, write
write : FileNum, Source
close : FileNum
```

The name of the file is `"randvals.dat"`. One write statement is sufficient to write the entire array to the disk. The close statement is the same for binary files and text files.

Next, the program opens the same file for reading and reads its contents into another array. One read statement is sufficient to read the entire array from the disk.

```
open : FileNum, FileName, read
read : FileNum, Dest
close : FileNum
```

Finally, the program compares the arrays, using exact equality:

```
var  DiffCount := 0
for N : 1 .. Size
   if Source (N) ≠ Dest (N) then
     DiffCount += 1
   end if
end for
put DiffCount, " differences."
```

When the program is executed, it displays

    0 differences.

indicating that binary data was both written and read.

If Turing had converted the numbers to characters while executing the write statement and then had performed the opposite conversion while executing the read statement, it is unlikely that the numbers would be exactly equal.

The binary file does not contain type information. We can therefore read it back into a variable of another type. There is nothing to prevent us reading the file "randvals.dat" created by Example 11.1 as if it contained integers, but the result would be meaningless and useless. An approximate analogy to reading integer values from a file of real values would be to telephone someone by punching in their social security number.

In Example 11.1, the variables that the program reads and writes have the same type: they are both arrays of real numbers. The example represents the simplest and safest way of using binary files.

Reading Items

We do not have to read an entire file in one operation. We can read individual items from the file and, as with text files, we can detect the end of the file.

Example 11.2   Reading a File of Real Numbers

Suppose that we have a slightly more general situation than that of Example 11.1, in which there are files of varying sizes that we know contain real numbers. We can read such a file by first creating an array that we are sure is large enough. Then we read the file, storing one real number at a time in the array until we reach the end of the file.

```
var Data : array 1 .. 500 of real
var ActualSize := 0
open : FileNum, FileName, read
loop
    exit when eof (FileNum)
    ActualSize += 1
    read : FileNum, Data (ActualSize)
end loop
put ActualSize, " entries read."
```

When the loop terminates, the value of *ActualSize* tells us how many numbers were read. The numbers themselves are stored in locations $1, 2, \ldots, ActualSize$ of the array *Data*. If the file had been empty, *ActualSize* would be zero.

11.1.2   Random Access Binary Files

The examples in Sections 6.3 and 11.1.1 process files sequentially; the program reads or writes the file from beginning to end. This is a common way to use files, but it is not the only way. We can also read and write information at arbitrary positions in a binary file, rather as if it was an array on the disk. A file used in this way is called a *random access file*. The word "random" means not that the order is haphazard but that the components of the file may be accessed in any order.

Capabilities

We indicate our intention to access a file randomly by including the keyword **seek** in the **open** statement that opens the file. For example, the statement

> **open** : *Bin*, `"accounts.dat"`, **read**, **seek**

opens the file `accounts.dat` in random access mode.

The keywords at the end of the **open** statement are called *capabilities*. The capabilities in the **open** statement above are **read** and **seek**. We have already seen four capabilities. In Section 6.3 on page 181, the capabilities **get** and **put** are used with text files. In Section 11.1.1, the capabilities **read** and **write** are used with binary files.

Capabilities determine what the program can do with the file after it has been opened. There is a straightforward relationship between capabilities with which we open a file and the statements we can use to process it. For instance, we can use a **get** statement to process a file only if the file has been opened with capability **get**. The **put**, **read**, and **write** statements are restricted in the same way. The **close** statement, however, does not require any particular capabilities.

An **open** statement should include all of the capabilities we will need to process the file. Some combinations are illegal but, unfortunately, the legality is determined by the operating system rather than by Turing. For example, we can open a file with both **get** and **read** capabilities if Turing is running on some UNIX systems but not if Turing is running on a PC. Consequently, programs that use complex combinations of capabilities are not portable and should be avoided whenever possible. In this book, we use only combinations that run on all systems.

An **open** statement with the capability **seek** indicates that we want to use the file as a random access file. The capability **seek** is always used in conjunction with one or both of the capabilities **read** and **write**. If a file has been opened with **seek** capability, we can use **seek** and **tell** statements to process it. The **seek** statement moves the file to a specified position. The **tell** statement returns the current position of the file.

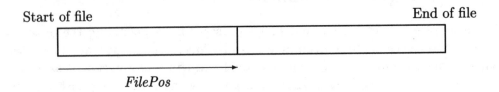

Start of file

End of file

FilePos

Figure 11.1   File Position

The file position is an integer whose value is the number of bytes between the beginning of the file and the first byte of the current component. Figure 11.1 represents the file as a horizontal band with a vertical line indicating the current position. The name of the variable containing the current position is *FilePos*, and the arrow indicates its value.

It is important to realize that the file position is *not* the number of logical components we store in the file but the number of bytes the components occupy.

Suppose we have opened `accounts.dat` with **read** and **seek** capabilities. The statement

> **seek** : *Bin*, 1500

positions the file 1,500 bytes from the beginning. If the file consisted of records with 150 bytes each, it would be in the correct position for reading or writing the tenth record.

The **tell** statement performs the converse operation: it reports the current position. The statements

> **var** *Pos* : int
> **tell** : *Bin*, *Pos*

set the integer variable *Pos* to the current position of the file. Since the number of bytes in a record may depend on the implementation, it is better to use **tell** to determine file positions than it is to calculate them.

Opening Files for Writing

When we open a file with **put** or **write** capability, Turing normally creates a new, empty file. If a file with the name given in the **open** statement exists already, Turing deletes it. If we want to open a random access file and then change a few of its components, deleting the file before we start is clearly the wrong thing to do. The capability **mod**, which stands for "modify", tells Turing *not* to delete an existing file with the same name before opening a new one.

After executing the statement

open : *Bin*, "accounts.dat", read, seek

we can read any component of the file **accounts.dat**, but we cannot write new information to it.

The statement

open : *Bin*, "accounts.dat", read, write, seek

first deletes the file **accounts.dat**, if it exists, and then creates a new file with that name. We can write records to the file in any order and subsequently read from them in any order.

The statement

open : *Bin*, "accounts.dat", read, write, seek, mod

looks for a file called **accounts.dat** and opens it for reading and writing. If the file does not exist, Turing creates it. We can read records from **accounts.dat** and write records to it in any convenient order.

11.1.3   A Random Access File for Pictures

Since most modern computers have plenty of memory, many applications that require random access can be implemented by using an array. Storing pictures, however, requires large amounts of memory, and so pictures may have to be stored on disk.

In the following example, we construct a simple program that could form the basis for a "picture management" package. We use the predefined procedures *takepic* and *drawpic* described in Section 7.3.

The pictures we store will not always be of the same size. Consequently, there is no easy way of finding where they are in the file and we cannot use **seek** to access them directly. To solve this problem, we use two files. The first is an *index file*, which contains the position and size of each picture. The second is the *picture file* itself.

We start by defining the maximum number of pictures we want to store and the names of the files in which we want to store them:

const *MaxPictures* := 50
const *IndexFileName* := "index.pic"
const *PicFileName* := "data.pic"

The procedure outlined below draws picture *Num* and returns its width, X, and height, Y. The picture is contained within the rectangle with lower left corner $(0, 0)$ and upper right corner X, Y. The complete procedure would include code for drawing each kind of picture.

```
procedure Draw (Num : int, var X, Y : int)
    case Num  of
        label 1 :
            X := 60
            Y := 40
            drawoval (15, 20, 15, 20, 1)
            drawoval (45, 20, 15, 20, 1)
        label 2 :
            [         ]        % Code for label 2 and other labels.
    end case
end Draw
```

We create the picture file by plotting each picture in turn and writing appropriate records to the index and picture files:

```
var Pos, X, Y, IndexFile, PicFile : int
open : IndexFile, IndexFileName, write
open : PicFile, PicFileName, write, seek
for Picture : 1 .. MaxPictures
    cls
    Draw (Picture, X, Y)
    var PictureData : array 1 .. sizepic (0, 0, X, Y) of int
    takepic (0, 0, X, Y, PictureData)
    cls
    tell : PicFile, Pos
    write : IndexFile, Pos, X, Y
    write : PicFile, PictureData
end for
close : IndexFile
close : PicFile
```

We read the files in a loop. During each iteration of the loop, the user enters a number. If the number is between 1 and *MaxPictures*, the program calls *ShowPicture*, declared on the following page, to plot the picture.

```
open : IndexFile, IndexFileName, read, seek
open : PicFile, PicFileName, read, seek
loop
    locate (1, 1)
    var PictureNum : int
    put "Enter picture number (0 terminates):  " ..
    get PictureNum
    if PictureNum = 0 then
        exit
    elsif PictureNum > MaxPictures then
        put "Number outside range"
    else
        ShowPicture (IndexFile, PicFile, PictureNum)
    end if
end loop
close : IndexFile
close : PicFile
```

The last step is to complete the procedure *ShowPicture*. To find the requested picture, *PictureNum*, the procedure first uses **seek** to position the index file at the beginning and then reads *PictureNum* records. We use this approach because it is independent of the size of a component of the index file. It would be faster to **seek** directly to $Size \times (PictureNum - 1)$, but to do this we would need to know $Size$, the size of a record in the index file.

The procedure *ShowPicture* reads the information from the index component and uses it to allocate the array *PictureData* to store the pixel information. Finally, the procedure reads the pixel information from the picture file and draws the picture at the center of the screen.

```
procedure ShowPicture (IndexFile, PicFile, PictureNum : int)
    var Pos, X, Y : int
    seek : IndexFile, 0
    for I : 1 .. PictureNum
        read : IndexFile, Pos, X, Y
    end for
    seek : PicFile, Pos
    var PictureData : array 1 .. sizepic (0, 0, X, Y) of int
    read : PicFile, PictureData
    cls
    drawpic ((maxx − X) div 2, (maxy − Y) div 2, PictureData, 0)
end ShowPicture
```

11.2   Subprogram Arguments

We have seen that we can pass values of any type to a subprogram. It is also possible to pass subprograms as arguments to other subprograms.

11.2.1   Plotting Mathematical Functions

Consider, for example, real-valued functions of a single real argument, such as $5x^2$, $2\sin x - 3\cos x$, and xe^{-x}. There are a number of operations we can apply to a function, f, of this kind, such as plotting its graph, finding values of x such that $f(x) = 0$, computing the derivative df/dx, and computing the integral $\int f(x)\,dx$. All these operations apply to the function f itself, not to a particular value, $f(x)$. Consequently, we should be able to pass the function as an argument.

Example 11.3   Passing a Function to a Plotting Procedure

Consider the task of plotting a function f. Assume that we are given limits, a and b, and the task is to use the entire screen to plot $f(x)$ for $a \le x \le b$.

The procedure *Plot* does the plotting. Its first parameter is the function to be plotted, written as a function header. In this case, the name of the functional parameter is F, it requires a real argument, and it returns a real value.

```
procedure Plot (function F (X : real) : real, Xa, Xb : real,
    NumPoints, Color : int)
```

The other parameters of *Plot* are: Xa and Xb, which determine the range of values to be plotted; *NumPoints*, the number of points at which the value of the function is to be calculated; and *Color*, the color of the graph.

The first thing *Plot* has to do is find the smallest and largest values of the function in the given interval. We calculate values of the function at the points we will eventually plot. Within the body of *Plot*, we can call the function F just as we call any other function.

```
const XRange := Xb − Xa
var YMin := F (Xa)
var YMax := F (Xa)
for Point : 1 .. NumPoints
    const Y := F (Xa + XRange * (Point/NumPoints))
    if YMin > Y then
        YMin := Y
    end if
```

```
   if YMax < Y then
      YMax := Y
   end if
end for
```

Using the values of *YMin* and *YMax*, we can scale values of the function so that *YMin* becomes 0 and *YMax* becomes *maxy*. Similarly, we scale X values so that *Xa* becomes 0 and *Xb* becomes *maxx*. The loop maintains a pair of adjacent points on the graph, (*XOld*, *YOld*) and (*XNew*, *YNew*), and draws a straight line between each pair.

```
const Yrange := YMax − YMin
var XOld, YOld : int
for Point : 0 .. NumPoints
   const P := Point/NumPoints
   const Y := F (Xa + XRange * P)
   const XNew := round (maxx * P)
   const YNew := round (maxy * (Y − YMin)/Yrange)
   if Point > 0 then
      drawline (XOld, YOld, XNew, YNew, Color)
   end if
   XOld := XNew
   YOld := YNew
end for
end Plot
```

As an example of the use of the procedure *Plot*, we plot an exponentially-damped sine wave defined by

```
function Damp (X : real) : real
   result exp (−X) * sin (40 * X)
end Damp
```

In the call to *Plot*, we provide the name of the function to be plotted as the first argument. We do *not* provide any arguments for *Damp*. We plot the function for the interval $0 \le X \le 5$, using as many points as the screen resolution provides:

$$Plot \, (Damp, 0, 5, maxx, White)$$

The procedure *Plot* is written in such a way that *Xb* does not have to be greater then *Xa*. The call

$$Plot \, (Damp, 5, 0, maxx, Yellow)$$

will plot the mirror image of the first call.

Predefined Subprograms

Turing does not allow the name of a predefined subprogram to be passed as an argument. The compiler rejects a call that contains the predefined function *sin*:

    Plot (*sin*, 0, 6.5, 100, *Green*) $\oslash$

This is only a minor inconvenience. If we need to plot a standard function, such as *sin*, we can declare our own version and pass it to the plotting function:

    function *MySine* (*X* : real) : real
      return *sin* (*X*)
    end *MySine*

    Plot (*MySine*, 0, 6.5, 100, *Blue*)

11.2.2   Solving Equations

Computers are often used to solve equations. It is usually possible to express an equation in the form $f(x) = 0$. The problem is then to find values of x that satisfy $f(x) = 0$. This problem is called *finding zeros* of the function f.

Example 11.4   A Function That Finds Zeros

The main difficulty in finding values of x for which $f(x) = 0$ is knowing where to look for the zero. In principle, $f(x)$ might be zero for any finite value of x, and we cannot try all of them.

The function that we give here has two requirements that simplify the search. First, the caller must provide two values, a and b, at which f has different signs: either $f(a) < 0$ and $f(b) > 0$ or $f(a) > 0$ and $f(b) < 0$. Second, $f(x)$ must be continuous in the interval $a \le x \le b$. Together, these requirements ensure that the equation $f(x) = 0$ has a solution in the given interval.

The method we use is called the *bisection method*. We divide the interval into two equal parts and continue halving it until we have a close approximation to the result we need. After each step, we obtain a new interval, half the size of the previous interval, that must contain the zero we are looking for. We stop halving either when we obtain an exact solution, which is unlikely, or when the interval is smaller than the error specified by the caller.

The function is called *FindZero*. Its parameters are the function whose zero we are to find, the end points of the interval, and a tolerance. If we let m denote the value returned by the function and t denote the tolerance specified by the caller, the function guarantees that the true solution lies between $m - t$ and $m + t$.

function *FindZero* (function $F(X : \text{real}) : \text{real}, Xa, Xb, Tolerance : \text{real}) : \text{real}$
   var $A := Xa$
   var $B := Xb$

The heart of the function is a loop that repeatedly halves the interval (A, B):

```
loop
   invariant sign (F (A)) ≠ sign (F (B))
   const M := (A + B)/2
   if abs (A − B) < Tolerance then
      result M
   end if
   const Fa := F (A)
   const Fb := F (B)
   const Fm := F (M)
   if Fm = 0 then
      result M
   elsif sign (Fa) = sign (Fm) then
      A := M
   else
      B := M
   end if
end loop
end FindZero
```

The invariant of the loop states that the value of the function at the ends of the interval have different signs, which implies that the zero lies within the interval, or possibly at one of its end points. The end points of the interval are A and B, and its midpoint is M.

There are two exit conditions: if $F(M)$ is zero, we have found the exact solution. Although this is unlikely to happen, we must check for it to maintain the invariant. It is more likely that the interval will become smaller than *Tolerance*, which will happen after a finite number of iterations.

We test *FindZero* by looking for a solution of $sin(X) = 0$ near 2π. Since we cannot pass the predefined function *sin* to *FindZero*, we use the function *MySine* declared on page 316.

```
const Pi := 3.1415926535
const Root := FindZero (MySine, 7, 5, 1e − 8)
put "The zero was found at ", Root
put "The error was ", abs (Root − 2 ∗ Pi)
```

Running this program yields the results shown below. The small size of the error is luck: we would expect the error to be a little smaller than the tolerance.

```
The zero was found at 6.283185
The error was 6.349765e-11
```

11.2.3   Data Structure Traversal

One of the important applications of subprogram arguments is to encapsulate the code for traversing a complex data structure. We first present an example of this technique and then discuss its limitations.

Example 11.5   Processing Nodes of a Binary Search Tree

Binary search trees, introduced in Section 9.4, provide an efficient way of storing keyed data. Most of the procedures that process binary search trees must traverse all or part of the tree. Procedures of this kind have a similar structure, and consequently a considerable amount of code is duplicated. We can reduce the duplication by first writing a procedure that traverses the tree and then passing other procedures to it.

We declare a binary tree in which each node contains a key and a probability:

```
const MaxKeyLength := 12
type KeyString : string (MaxKeyLength)
var Nodes : collection of forward NodeRecord
type NodeRecord :
   record
      Key : KeyString
      Probability : real
      Left, Right : pointer to Nodes
   end record
```

The next procedure is the most interesting one from the point of view of this example: its second parameter is a procedure, *ProcessNode*.

```
procedure TreeWalk (Tree : pointer to Nodes,
      procedure ProcessNode (Node : NodeRecord))
   if Tree ≠ nil (Nodes) then
      TreeWalk (Nodes (Tree).Left, ProcessNode)
      ProcessNode (Nodes (Tree))
      TreeWalk (Nodes (Tree).Right, ProcessNode)
   end if
end TreeWalk
```

The procedure *TreeWalk* traverses the binary search tree recursively, calling *ProcessNode* at each node of the tree. Thus *TreeWalk* encapsulates the method of traversing the tree. We can use it without having to know the details of the organization of the tree.

The procedure *ShowNode* provides a simple application for *TreeWalk*. It displays the value of the node that *TreeWalk* passes to it.

```
procedure ShowNode (Node : NodeRecord)
    put Node.Key, repeat (" ", MaxKeyLength + 5 − length (Node.Key)),
        Node.Probability : 4 : 4
end ShowNode
```

The effect of the call

```
TreeWalk (Tree, ShowNode)
```

is to display the key and probability at each node of *Tree*. The keys appear in alphabetical order.

The remaining code illustrates applications of *TreeWalk*. We use the procedure *MakeTree* to build a tree that we can use for testing.

```
procedure MakeTree (Key : KeyString, Probability : real,
        var Tree : pointer to Nodes)
    if Tree = nil (Nodes) then
        new Nodes, Tree
        Nodes (Tree).Key := Key
        Nodes (Tree).Probability := Probability
        Nodes (Tree).Left := nil (Nodes)
        Nodes (Tree).Right := nil (Nodes)
    elsif Key < Nodes (Tree).Key then
        MakeTree (Key, Probability, Nodes (Tree).Left)
    elsif Key > Nodes (Tree).Key then
        MakeTree (Key, Probability, Nodes (Tree).Right)
    end if
end MakeTree
```

The procedure *RandomKey* generates a key consisting of a random number of random letters.

```
procedure RandomKey (var Key : KeyString)
    Key := ""
    var KeyLength : int
    randint (KeyLength, 1, MaxKeyLength)
    for : 1 .. KeyLength
```

```
        var Letter : int
        randint (Letter, 0, 25)
        Key += chr (ord ("A") + Letter)
    end for
end RandomKey
```

The main program constructs a random tree containing twenty nodes with random keys and probabilities. It uses *ShowNode* to display the nodes on the screen.

```
var RandomTree := nil (Nodes)
for : 1 .. 20
    var Key : KeyString
    RandomKey (Key)
    var Probability : real
    rand (Probability)
    MakeTree (Key, Probability, RandomTree)
end for
TreeWalk (RandomTree, ShowNode)
```

Suppose that we need to know the sum of all the probabilities in a tree. The procedure *SumNodes* adds the probability at a node into the nonlocal sum *Total*.

```
var Total : real := 0
procedure SumNodes (Node : NodeRecord)
    Total += Node.Probability
end SumNodes
```

We find the sum of the probabilities by initializing *Total* and passing *SumNodes* to *TreeWalk*. The program displays the required total.

```
TreeWalk (RandomTree, SumNodes)
put "Total is ", Total
```

The example demonstrates both the strengths and the weaknesses of subprogram arguments. The advantage is that we need to write the recursive code for traversing the tree only once, in the procedure *TreeWalk*. If the data structure were even more complex than a binary search tree, the saving would be even greater. Furthermore, if we subsequently decide to change the structure and rewrite *TreeWalk* accordingly, the code that uses it will work without change.

The disadvantage is that the parameter *ProcessNode* has a fixed type. In the example, the argument corresponding to *ProcessNode* must be a procedure with one parameter that is a node record. In order to find the total of the probabilities, we had to use a nonlocal variable, *Total*, although it would have been better style to write *SumNodes* as a function returning a real value.

11.3 Summary

Numbers in parentheses refer to sections where material appears.

▶ Binary files contain data in the same form in which it is stored in memory (11.1).

▶ The **open** statement opens a binary file and the **close** statement closes it (11.1.1).

▶ A sequential binary file may be opened for reading with capability **read** or for writing with capability **write** (11.1.1).

▶ The amount of data read by a **read** statement or written by a **write** statement is determined by the arguments of the statement (11.1.1).

▶ Turing does not check that the data in the file is of the type required by the **read** statement (11.1.1).

▶ The predefined function *eof* returns **true** when there is no data left to be read from the file (11.1.1).

▶ The **open** statement must include capabilities specifying the operations that can be performed on the file (11.1.2).

▶ An **open** statement with the capabilities **seek**, **tell**, or **mod** indicates that the file will be accessed randomly (11.1.2).

▶ The **tell** statement reports the current file position, measured in bytes from the beginning of the file (11.1.2).

▶ The **seek** statement moves the file to the position specified by the argument (11.1.2).

▶ An index file may be used to locate items of varying size in a binary file (11.1.3).

▶ The arguments of a subprogram may be subprograms (11.2).

▶ Predefined subprograms may not be passed as arguments to subprograms (11.2.1).

▶ Subprogram arguments are useful for mathematical operations on functions (11.2.2) and for data structure traversal (11.2.3).

11.4   Exercises

11.1 By expanding on the ideas presented in Section 11.1.3, write a program that maintains a collection of images on the disk. Use *takepic* and *drawpic* to collect and recreate the images, and use a binary file to store the images.

11.2 We cannot store a binary search tree in a binary file because binary search trees contain pointers. Nevertheless, we can apply the method of binary search to finding information in a binary file. Write a program that stores records with keys in a binary file and then uses binary search to locate a record with a given key.

11.3 By avoiding duplicated calculations, improve the plotting function that appears in Example 11.3 on page 314. While finding the maximum and minimum values of the function, *Plot* should store the computed values in an array. It can then plot the stored values directly, without recalculating the function.

11.4 Write a procedure that accepts as an argument a real-valued function r and plots the function in polar coordinates. Assume that the function r has an argument θ that varies from 0 to 2π. Plot points at $x = r(\theta)\cos\theta$ and $y = r(\theta)\sin\theta$ with suitable scaling.

11.5 Write a function that returns an approximate value of the derivative of a function at a given point. Use the fact that for small values of h:

$$f'(x) \approx \frac{f(x+h) - f(x-h)}{2h}.$$

Test your function using the fact that the derivative of e^x is e^x. It is difficult to get consistently accurate results because it is necessary to compute the difference of numbers that are almost equal, an operation that is likely to lose precision.

11.6 Write a function that returns an approximate value of the integral of a function over a given interval. The header of the function should be

function *Integrate* (function $F(X : \text{real}) : \text{real}, A, B : \text{real}) : \text{real}$

The call

$Integrate\,(F, A, B)$

should compute

$$\int_a^b f(x)\,dx.$$

There are several ways of writing this function. All of them start by dividing the interval from $x = a$ to $x = b$ into n equal parts. Let $h = (b - a)/n$, and define $x_i = a + ih$ for $0 \le i \le n$. Thus $x_0 = a, x_1 = a + h, \ldots, x_n = b$. We write f_i to stand for $f(x_i)$.

(a) The *rectangular formula* is the simplest formula for estimating an integral. It approximates the function f as a sequence of horizontal segments:

$$\int_a^b f(x)\,dx \approx h\,(f_0 + f_1 + \cdots + f_{n-1}).$$

(b) The *trapezoidal rule* approximates the function as a sequence of straight lines:

$$\int_a^b f(x)\,dx \approx \frac{h}{2}\,(f_0 + 2f_1 + \cdots + 2f_{n-1} + f_n).$$

(c) *Simpson's rule* is more accurate than either the rectangular or the trapezoidal rule:

$$\int_a^b f(x)\,dx \approx \frac{h}{3}\,(f_0 + 4f_1 + 2f_2 + \cdots + 2f_{n-2} + 4f_{n-1} + f_n).$$

Chapter 12

Object Oriented Turing

The concepts that underlie object oriented programming emerged more than twenty years ago with languages such as Simula (1967) and Smalltalk (1976). The object oriented style of programming, however, has seen widespread use only since the middle of the 1980s. Software practitioners now use both pure object oriented languages, such as Eiffel and Smalltalk, and languages with object oriented extensions, such as C++ and Object Oriented Turing (OOT).

The object oriented extensions of Turing do not change the appearance of Turing programs to any great extent, but they have a profound effect on the kinds of programs we can write and the way in which we design programs. Object oriented techniques allow us to write program components that are more abstract and more reusable than the components we have seen previously.

OOT is a general-purpose language that is suitable for a wide range of applications, including systems programming. As well as object oriented features, OOT provides concurrent programming constructs and a variety of predefined types. In this chapter we discuss the object oriented features of OOT.

The programs presented in previous chapters run with any version of Turing. The programs described in this chapter can be run only with OOT.

12.1   Classes and Objects

Every new paradigm of programming imposes its own vocabulary. Object oriented programming is no exception. Some of the words we define in this section are new names for familiar concepts. These new names emphasize the metaphors that underlie the object programming paradigm.

An *object* is a data structure rather like a record. Instead of accessing the components of an object directly, we access them by calling functions and procedures. The functions and procedures are called *methods* of the object. The use of methods ensures that only meaningful operations are applied to the object. By using methods, we can guarantee the integrity of the object in ways that we could not if its components were directly accessible to its users.

A *class* defines the behavior of a family of objects. Each object in the family is called an *instance* of the class. The definition of a class is similar to the definition of a module. A class definition, like a module definition, contains import and export lists as well as declarations of types, constants, variables, functions, and procedures. Each instance of the class has its own copy of the variables declared in the class. For this reason, the variables declared in a class are called *instance variables* of the class.

The relationship between an object and its class is similar to the relationship between a variable and its type. When we say that a variable X has type T, we mean that T determines the range of values that X can assume. Similarly, when we say that an object O is an instance of a class C, we mean that C determines the *behavior* of O. Just as a conventional program may contain many variables of a particular type, an object oriented program may contain many instances of a particular class.

Although the methods of an object are ordinary functions and procedures, they are called with a special syntax that mentions both the object and the method. To call method M of object O, we write $O{\rightarrow}M$. This expression is called a *message*, and we can read it as: Ask object O to execute method M. The object O is called the *receiver* of the message.

12.1.1   Declaring a Class

Almost any computational entity can be turned into an object. Histograms, introduced in Example 5.4, provide a simple basis for the illustration of object oriented techniques.

Example 12.1   A Class for Histograms

We introduce a class with the keyword class and the name of the class. Like a module, a class begins with an import list and an export list. The class *Histogram* does not import anything, but it exports three methods.

> class *Histogram*
> > export *Initialize, Put, Show*

We use conventional variable declarations to introduce data for a histogram:

> var *Store* : array 0 .. 100 of int
> var *X, Y* : int

The value of the *I*th component of *Store* is the number of times the value *I* has been observed. The coordinate pair (X, Y) gives the position at which the histogram will appear on the screen.

The procedure *Initialize* assigns the position (X, Y) of the histogram and sets all components of the array *Store* to zero:

> procedure *Initialize* (*InitX, InitY* : int)
> > $X := InitX$
> > $Y := InitY$
> > for *I* : 0 .. 100
> > > *Store* $(I) := 0$
> > end for
> end *Initialize*

The procedure *Put* checks the value of *I* and increments the component *I* of the histogram:

> procedure *Put* (*I* : int)
> > pre $0 \leq I$ and $I \leq 100$
> > *Store* $(I) += 1$
> end *Put*

Finally, the procedure *Show* displays the histogram on the screen at the chosen position (X, Y). It does not display counts greater than 50.

> procedure *Show*
> > *drawbox* $(X, Y, X + 110, Y + 60, black)$
> > for *x* : 0 .. 100
> > > for *y* : 0 .. 50
> > > > if *Store* $(x) \geq y$ then
> > > > > *drawdot* $(X + x + 5, Y + y + 5, blue)$
> > > > end if

```
        end for
      end for
    end Show
```

We conclude the definition of a class in the same way we conclude the definition of a module, with an **end** statement:

    end *Histogram*

After Turing has processed the declaration of a class, we can use the name of the class in most of the ways that we can use a type identifier. In the following three statements we declare a variable, H, allocate memory for an instance of the class *Histogram*, and initialize the histogram.

    var H : **pointer to** *Histogram*
    new *Histogram*, H
    Histogram (H). *Initialize* $(0, 0)$

Turing provides abbreviations for all three of these statements. In abbreviated form, the statements look like this:

    var H : ↑*Histogram*
    new H
    $H \rightarrow Initialize$ $(0, 0)$

In this chapter, we use the full form "**pointer to**" rather than the abbreviation "↑". We use the abbreviated forms of the second and third statements.

The following program uses the histogram. The **for** statement simulates 2,000 random observations. The final statement displays the histogram after the observations have been recorded.

    for : 1 .. 2000
      var R : **int**
      randint $(R, 0, 100)$
      $H \rightarrow Put$ (R)
    end for
    $H \rightarrow Show$

The statements $H \rightarrow Put$ (R) and $H \rightarrow Show$ are *messages*. The syntax suggests that we are telling the object H to perform the tasks *Put* (R) and *Show*. This distinguishes messages from ordinary procedure calls that do not specify particular objects.

The histogram that H points to is an object. It is an *instance* of the class *Histogram*. Turing does not allow the direct declaration of objects. For example, the OOT compiler would not accept the declaration

> var X : *Histogram* $\oslash$

Consequently, all objects must be introduced indirectly, with a pointer variable and a new statement that allocates memory for the object.

12.1.2   Classes as Generators

We could have achieved the effect of Example 12.1 without introducing a class. The important property of classes, however, is that they allow us to introduce as many objects — histograms in this case — as we need. In this sense, classes are *generators* of objects.

Example 12.2   Multiple Instances of a Class

In this example, we use the declaration of the class *Histogram* given in Example 12.1. We declare three instances of the class and use them to illustrate different probability distributions. The first experiment uses a quadratic function to generate random observations and store them in the histogram *Quad*:

```
var Quad : pointer to Histogram
new Quad
Quad→Initialize (0, 150)
for : 1 .. 1000
   var R : real
   rand (R)
   Quad→Put (round (100.0 * R * R))
end for
```

The second experiment uses summation to obtain an approximately binomial distribution stored in *Bin*:

```
var Bin : pointer to Histogram
new Bin
Bin→Initialize (0, 75)
for : 1 .. 100
   var I := 0
   for : 0 .. 20
      var R : int
      randint (R, 0, 5)
      I += R
```

```
      Bin→Put (I)
        end for
      end for
```

The third experiment generates a "negative exponential" distribution in the histogram *Exp*. We make use of the fact that if $e^{-5} \leq R \leq 1$, then $-5 \leq ln(R) \leq 0$.

```
      var Exp : pointer to Histogram
      new Exp
      Exp→Initialize (0, 0)
      for : 1 .. 1000
        var R : real
        rand (R)
        if R ≥ exp (−5.0) then
            Exp→Put (round (−20.0 ∗ ln (R)))
        end if
      end for
```

The following statements display the completed histograms. The position of each histogram on the screen is determined by the arguments passed to its initialization procedure.

```
      Quad→Show
      Bin→Show
      Exp→Show
```

The example demonstrates that each of the objects, *Quad*, *Bin*, and *Exp*, is a distinct entity with its own data.

We could write this program using modules instead of classes. For example, we could define a module, *HistMod*, that exports a type, *HistType*, and we could declare *Quad*, *Bin*, and *Exp* as variables of this type. We would have to write statements such as

```
      HistMod.Put (Quad, I)
```

rather than the simpler statement

```
      Quad→Put (I)
```

12.1.3   Dynamic Object Declaration

The class declaration provides a simple and natural way of declaring the instance variables of an object. Reducing the length and complexity of code is one of the advantages of object oriented programming. The next example illustrates the use of objects in a dynamic setting.

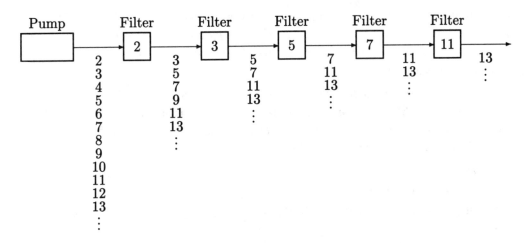

Figure 12.1   Pumping Numbers and Filtering Primes

Example 12.3   Using Filters to Generate Primes

Figure 12.1 shows a "machine" that generates prime numbers. The machine consists of a pump and several filters. Each filter is labeled with a number. The pump sends a stream of numbers, shown in a vertical column below the arrow in Figure 12.1, to the filter labeled "2". A filter displays the first number it receives. For each subsequent number, it makes a decision: if the number is a multiple of its label, it does nothing; otherwise, it sends the number to the next filter.

The filter labeled "2", for example, receives the numbers $2, 3, 4, 5, \ldots$. It displays "2" and then sends $3, 5, 7, \ldots$ to the filter labeled "3". It does not send $4, 6, 8, \ldots$, because these numbers are multiples of 2. Similarly, filter "3" receives $3, 5, 7, 9, \ldots$, displays "3", and sends $5, 7, 11, 13, \ldots$ to filter "5".

What happens when the pump emits "13"? The number 13 passes through filters $2, 3, 5, 7$, and 11. Since filter "11" has nowhere to send "13" in Figure 12.1, the machine creates a new filter labeled "13". As the pump continues to send numbers into the chain of filters, a new filter is created each time a number reaches the last filter in the chain. If this number was a multiple of a prime p, it would have been absorbed by the filter labeled "p". Since the number has reached the end of the chain, it cannot be a multiple of any prime, and therefore it must be a prime itself. In this way, the machine builds a sequence of filters, each one labeled with a prime number. As it does so, it prints a list of prime numbers.

To simulate the machine, we could write a program using a linked list and the list manipulation techniques of Chapter 9. For this example, however, we use objects to represent the filters. We declare a class *Filter* and construct instances of this class as we need them.

The task of a filter is to receive numbers and process them in the way we have described. Each filter performs essentially the same task. Filters differ only in their labels. We can therefore define a class to describe the behavior of a filter. Each filter will be an instance of the class:

> class *Filter*
>> export *Start, Check*

Each filter must have a label, which is an integer, and a pointer to the next filter in the chain:

>> var *Prime* : int
>> var *Next* :   pointer to *Filter*

When we create a new filter, we must initialize both of its instance variables. The initial value of *Prime* will be supplied by the caller, and the initial value of *Next* will be nil. After initializing its variables, the filter displays its prime number.

>> procedure *Start* (*P* : int)
>>> *Prime* := *P*
>>> *Next* := nil
>>> put *Prime*
>> end *Start*

After it has been created, a filter must check numbers sent to it. The procedure *Check* performs this task.

>> procedure *Check* (*N* : int)
>>> if *N* mod *Prime* ≠ 0 then
>>>> if *Next* = nil then
>>>>> new *Next*
>>>>> *Next*→*Start* (*N*)
>>>> else
>>>>> *Next*→*Check* (*N*)
>>>> end if
>>> end if
>> end *Check*

> end *Filter*

There are three cases to consider. If *N* is a multiple of *Prime*, there is nothing to do. Otherwise, the action taken depends on whether the filter has a successor. If

Next is a null pointer, the filter does not have a successor. In this case, *Check* creates a new filter, using new, and initializes it, using *Start*. If the successor exists, *Check* asks it to check the number N.

The role of the pump is performed by the main program, which first creates the filter labeled "2" and then sends the numbers $3, 4, 5, \ldots$ to it.

```
var Filt : pointer to Filter
new Filt
Filt→Start (2)
var N := 3
loop
    Filt→Check (N)
    N += 1
end loop
```

When we run this program, it displays a list of prime numbers:

```
2
3
5
7
. . .
```

Discussion

Although the examples of this section are quite simple, they illustrate two characteristics typical of object oriented programs. The first characteristic is that methods tend to be quite short. Even in large programs, many methods consist of only two or three lines of code. This occurs because objects, even complex objects, are required to perform simple tasks such as changing the value of an instance variable.

The second characteristic is that methods tend to have fewer parameters than conventional functions and procedures. This is because the object provides a convenient place to store variables that would otherwise be passed as arguments. For example, each instance of class *Histogram* stores screen coordinates that determine where it will appear on the screen. Consequently, the method *Show* does not have to pass the coordinates as arguments.

Both of these characteristics reflect one of the principal goals of object oriented design: an object should have *responsibilities*. A histogram object is responsible for its position on the screen. Informally, we can say that a histogram knows how to display itself.

12.2   Inheritance

The word "inheritance" has several distinct but related meanings in English. Its use in object oriented programming is loosely related to the phenomena of inheritance in families. Just as children inherit characteristics or properties from their parents, a "child class", C, inherits features from its "parent class", P. The class C has more features than the class P and is accordingly more specialized.

As an example, consider the class *Dog*. Instances of this class are dogs. They have four legs and they bark. The class *Spaniel* inherits these features from the class *Dog* and adds the new feature of large, drooping ears. We say that a spaniel "is a kind of" dog.

We can also move in the direction of increasing generality. A more general class that includes dogs is the class of mammals. We say that a dog "is a kind of" mammal. In general, if it makes sense to say that "a C is a kind of P" then it is likely that C inherits some of the features of P.

Example 12.4 provides a simple illustration of the use of inheritance in object oriented programming.

Example 12.4   Inheritance in Graphics Programming

Consider a program that manipulates simple graphical objects such as circles, squares, and triangles. Each kind of object should be able to respond to messages such as *Draw*, *Erase*, and *Move*. Figure 12.2 summarizes, in tabular form, the operations the program must provide.

The conventional way to write the program would make use of the techniques described in Chapter 8. We would declare a union type with variants for circles, squares, and triangles. The procedure *Draw* would contain a **case** statement to choose the drawing algorithm appropriate for the object. In other words, we would organize the program according to the rows of Figure 12.2.

	Circle	*Square*	*Triangle*
Draw	draw a circle	draw a square	draw a triangle
Erase	erase a circle	erase a square	erase a triangle
Move	move a circle	move a square	move a triangle

Figure 12.2   Operations for a Graphics Program

The object oriented approach to the problem splits up the procedures according to the columns of Figure 12.2. We declare a class *Circle*, a class *Square*, and a class *Triangle*. Each class has three methods: *Draw*, *Erase*, and *Move*. For example, here is the class *Circle*:

```
class Circle
    export Make, Draw, Erase, Move
    var X, Y, Radius : int
    procedure Make (InitX, InitY, InitRadius : int)
        X := InitX
        Y := InitY
        Radius := InitRadius
    end Make
    procedure Draw
        drawoval (X, Y, Radius, Radius, black)
    end Draw
    procedure Erase
        drawoval (X, Y, Radius, Radius, white)
    end Erase
    procedure Move (DeltaX, DeltaY : int)
        Erase
        X += DeltaX
        Y += DeltaY
        Draw
    end Move
end Circle
```

We can anticipate that the class *Square* will be quite similar to the class *Circle*. The details of how to draw circles and squares are different, but the general ideas of drawing, erasing, and moving are the same.

For example, to make something appear on a white screen, we can draw it in black. To erase it, we can draw it in white. Suppose we declare the method *Redraw* in the class *Circle* as follows:

```
procedure Redraw (Col : int)
    drawoval (X, Y, Radius, Radius, Col)
end Redraw
```

With this definition, we can declare *Draw* and *Erase* as follows:

```
procedure Draw
    Redraw (black)
end Draw
```

```
procedure Erase
    Redraw (white)
end Erase
```

The interesting point is that these definitions of *Draw* and *Erase* are independent of the particular object that we are drawing or erasing. They could be declared in a parent class and inherited by the classes *Circle*, *Square*, and *Triangle*.

We can apply the same idea to the procedure *Move*, declaring it as

```
procedure Move (DeltaX, DeltaY : int)
    Erase
    ChangePos (DeltaX, DeltaY)
    Draw
end Move
```

in which the method *ChangePos* performs the actions required by a specific shape and the methods *Erase* and *Draw* work for any shape.

The class *Shape* is the parent of the classes *Circle*, *Square*, and *Triangle*. We declare it as

```
class Shape
    export Draw, Erase, Move
    deferred procedure Redraw (Col : int)
    deferred procedure ChangePos (DeltaX, DeltaY : int)
    procedure Draw
        Redraw (black)
    end Draw
    procedure Erase
        Redraw (white)
    end Erase
    procedure Move (DeltaX, DeltaY : int)
        Erase
        ChangePos (DeltaX, DeltaY)
        Draw
    end Move
end Shape
```

The keyword **deferred** indicates that the method is a feature of the class but that it has not been declared yet. We can create instances of *Shape*, but we cannot do anything with them because some of their methods are undefined. Classes such as *Shape*, which contain methods without implementations, are called *abstract classes*. If all of the methods of a class have implementations, the class is called a *concrete class*.

The child class *Circle* inherits *Draw*, *Erase*, and *Move* from the class *Shape*, but it provides its own definitions of *Make*, *Redraw*, and *ChangePos*. Turing requires the keyword **body** before the redefinition of a function or procedure that was declared in the parent class.

```
class Circle
    inherit Shape
    export Make
    var X, Y, Radius : int
    procedure Make (InitX, InitY, InitRadius : int)
        X := InitX
        Y := InitY
        Radius := InitRadius
    end Make
    body procedure Redraw (Col : int)
        drawoval (X, Y, Radius, Radius, Col)
    end Redraw
    body procedure ChangePos (DeltaX, DeltaY : int)
        X += DeltaX
        Y += DeltaY
    end ChangePos
end Circle
```

The export list of the class *Circle* consists only of the name *Make*. The class also exports *Draw*, *Erase*, and *Move* by inheritance from class *Shape*.

The classes *Square* and *Triangle* are constructed in the same way as the class *Circle*. First, we declare the class *Square*.

```
class Square
    inherit Shape
    export Make
    var X, Y, Size : int
    procedure Make (InitX, InitY, InitSize : int)
        X := InitX
        Y := InitY
        Size := InitSize
    end Make
```

```
body procedure Redraw (Col : int)
    drawline (X, Y, X + Size, Y, Col)
    drawline (X + Size, Y, X + Size, Y + Size, Col)
    drawline (X + Size, Y + Size, X, Y + Size, Col)
    drawline (X, Y + Size, X, Y, Col)
end Redraw
body procedure ChangePos (DeltaX, DeltaY : int)
    X += DeltaX
    Y += DeltaY
end ChangePos
end Square
```

Next, we declare the class *Triangle*.

```
class Triangle
    inherit Shape
    export Make
    var X, Y : array 1 .. 3 of int
    procedure Make (InitX, InitY : array 1 .. 3 of int)
        for I : 1 .. 3
            X (I) := InitX (I)
            Y (I) := InitY (I)
        end for
    end Make
    body procedure Redraw (Col : int)
        drawline (X (1), Y (1), X (2), Y (2), Col)
        drawline (X (2), Y (2), X (3), Y (3), Col)
        drawline (X (3), Y (3), X (1), Y (1), Col)
    end Redraw
    body procedure ChangePos (DeltaX, DeltaY : int)
        for I : 1 .. 3
            X (I) += DeltaX
            Y (I) += DeltaY
        end for
    end ChangePos
end Triangle
```

If we have an instance of the class *Circle*, we can send it any of the messages *Make*, *Draw*, *Erase*, or *Move*. The first is declared in the class *Circle* and the others are inherited from the class *Shape*.

We cannot send a *Redraw* or a *ChangePos* message to a *Circle* object because these names are not exported. When we send a *Draw* message, however, the *Draw* method in the parent class, *Shape*, calls the *Redraw* method in the child, *Circle*. Using inheritance in this way, we can separate the general properties of the parent, *Shape*, from the particular implementations of its children, *Circle*, *Square*, and *Triangle*.

The following program constructs one instance of each shape and moves the shapes across the screen in different directions.

```
var S : pointer to Square
new S
S→Make (50, 50, 50)
S→Draw


var C : pointer to Circle
new C
C→Make (200, 20, 20)
C→Draw


var T : pointer to Triangle
new T
const X : array 1 .. 3 of int := init (5, 30, 5)
const Y : array 1 .. 3 of int := init (180, 240, 240)
T→Make (X, Y)
T→Draw


for : 1 .. 150
   delay (20)
   S→Move (3, 1)
   C→Move (−1, 1)
   T→Move (2, −1)
end for
```

This small example illustrates both strengths and weaknesses of object oriented programming. The program shows how we can use inheritance to provide a uniform interface to objects of different classes. It also shows that long calling sequences may be needed to obtain the benefits of inheritance.

Extension by Inheritance

Inheritance is the central abstraction mechanism of object oriented programming. When we notice that classes have similar features, we can abstract their common features into a parent class. Conversely, if a class has some, but not all, of the features we need for a particular application, we can create a new class that inherits the existing features and adds new features.

Consider two ways of extending the graphics program of Example 12.4. The first extension consists of adding a method, such as *Rotate*, to the program. This extension corresponds to adding a row to the table of Figure 12.2 on page 334, as shown in Figure 12.3. We can implement the extension by adding a deferred method, *Rotate*, to the class *Shape* and an implementation for *Rotate* to each of the classes *Circle*, *Square*, and *Triangle*. Each class must then be recompiled.

Another kind of extension would be to add a new shape to the program. This corresponds to adding a new column to the table of Figure 12.2, as shown in Figure 12.4. In this case, all we have to do is write a declaration for the new class, *Rectangle*, and compile it. We do not have to alter, or even to recompile, existing code.

Consider how awkward it would be to add the shape *Rectangle* to a graphics program coded in the conventional style. We would have to add an additional clause to each of the case statements in each of the procedures *Draw*, *Erase*, and *Move*. We would be changing existing code, which is always a more risky operation than adding new code to a program.

$\vdots$	$\vdots$	$\vdots$	$\vdots$
Rotate	rotate a circle	rotate a square	rotate a triangle

Figure 12.3   Adding a Method to the Graphics Program

...	*Rectangle*
...	draw a rectangle
...	erase a rectangle
...	move a rectangle

Figure 12.4   Adding a Class to the Graphics Program

12.3 Frameworks

Turing, like most programming languages, has a large number of predefined functions and procedures. We can use these predefined subprograms, together with subprograms that we write ourselves, to construct a *library*. The main program obtains basic services by calling subprograms from the library, as shown in Figure 12.5. The structure of the system is determined by the main program; the library is a collection of individual components.

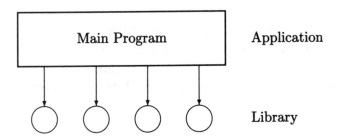

Figure 12.5   A Program Using Components from a Library

Using object oriented techniques, we can reverse the relationship between the library and the main program. Instead of the application calling the library, the library calls the application. A library of this kind is referred to as a *framework*. A framework is a coherent collection of classes that contain deferred methods. The deferred methods are "holes" that we fill in with methods that are specific to the application. The organization of a program constructed from a framework is shown in Figure 12.6. The structure of the system is determined by the framework; the application is a collection of individual components.

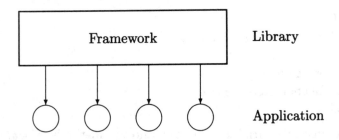

Figure 12.6   A Program Using a Framework from a Library

12.3.1   The MVC Framework

The framework that we describe in this section is a modified and simplified version of Smalltalk's model-view-controller (MVC) framework. The MVC framework is an abstract description of a simulation program. The *model* is a program that simulates some real-world entity such as a radiator in a house, a flying object, the cruise-control mechanism of a car, or a bus service. The *view* is a program that displays the results of the simulation on the screen in forms such as numbers, graphs, meters, and barcharts. The *controller* provides the link between the model and the view.

The organization of the components of the MVC framework appears in Figure 12.7. The arrows indicate that the controller can send messages to the model and the view. The dashed line represents a data link between the model and the view. In our simple version of the framework, there is no direct link between the model and the view.

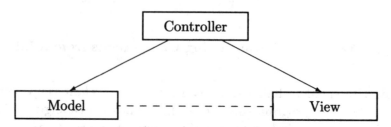

Figure 12.7   The Model-View-Controller Framework

Constructing the MVC Framework

The first step in the construction of the MVC framework is the declaration of the class *Model*.

```
class Model
    export Update, Report, Finished
    var Finished := false
    deferred procedure Update
    deferred function Report : real
end Model
```

A model has an instance variable, *Finished*, and two methods, *Update* and *Report*. When a model receives an *Update* message, it calculates new values of its instance variables. In response to a *Report* message, it returns the value of one of its instance variables. A complete MVC framework would allow the model to report the values of several variables. The declarations of *Update* and *Report* are deferred. We will give them bodies when we introduce an actual model.

The class *View* has only one method, *Update*, and one instance variable, *Finished*. The task of *Update* is to display the number *Val* in some way on the screen. We assume that *Val* ranges between 0 and 100.

```
class View
    export Update, Finished
    var Finished := false
    deferred procedure Update(Val : real)
end View
```

Either a model or a view can set its own variable *Finished* to true. When the controller notices this event, the simulation terminates.

A controller has a pointer to a model, *M*, and a pointer to a view, *V*. Its method, *Make*, initializes the controller by providing values for each instance variable. The method *Run* performs the simulation. During each iteration, *Run* determines whether the model or the view has finished and, if they have not, it sends an *Update* message to each.

```
class Controller
    import Model, View
    export Make, Run
    var M : pointer to Model
    var V : pointer to View

    procedure Make (InitM : pointer to Model, InitV : pointer to View)
        M := InitM
        V := InitV
    end Make

    procedure Run
        loop
            exit when M→Finished or V→Finished
            M→Update
            V→Update (M→Report)
        end loop
    end Run

end Controller
```

Using the MVC Framework

In order to use the MVC framework, we provide concrete classes that inherit from *Model* and *View*. The class *Heater* inherits from *Model* and simulates a room heater controlled by a thermostat:

```
class Heater
   inherit Model
   var Temp := 70.0
   var On := false
```

The variable *Temp* refers to the temperature of the room being heated. The variable *On* is true if the radiator is switched on.

The first statement of the method *Update* models the cooling of the room as it loses heat to the outside. The second statement models the heating of the room that occurs if the radiator is on. We have incorporated two assumptions into the program: the outside temperature is 50°F and the temperature of the radiator is 150°F. The two conditional statements simulate the thermostat, turning the radiator off when the room temperature rises to 75°F and turning it on when the temperature falls to 65°F. These temperatures are too far apart to be realistic thermostat settings. We use them in the simulation so that changes in the room temperature are easy to see.

```
body procedure Update
   Temp += 0.005 * (50.0 − Temp)
   if On then
      Temp += 0.005 * (150.0 − Temp)
   end if
   if On and Temp > 75 then
      On := false
   end if
   if not On and Temp < 65 then
      On := true
   end if
end Update
```

The function *Report* returns the current value of the room temperature. It completes the definition of the class *Heater*.

```
body function Report
   result Temp
end Report

end Heater
```

The class *DigitalView* is a simple view; it displays the value of a real number as a string of digits on the screen.

```
class DigitalView
   inherit View
   body procedure Update (Val : real)
      locate (5, 20)
      put Val : 10 : 3
   end Update
end DigitalView
```

The following program uses the classes we have defined so far to display the temperature of the room as a number on the screen.

```
var M : pointer to Heater
var V : pointer to DigitalView
var C : pointer to Controller
new M
new V
new C
C→Make (M, V)
C→Run
```

Adding Models and Views

A simple example such as the heating system does not demonstrate the range and flexibility of the object oriented paradigm. To obtain a convincing demonstration, we introduce two additional classes.

If a ball is thrown straight up, it rises for a while and then falls to the ground. As Newton showed, the ball moves with constant acceleration due to the earth's gravity. We can compute the motion approximately from the equations

$$Vel_i \quad = \quad Vel_{i-1} + Accel \times (T_i - T_{i-1})$$

and

$$Height_i \quad = \quad Height_{i-1} + Vel_i \times (T_i - T_{i-1})$$

in which Vel_i is the velocity of the ball at time T_i, $Height_i$ is the height of the ball at time T_i, and $Accel$ is the constant acceleration due to gravity. We perform the calculation repeatedly using a small, constant time interval, $Dt = T_i - T_{i-1}$. The calculation is performed by an instance of the class *Projectile*, simulating the vertical motion of the ball.

```
class Projectile
  inherit Model
  const Dt := 0.1
  const Grav := −1.0
  var Vel := 10.0
  var Pos := 0.0
  body procedure Update
    Vel += Grav * Dt
    Pos += Vel * Dt
    if Pos < 0.0 then
      Finished := true
    end if
  end Update
  body function Report
    result Pos
  end Report
end Projectile
```

The second class, *GraphicalView*, plots a graph of the room temperature as it changes with time.

```
class GraphicalView
  inherit View
  const Scale := maxy/100.0
  var X := 0
  body procedure Update (Val : real)
    if X > maxx then
      Finished := true
    end if
    drawdot (X, round (Scale * Val), red)
    X += 1
  end Update
end GraphicalView
```

Choosing Options at Run-Time

It would be straightforward to write programs, like the heating simulation, that provide different combinations of the model and the view. It is more interesting, however, to allow the user to select a model and a view at run-time.

We construct the program as a loop that alternately asks the user to make selections and runs the appropriate simulation. The first step is to determine whether the user wants a digital view or a graphical view.

```
loop
  var Reply : string (1)
  cls
  put "\nDo you want a (d)igital view or a (g)raphical view?  " ..
  getch (Reply)
  var V : pointer to View
  if Reply = "d" then
    var Vd : pointer to DigitalView
    new Vd
    V := Vd
  elsif Reply = "g" then
    var Vg : pointer to GraphicalView
    new Vg
    V := Vg
  else
    V := nil
  end if
```

Next, the program asks the user to choose a model.

```
  put "\nDo you want to simulate a (p)rojectile or a (h)eater?  " ..
  getch (Reply)
  var M : pointer to Model
  if Reply = "p" then
    var Mp : pointer to Projectile
    new Mp
    M := Mp
  elsif Reply = "h" then
    var Mh : pointer to Heater
    new Mh
    M := Mh
  else
    M := nil
  end if
```

If the user has not made appropriate selections, the program issues a warning message. Otherwise, it runs the simulation.

```
  if V = nil or M = nil then
    put "Please enter the letters suggested!"
```

```
else
    cls
    var C : pointer to Controller
    new C
    C→Make (M, V)
    C→Run
end if
put "\nAgain?   " ..
getch (Reply)
exit when Reply ≠ "y"
end loop
```

Discussion

The assignments to V and M are the key to understanding how the program works. Consider the first such assignment, $V := Vd$. At this point in the program, the user has chosen a digital view, the program has constructed an instance of the class $DigitalView$, and Vd is a pointer to it. After executing the assignment $V := Vd$, the pointer V references this digital view.

The final section of the code passes the pointer V to the controller C in the message $C→Make(M, V)$. The controller is expecting a view, and it receives a view. The controller does not know what kind of view it has been given, but this is unimportant because all views accept the message $Update$. In a similar way, the controller is given a pointer to a model, M, without knowing what kind of model it is. Again, this does not matter because all models recognize the messages $Update$ and $Report$.

Another interesting feature of the example is the way in which a simulation terminates. If the model is a projectile, the simulation terminates when the projectile hits the ground. If the view is graphical, the simulation terminates when the time coordinate reaches the end of the horizontal axis. A graphical view of a projectile may be terminated by either the view or the model. A digital view of a heating system has no natural termination condition, and the simulation runs until the user interrupts it.

The MVC framework demonstrates polymorphism. We know that the method Run in class $Controller$ calls the methods $Update$ and $Report$. But we do not know, until the program executes, which version of these methods will actually be used. A method name is called $polymorphic$ if the code associated with it is not determined until the program is executed.

The object oriented paradigm of programming derives much of its power from polymorphism. We can write methods such as *Run* without knowing what *Update* and *Report* will do. We can even provide new versions of *Update* and *Report*, in new views and models, long after we have written the class *Controller*.

12.4 Ancestors and Descendants

If C is a class, the following classes are ancestors of C, if they exist: the class C itself; P, the parent class of C; the ancestors of P. Similarly, the descendants of C include C itself, its children, the children of its children, and so on.

In some object oriented languages, a class can have more than one parent. These languages provide *multiple inheritance*. OOT provides only *single inheritance*; a class can have only one parent.

Assignment

Assignments to objects have the same effect as assignments to pointers because all objects are represented as pointers. If X and Y are pointers to instances of the same class, the assignment

$$X := Y$$

is legal. After it has been executed, X and Y point to the same object.

Suppose that the class *Mammal* is an ancestor of the class *Dog*. We declare

    var M: pointer to *Mammal*
    var D: pointer to *Dog*

We allocate memory for the objects M and D and initialize them. The assignment

$$M := D$$

makes M point to an instance of class *Dog*. This is reasonable because a dog is a kind of mammal. Turing allows this assignment. In fact, we have already used similar assignments in Section 12.3.

The assignment

$$D := M$$

does not make sense. All that we know is that M is a pointer to a mammal; it might point to an aardvark or a zebra. It is not safe to assign the value of M to D, and Turing does not allow such assignments.

The general rule is that if X and Y are pointers to objects, the assignment

$$X := Y$$

is legal only if the class of X is an ancestor of the class of Y. The special case in which X and Y belong to the same class is legal because every class is its own ancestor.

The Class *anyclass*

OOT provides a predefined class, *anyclass*, which is the ancestor of all classes. The class *anyclass* has no variables or methods and is useful only for heterogeneous collections. Suppose that we declare

    var *Bucket* : array 1 .. 100 of pointer to *anyclass*

We can use the variable *Bucket* as a receptacle for objects of all kinds. The array *Bucket* is called a *heterogeneous collection*. For example, we could store models and views in *Bucket* and use them later for simulations.

It is easy enough to put an object in the *Bucket*:

    var P : pointer to *Projectile*
    new P
    Bucket $(1) := P$

A problem arises, however, when we remove objects from the *Bucket*. How do we know which messages we can send to *Bucket* (3), for instance? OOT provides the predefined function *objectclass* for this purpose. The condition

    $objectclass\,(Bucket\,(3)) > Model$

is **true** if the class of *Bucket* (3) is a descendant of the class *Model*. We can use *objectclass* in statements such as

    if $objectclass\,(M) > Model$
        and $objectclass\,(V) > View$ then
        $V \rightarrow Update\,(M \rightarrow Report)$

Conclusion

Object oriented programming has entered the arena of software development with considerable fanfare. Some people have heralded the introduction of object oriented programming languages as "the end of history"; others have claimed that object orientation is no more than a passing fad.

The truth lies somewhere between. Programming languages and programming techniques will continue to evolve. The fundamental concepts of object oriented programming — objects, classes, and inheritance — will continue to be important, although syntax and semantic details will undoubtedly vary.

12.5   Summary

Numbers in parentheses refer to sections where material appears.

▶   A *class* contains declarations of instance variables and methods (12.1).

▶   An *object* is an instance of a class and can execute any of the methods declared in its class (12.1).

▶   A *method* is a procedure or function declared within a class (12.1).

▶   An *instance variable* is a variable declared within a class. Each instance of the class has its own copy of the instance variable (12.1).

▶   A *feature* is either an instance variable or a method (12.1).

▶   The *message* $P{\rightarrow}M$ specifies that the object P should execute its method M (12.1).

▶   Variables can be used to store pointers to objects but not to store the objects themselves (12.1.1).

▶   Before an object can be used, the program must execute a **new** statement to allocate memory for it (12.1.1).

▶   We can create as many instances of a class as necessary, either statically (12.1.2) or dynamically (12.1.3).

▶   A class C may *inherit* features from another class P, in which case P is the *parent* of C and C is the *child* of P (12.2).

▶   A method may be declared as **deferred** in a parent class and subsequently instantiated in a child class (12.2).

▶   A *framework* is a coherent collection of classes that contain deferred methods (12.3). Programs can be constructed by defining classes that inherit from the classes in the framework.

▶   The effect of a procedure call $P(\dots)$ depends only on the name P. In contrast, the effect of a message $O{\rightarrow}M(\dots)$ depends on the class of O and the name M (12.3). This phenomenon is called *polymorphism*.

▶   The *ancestors* of a class consist of the class itself, its parent, the parent of its parent, and so on (12.4). The class *anyclass* is the ancestor of all classes.

▶   The *descendants* of a class consist of the class itself, its children, the children of its children, and so on (12.4).

▶   The predefined function *objectclass* can be used to determine whether a class is an ancestor or descendant of another class (12.4).

12.6 Exercises

12.1 Modify the classes *Model* and *View* so that the view can display more than one variable of the model. The information could be passed either as an array or as a linked list of real numbers.

12.2 In some versions of the MVC framework, one of the instance variables of the view is a pointer to the model. This pointer enables the view to interrogate the model directly, without involving the controller. Modify the MVC framework to follow this convention.

12.3 Design a heating system that is more realistic than the system of Section 12.3. Include a furnace and several rooms, each with a thermostat and a radiator. Write an object oriented program with objects that correspond to the objects of the design.

12.4 Using Example 10.3 as a guide, write a class whose instances are rational numbers. The object oriented style introduces an asymmetry into binary operations in classes that provide binary operations. The addition of rationals P and Q must be expressed as a message to one of them, such as $P \rightarrow Add(Q)$.

12.5 Design and implement a framework for playing two-person games. The framework should include a class *Player* with one child class that computes the move and another child class that interacts with a person to obtain the move.

12.6 Object oriented techniques can be used to good effect in solving problems such as that in Exercise 11.1. Write an object oriented program that uses a binary file to store pictures. Each picture should be an object.

12.7 Construct a class whose instances are sets of integers. The class should include the following methods.

procedure *Insert* (N : int)	%	Add N to the set.
procedure *Remove* (N : int)	%	Remove N from the set.
function *Member* (N : int) : *bool*	%	Return true if N is in the set.

12.8   Write an abstract class *Stack* with the following deferred methods:

> procedure *Initialize*
> function *Empty* : bool
> procedure *Push* (*P* : pointer to *anyclass*)
> procedure *Pop* (var *P* : pointer to *anyclass*)

Write two classes that inherit from *Stack*. One class should implement the methods using an array and the other should implement the methods using a linked list.

Appendixes

A.   Turing Keywords

* addressint	decreasing	get	* nat	procedure	* signal
all	* deferred	if	* nat1	* process	skip
and	div	* implement	* nat2	put	string
* anyclass	else	import	* nat4	* quit	tag
array	elsif	in	new	read	tell
assert	end	* inherit	nil	real	then
begin	enum	init	not	* real4	to
bind	exit	int	of	* real8	true
body	export	* int1	opaque	record	type
boolean	external	* int2	open	* register	* unchecked
case	false	* int4	or	* rem	union
* char	fcn	invariant	* pause	result	* unit
* checked	for	label	pervasive	return	var
* class	* fork	loop	pointer	seek	* wait
close	forward	mod	post	set	when
collection	free	module	pre	* shl	write
const	function	* monitor	proc	* shr	* xor

An asterisk indicates that the keyword is available only in OOT.

B. Expression Operators

Turing	This Book	Short Form	Precedence	Function
**	**		1	Exponentiation
^	↑		1	Dereference
+	+		2	Unary plus
−	−		2	Unary minus
*	*		3	Multiplication
/	/		3	Division
+	+		4	Addition
−	−		4	Subtraction
=	=		5	Equal
not=	≠	~=	5	Not equal
<	<		5	Less than
<=	≤		5	Less than or equal
>	>		5	Greater than
>=	≥		5	Greater than or equal
in	in		5	Set membership
not in	not in	~in	5	Set nonmembership
not	not	~	6	Logical negation
and	and	&	7	Logical conjunction
or	or	|	8	Logical disjunction
=>	⇒		9	Logical implication

The symbol "^" (dereference) and the abbreviation "|" are available only in OOT.

C. Assignment Operators

Turing	This Book	Function
:=	:=	Assign
+=	+=	Add and assign
-=	−=	Subtract and assign
*=	*=	Multiply and assign

D.   Predefined Functions and Procedures

"Δ" indicates that the function or procedure may not have the same effect on all systems. "OOT" indicates that the function or procedure is available only in Object Oriented Turing.

abs (*X* : *T*) : *T*

> This function returns the absolute value of *X*. The type of the result is the same as the type of the argument and must be int (or a subrange) or real.

arctan (*X* : real) : real

> This function returns the inverse tangent of the ratio *X*. The result is in radians. 1 radian = 180/π degrees.

arctand (*X* : real) : real

> This function returns the inverse tangent of the ratio *X*. The result is in degrees.

ceil (*X* : real) : int

> This function returns the result of converting the real value *X* to the smallest integer that is not smaller than *X*. That is, *ceil* "rounds up". For example, *ceil* (6.7) = 7 and *ceil* (−6.7) = −6. Turing reports an error if it cannot represent the correct result. See *floor* and *round*.

chr (*I* : int) : string (1)

> This function returns the result of converting the integer *I* to a character. Turing allows all values of *I* in the range 0 .. 255 except 0 and 128. OOT allows all values in the range 0 .. 255. The function *chr* is the inverse of *ord* for characters.

clock (*C* : int)   Δ

> This procedure sets *C* to the number of milliseconds that have elapsed since the program started.

cls   Δ

> This procedure erases any text or graphics from the screen and turns the entire screen to the current background color, which is set by *colorback*.

color (*C* : int) △

This procedure determines the color of displayed characters.

colorback (*C* : int) △

This procedure determines the color of the background on which characters are displayed. In graphics mode, *colorback* does not have any effect until *cls* has been called.

cos (*X* : real) : real

This function returns the cosine of its argument. The argument is in radians. 1 radian = $180/\pi$ degrees.

cosd (*X* : real) : real

This function returns the cosine of its argument. The argument is in degrees.

date (*D* : string) △

This procedure sets *D* to the current date. The string has nine characters, for instance "04␣Jun␣95".

delay (*D* : int) △

This procedure suspends execution of the program for approximately *D* milliseconds.

drawarc (*X*, *Y*, *XR*, *YR*, *IA*, *FA*, *C* : int) △

This procedure draws an arc on the screen. The arc has center (*X*, *Y*), X-radius *XR*, Y-radius *YR*, initial angle *IA*, final angle *FA*, and color *C*. The radius units are pixels and the angles are in degrees. An angle of zero indicates the positive X-axis, and angles increase in the counterclockwise direction.

drawbox (*X1*, *Y1*, *X2*, *Y2*, *C* : int) △

This procedure draws a rectangle on the screen. The rectangle has its left bottom corner at (*X1*, *Y1*) and its right top corner at (*X2*, *Y2*). The values *X1* and *X2* are X-coordinates and the values *Y1* and *Y2* are Y-coordinates. The rectangle has color *C*.

drawdot (*X*, *Y*, *C* : int) △

This procedure draws a dot on the screen. The dot is displayed at coordinate (*X*, *Y*) and has color *C*.

drawfill $(X, Y, FillColor, BorderColor :$ int)   △

> This procedure paints an enclosed area on the screen. The coordinate (X, Y) must be inside the area to be painted. The color of the paint used for filling is *FillColor*. The area must have a border of color *BorderColor*.

drawfillarc $(X, Y, XR, YR, IA, FA, C :$ int)   OOT, △

> This procedure has the same effect as *drawarc*, but the arc it draws is filled with solid color.

drawfillbox $(X1, Y1, X2, Y2, C :$ int)   △

> This procedure has the same effect as *drawbox*, but the rectangle it draws is filled with solid color.

drawfilloval $(X, Y, XR, YR, C :$ int)   △

> This procedure has the same effect as *drawoval*, but the oval it draws is filled with solid color.

drawfillpolygon $(X, Y :$ array $1 .. *$ of int, $N :$ int, $C :$ int)   OOT, △

> This procedure draws a filled polygon with N vertices. The coordinates of the vertices are $(X(1), Y(1)), \ldots, (X(N), Y(N))$. The polygon is filled with color C.

drawline $(X1, Y1, X2, Y2, C :$ int)   OOT, △

> This procedure draws a line from $(X1, Y1)$ to $(X2, Y2)$. The color of the line is C.

drawoval $(X, Y, XR, YR, C :$ int)   △

> This procedure draws an oval. The center of the oval is at (X, Y), its X-radius is XR, its Y-radius is YR, and its color is C.

drawpic $(X, Y :$ int, $B :$ array $1 .. *$ of int, $D :$ int)   △

> This procedure draws the rectangular image stored in the buffer B with its lower left corner at (X, Y). The parameter D determines the way in which the picture will be drawn on the screen: if $D = 0$, the picture will be copied to the screen, and if $D = 1$, the picture will be "exclusive-ored" to the screen. See *sizepic* and *takepic*.

eof $(S :$ int) : boolean

> This function returns true if no more characters can be read from the input stream S. If S is omitted, *eof* detects the end of the standard input file.

erealstr $(R : \text{real}, W, F, E : \text{int}) : \text{string}$

> This function converts a real number R to a string. The string returned by *erealstr* (R, W, F, E) is the same as the string displayed by put $R{:}W{:}F{:}E$. The integers W, F, and E provide formatting information. The integers W, F, and E may be zero but must not be negative. The width W determines the overall length of the result. The result will not contain less than W characters but may contain more. The fraction width F determines the number of digits after the decimal point. The exponent width E determines the width of the exponent. Turing will use more than E exponent digits for accuracy if necessary. See *frealstr* and *realstr*.

exp $(X : \text{real}) : \text{real}$

> This function computes e^X. It is the inverse of *ln*. On a PC, a value of X larger than about 709 will cause real overflow.

fetcharg $(I : \text{int}) : \text{string}$ △

> This function returns the Ith argument on the command line. If $I = 0$, the result is the name of the program. The function fails if I is larger than *nargs*, the number of arguments on the command line. See *nargs*.

floor $(R : \text{real}) : \text{int}$

> This function returns the largest integer that is not greater than the real number R. That is, *floor* "rounds down". For example, *floor* $(3.99) = 3$ and *floor* $(-500.1) = -501$. Turing reports an error if it cannot represent the correct result. See *ceil* and *round*.

frealstr $(R : \text{real}, W, F : \text{int}) : \text{string}$

> This function converts a real number to a string consisting of an integer and a fraction but no exponent. The integers W and F, which determine the format of the string, must not be negative. The string returned by *frealstr* (R, W, F) is the same as the string displayed by put $R{:}W{:}F$. The value of W determines the minimum width of the string. Turing uses more than W characters if necessary to retain accuracy. The value of F determines the number of digits after the decimal point. See *erealstr* and *realstr*.

getch $(\text{var } ch : \text{string}(1))$ △

> This procedure waits until the user presses a key. It then assigns the corresponding key code to ch. See Appendix G, *Values Returned by getch*.

getenv (*S* : string) : string   Δ

This function returns the value of the environment variable *S*.

hasch : boolean   Δ

This function returns true if the user enters a character the program has not yet read. Note that *hasch* does not read the character: if *hasch* has returned true, it will continue to do so until the program calls *getch* or executes a **get** statement.

index (*S*, *P* : string) : int

This function returns the first position at which the pattern *P* occurs in the string *S*. If the pattern does not occur in the string, *index* returns 0.

intreal (*I* : int) : real

This function converts the integer *I* to the corresponding real value. It is not needed often because Turing normally performs the conversion automatically.

intstr (*I*, *W* : int) : string

This function converts the integer value *I* to a string. The argument *W* is optional. The value of *W* determines the minimum length of the result. The result will have more than *W* characters if necessary to maintain accuracy. See *strint*.

length (*S* : string) : int

This function returns the length of the string *S*. The empty string, "", has length 0.

ln (*X* : real) : real

This function returns the natural logarithm, or logarithm to the base *e*, of its real argument, *X*. It is the inverse of *exp*: $ln(exp(X)) = X$. The argument must be a positive, nonzero, real number.

locate (*R*, *C* : int)   Δ

This procedure moves the cursor to row *R* and column *C* of the screen. The call *locate* (1, 1) will move the cursor to the top left corner of the screen.

locatexy (*X*, *Y* : int)   Δ

This procedure moves the cursor to a position on the graphics screen close to (*X*, *Y*).

max $(X, Y : T) : T$

> This function returns the larger of X and Y. The arguments X and Y must have the same type, which must be either int or real. The result has the same type as the arguments. See *min*.

maxcol : int   △

> This function returns the number of text columns that can be displayed on the screen. The usable columns are numbered 1 .. *maxcol*. See *maxrow*.

maxcolor : int   △

> This function returns the largest number that can be used to select a color. The usable colors are numbered 0 .. *maxcolor*.

maxint : int   △

> This function returns the value of the largest integer Turing can represent.

maxrow : int

> This function returns the number of text rows that can be displayed on the screen. The usable rows are numbered 1 .. *maxrow*. See *maxcol*.

maxx : int   △

> This function returns the largest number that can be used as the X-coordinate of a graphic image. The usable coordinates are 0 .. *maxx*. See *maxy*.

maxy : int   △

> This function returns the largest number that can be used as the Y-coordinate of a graphic image. The usable coordinates are 0 .. *maxy*. See *maxx*.

min $(X : T) : T$

> This function returns the smaller of X and Y. The arguments X and Y must have the same type, which must be either int or real. The result has the same type as the arguments. See *max*.

nargs : int   △

> This function returns the number of arguments that have been passed to the program from the command line. See *fetcharg*.

objectclass $(P :$ pointer to *anyclass*$) :$ class   OOT

> This attribute returns the class of the object to which P points. It can be used only to compare classes.

ord $(X : T)$: int

> This function returns the integer code of a value of an enumerated or character type. The values of an enumerated type are numbered from left to right using the codes $0, 1, \ldots$. For characters, *ord* is the inverse of *chr*; if C is a character, $chr\,(ord\,(C)) = C$.

play $(S :$ string$)$ Δ

> This procedure plays the tune described by the string S. See Appendix H, *The Procedure play*.

playdone : boolean   Δ

> This function returns **true** when the sounds produced by *play* have ended.

pred $(X : T) : T$

> This function returns the predecessor of its argument. The type of the argument must be an integer, a subrange, or an enumeration. The type of the result is the same as the type of the argument. For integers and subranges, $pred\,(N) = N - 1$. For enumerations, $pred\,(X)$ is the item that precedes X in the declaration. The inverse of *pred* is *succ*.

rand (var R : real)

> This procedure generates a pseudorandom real value and assigns it to R. The value is uniformly distributed over the range $0 < R < 1$. See *randomize*.

randint (var I : int, L, H : int)

> This procedure generates a pseudorandom integer value bounded by L and H and assigns it to I. After the call, $L \le I \le H$. Turing reports an error if $L > H$. See *randomize*.

randnext (var R : real, $Q : 1 .. 10$)

> This procedure generates the next pseudorandom value in the sequence Q and assigns it to R. See *randseed*.

randomize

> Turing generates pseudorandom numbers in a fixed, very long sequence. The effect of *randomize* is to start the pseudorandom number sequence at a different place each time the program is run.

randseed (I : int, Q : 1 .. 10)

Turing maintains seeds for ten pseudorandom number sequences. The call *randseed* (I, Q) sets the seed of sequence Q to the value I. See *randnext*.

realstr (R : real, W : int) : string

This function converts a real number to a string with an integer part, a fraction part, and an exponent unless $10^{-3} < |R| < 10^6$. The integer W, which determines the minimum length of the string, must not be negative. The string returned by *realstr* (R, W) is equal to the string displayed by put R:W. See *erealstr* and *frealstr*.

repeat (S : string, N : int) : string

This function returns a string consisting of N copies of the string S. If $N \leq 0$, the result is the empty string, "".

round (R : real) : int

This function returns the integer closest in value to the real argument. Turing reports an error if it cannot represent the correct result. See *ceil* and *floor*.

self : pointer to *anyclass*   OOT

This function returns a pointer to the current object. During the evaluation of $O{\rightarrow}M$ (...), calls to *self* within the body of M will return a pointer to O.

setscreen (S : string)   Δ

This procedure controls a variety of screen attributes. See Appendix I, *The Procedure setscreen*.

sign (R : real) : -1 .. 1

The call *sign* (R) returns -1 if R is negative, 0 if R is zero, or 1 if R is positive.

sin (X : real) : real

This function returns the sine of its argument. The argument is in radians. 1 radian = $180/\pi$ degrees.

sind (X : real) : real

This function returns the sine of its argument. The argument is in degrees.

sizepic $(X1, Y1, X2, Y2 : \text{int}) : \text{int}$ △

This function returns the amount of storage required to store a rectangular screen image defined by its bottom left corner, $(X1, Y1)$, and its top right corner, $(X2, Y2)$. The unit of storage is 4 bytes, the space required to store an integer. The function is usually used in an array declaration, as in

var *Buffer* : array 1 .. *sizepic* $(0, 0, 20, 10)$ of int

The value returned by *sizepic* depends on the screen mode. See *drawpic* and *takepic*.

sound $(F, T : \text{int})$ △

The procedure *sound* creates a sound at frequency F Hertz (cycles per second) for a time T milliseconds.

sqrt $(R : \text{real}) : \text{real}$

This function returns the square root of its argument. The argument must be a positive real number.

strint $(S : \text{string}, B : \text{int}) : \text{int}$

This function converts the string S to the corresponding integer value. The argument B is the base for conversion. It is required that $2 \le B \le 36$. If B is omitted, base 10 is used. The string must consist of zero or more leading blanks, an optional sign ("+" or "−"), and digits that are valid for the chosen base. For bases larger than 10, Turing uses upper case letters as digits, with $A = 10, B = 11, \ldots, Z = 35$. See *intstr*.

strreal $(S : \text{string}) : \text{real}$

This function converts a string to a real number. The string must consist of zero or more blanks, an optional sign ("+" or "−"), and an integer or real constant.

succ $(X : T) : T$

This function returns the successor of its argument. The type of the argument must be an integer, a subrange, or an enumeration. The type of the result is the same as the type of the argument. For integers and subranges, $pred(N) = N + 1$. For enumerations, $succ(X)$ is the item that follows X in the declaration. The inverse of *succ* is *pred*.

sysclock $(C : \text{int})$ △

This procedure sets C to the number of milliseconds used by the current process.

takepic (*X1, Y1, X2, Y2* : int, var *B* : array 1 .. * of int) Δ

This procedure copies the pixels in a rectangular area of the screen into the buffer *B*. The area is defined by its bottom left corner, (*X1, Y1*), and its top right corner, (*X2, Y2*). The function *sizepic* should be used to determine the size of the buffer. See *drawpic* and *sizepic*.

time (*S* : string) Δ

This procedure sets the string *S* to the current time in the form "11:04:30", in which the digit groups denote hours, minutes, and seconds, respectively. The result always has exactly eight characters.

wallclock (*C* : int) Δ

This procedure sets *C* to the number of seconds that have elapsed since midnight, Greenwich Mean Time, December 31, 1969.

whatcolor : int Δ

This function returns the current foreground color, the color in which characters are displayed.

whatcolorback : int Δ

This function returns the current background color.

whatdotcolor (*X, Y* : int) : int Δ

This function returns the color of the pixel at (*X, Y*).

whattextchar : string (1) Δ

This function returns the character displayed at the current cursor position.

whattextcolor : int Δ

This function returns the color of the character at the current cursor position.

whattextcolorback : int Δ

This function returns the background color of the character at the current cursor position.

E. Codes for the ASCII Graphic Character Set

32	␣	48	0	64	@	80	P	96	`	112	p
33	!	49	1	65	A	81	Q	97	a	113	q
34	"	50	2	66	B	82	R	98	b	114	r
35	#	51	3	67	C	83	S	99	c	115	s
36	$	52	4	68	D	84	T	100	d	116	t
37	%	53	5	69	E	85	U	101	e	117	u
38	&	54	6	70	F	86	V	102	f	118	v
39	'	55	7	71	G	87	W	103	g	119	w
40	(	56	8	72	H	88	X	104	h	120	x
41	)	57	9	73	I	89	Y	105	i	121	y
42	*	58	:	74	J	90	Z	106	j	122	z
43	+	59	;	75	K	91	[	107	k	123	{
44	,	60	<	76	L	92	\	108	l	124	|
45	-	61	=	77	M	93	]	109	m	125	}
46	.	62	>	78	N	94	^	110	n	126	~
47	/	63	?	79	O	95	_	111	o		

F.   ASCII Codes for Border Characters

Function	Single Border	Double Border
Horizontal line	196	205
Vertical line	179	186
Top left corner	218	201
Top right corner	191	187
Bottom left corner	192	200
Bottom right corner	217	188

G.   Values Returned by *getch*

0		32	␣	64	@	96	'
1	Ctrl A	33	!	65	A	97	a
2	Ctrl B	34	"	66	B	98	b
3	Ctrl C	35	#	67	C	99	c
4	Ctrl D	36	$	68	D	100	d
5	Ctrl E	37	%	69	E	101	e
6	Ctrl F	38	&	70	F	102	f
7	Ctrl G	39	'	71	G	103	g
8	Ctrl H	40	(	72	H	104	h
9	Ctrl I	41	)	73	I	105	i
10	Ctrl J	42	*	74	J	106	j
11	Ctrl K	43	+	75	K	107	k
12	Ctrl L	44	,	76	L	108	l
13	Ctrl M	45	-	77	M	109	m
14	Ctrl N	46	.	78	N	110	n
15	Ctrl O	47	/	79	O	111	o
16	Ctrl P	48	0	80	P	112	p
17	Ctrl Q	49	1	81	Q	113	q
18	Ctrl R	50	2	82	R	114	r
19	Ctrl S	51	3	83	S	115	s
20	Ctrl T	52	4	84	T	116	t
21	Ctrl U	53	5	85	U	117	u
22	Ctrl V	54	6	86	V	118	v
23	Ctrl W	55	7	87	W	119	w
24	Ctrl X	56	8	88	X	120	x
25	Ctrl Y	57	9	89	Y	121	y
26	Ctrl Z	58	:	90	Z	122	z
27	Ctrl [	59	;	91	[	123	{
28	Ctrl \	60	<	92	\	124	|
29	Ctrl]	61	=	93	]	125	}
30	Ctrl ^	62	>	94	^	126	~
31	Ctrl _	63	?	95	_	127	

128	Alt 9	160	Alt D	192	F6	224	Ctrl F3
129	Alt 0	161	Alt F	193	F7	225	Ctrl F4
130	Alt -	162	Alt G	194	F8	226	Ctrl F5
131	Alt =	163	Alt H	195	F9	227	Ctrl F6
132	Ctrl PgUp	164	Alt J	196	F10	228	Ctrl F7
133		165	Alt K	197		229	Ctrl F8
134		166	Alt L	198		230	Ctrl F9
135		167		199	Home	231	Ctrl F10
136		168		200	↑	232	Alt F1
137		169		201	PgUp	233	Alt F2
138		170		202		234	Alt F3
139		171		203	←	235	Alt F4
140		172	Alt Z	204		236	Alt F5
141		173	Alt X	205	→	237	Alt F6
142		174	Alt C	206		238	Alt F7
143	Shift TAB	175	Alt V	207	End	239	Alt F8
144	Alt Q	176	Alt B	208	↓	240	Alt F9
145	Alt W	177	Alt N	209	PgDn	241	Alt F10
146	Alt E	178	Alt M	210	Ins	242	
147	Alt R	179		211	Del	243	Ctrl ←
148	Alt T	180		212	Shift F1	244	Ctrl →
149	Alt Y	181		213	Shift F2	245	Ctrl End
150	Alt U	182		214	Shift F3	246	Ctrl PgDn
151	Alt I	183		215	Shift F4	247	Ctrl Home
152	Alt O	184		216	Shift F5	248	Alt 1
153	Alt P	185		217	Shift F6	249	Alt 2
154		186		218	Shift F7	250	Alt 3
155		187	F1	219	Shift F8	251	Alt 4
156		188	F2	220	Shift F9	252	Alt 5
157		189	F3	221	Shift F10	253	Alt 6
158	Alt A	190	F4	222	Ctrl F1	254	Alt 7
159	Alt S	191	F5	223	Ctrl F2	255	Alt 8

H. The Procedure *play*

The procedure *play* plays the tune described by the string S. The argument of *play* is a string that may contain blanks, which Turing ignores, and the characters a, b, c, d, e, f, g, p, +, -, 1, 2, 4, 8, 6, <, and >.

The letters a, ..., g select the corresponding notes of the diatonic scale, or white piano keys. Either lower case letters or upper case letters may be used.

The letter p indicates a rest, or pause.

The symbol + sharpens the previous note and - flattens it. For instance, f+ plays $F\sharp$ and e- plays $E\flat$.

The symbol > transposes the notes following it up one octave, and the symbol < transposes them down one octave. To play the scale of G, for example, we write *play* ("gab > cdef+g f+edc < bag").

Numbers indicate note durations: 1 gives a whole note, 2 gives a half note, 4 gives a quarter note, 8 gives an eighth note, and 6 gives a sixteenth note. If no duration is provided, Turing plays quarter notes. Since the duration of a whole note is about 2.6 seconds, the tempo is relatively sedate.

Turing remembers the octave in which the last note was played. Suppose that we execute the following statements, in which the box represents code that might do several things but does not call *play*.

    play ("4 g a b > c d e f+ g")
    [   ]
    play ("4 g a b > c d e f+ g")

Although the argument of *play* is the same in each case, the second scale will be played an octave higher than the first scale. To avoid confusion, it is best to follow the policy that every call to *play* should end in the middle octave. This implies, for example, that to play an isolated high note, we might write something like

    play (">>> c <<<")

I. The Procedure *setscreen*

The procedure *setscreen* controls a variety of screen attributes. These are described below. When a Turing program starts, it behaves as if the following calls had been executed:

> *setscreen* (`"text"`)
> *setscreen* (`"cursor"`)
> *setscreen* (`"echo"`)
> *setscreen* (`"line"`)

Turing automatically calls *setscreen* to change the screen mode if it encounters an operation that cannot be performed in the current mode. For example, a call to *locate* will automatically switch the screen from `text` mode to `screen` mode, and a call to any pixel graphics procedure or function will switch the screen to `graphics` mode.

Screen Attributes

`"text"`   In `text` mode, Turing writes characters to the current cursor position on the screen. A character displayed at the bottom right corner of the screen or a new-line character on the last row makes the screen scroll.

`"screen"`   In `screen` mode, Turing writes characters at any position on the screen. The predefined procedure *locate* moves the cursor. Turing will automatically select screen mode if *locate* is called.

`"graphics"` In `graphics` mode, Turing uses pixel graphics. Turing will automatically select this mode if the program calls any of the graphics functions or procedures. For example, evaluating *maxx* will select `graphics` mode.

`"cursor"`   Turing will display the cursor in `text` and `screen` modes. The cursor is never displayed in `graphics` mode.

`"nocursor"` Turing will hide the cursor in `text` and `screen` modes.

`"echo"`   Whenever the user presses a key, Turing displays a character on the screen. All keys, including keys for nongraphic characters such as ESC and F1, cause a character to be displayed.

`"noecho"` Turing does not display a character on the screen when the user presses a key. This mode is useful for interactive programs.

J. Colors for the IBM PC and Compatibles

Code	Color	OOT
0	Black	White
1	Blue	
2	Green	
3	Cyan	
4	Red	
5	Magenta	
6	Brown	
7	Light gray	Black
8	Dark gray	
9	Light blue	
10	Light green	
11	Light cyan	
12	Light red	
13	Light magenta	
14	Yellow	
15	White	Light gray

K. Installing WinOOT

The disk accompanying this book contains a version of Object Oriented Turing, called WinOOT, that runs on a PC with Microsoft Windows. The disk contains a substantial amount of information about Turing in general and WinOOT in particular. There may be discrepancies between the information on the disk and the information provided by this book. The disk is probably more up to date and therefore more reliable than the book.

1. Start Windows.

2. Select Run from the File menu. Windows should open a dialogue box called Run.

3. Put the WinOOT disk in the floppy disk drive A: of your computer. In the box labeled Command Line: in the Run dialogue box, enter the text a:\setup. If your floppy disk drive is B:, enter the text b:\setup instead.

4. Use the mouse to click on OK in the Run dialogue box.

5. The WinOOT installation program should display a dialogue box called OOT for Windows Installation. If you click on OK, the installation program will install WinOOT on the drive c:\winoot. If you prefer another drive or directory name, make the appropriate changes in the dialogue box before clicking on OK.

6. The installation program should display a second window that monitors the progress of the installation.

7. When installation is complete, you must exit and then restart Windows before going on to the next step. When Windows restarts, it will load drivers that are needed by WinOOT.

8. If the installation is successful, there should be a new program group called OOT for Windows in the Program Manager window. To start WinOOT, double click on the icon labeled OOT for Windows.

9. WinOOT displays a dialogue box called Object Oriented Turing for Windows with a number of options. To start WinOOT, click on Start Up OOT.

10. WinOOT should open three windows: the Control Panel, the Directory Viewer, and the File Editor.

L. Running WinOOT

The **Control Panel** provides overall control of WinOOT. You can use it to open and close other windows, to run programs, and to obtain information about using WinOOT.

The **Directory Viewer** provides access to all the files on your system. Double clicking on the name of a file or a directory selects that file or directory. Clicking on the name of a selected file causes WinOOT to open a **File Editor** window for the file. Although you will usually open files containing Turing programs, you can use the Turing editor to view or edit any file that contains text.

The **Directory Viewer** displays directory names in square brackets. If you click on a directory name, the **Directory Viewer** displays the files in that directory. The directory above the current directory is displayed as [..]. For example, if the current directory is c:\winoot\demos, clicking on [..] will change the current directory to c:\winoot. You can select disk drives other than c: by clicking on [-a-] or [-b-].

The **File Editor** window allows you to enter and execute Turing programs. The **Help** menu provides information about all aspects of the **File Editor** window, including the editing commands.

When you have entered a Turing program into the **File Editor** window, you can run it by clicking on the button labeled **Run**. While the program is running, the label on this button turns to **Stop**; clicking on it stops the program.

Special Keys

The **File Editor** recognizes the following keys.

Moving the Cursor

↑	Move cursor up.
↓	Move cursor down.
←	Move cursor left.
→	Move cursor right.
Home	Move cursor to start of line.
End	Move cursor to end of line.
PgUp	Move cursor up one page.
PgDn	Move cursor down one page.

Ctrl-←	Move cursor left one word.
Ctrl-→	Move cursor right one word.
Ctrl-Home	Move cursor to start of file.
Ctrl-End	Move cursor to end of file.
Ctrl-U, Ctrl-PgUp	Move cursor up half a page.
Ctrl-D, Ctrl-PgDn	Move cursor down half a page.
Ctrl-F	Move forward to next error.
Ctrl-B	Move backward to previous error.

Inserting and Deleting Characters

Del	Delete character at cursor.
Backspace	Delete character to left of cursor.
Ctrl-E	Delete to end of line.
Ctrl-K	Delete this line.
Ctrl-J	Join this line and the next.
Ctrl-Y	Insert a blank line.

Block Operations

Ctrl-C	Copy from text to buffer.
Ctrl-V	Paste buffer into text.
Ctrl-X	Move text to buffer.
Ctrl-Shift-%	Comment selected block.
Ctrl-5	Uncomment selected block.

Miscellaneous Operations

Ctrl-L	Open search/replace dialogue box.
Ctrl-Z	Undo last change.
Ctrl-I	Paragraph the program.
Ctrl-R	Run the program.
Ctrl-S	Save file.
Ctrl-A	Save file with a new name.

On-Line Help

The keys F8 and F9 access WinOOT's on-line help system.

F8

> Position the cursor within, or just after, the name of a predefined subprogram, and press F8. WinOOT displays the parameter list of the subprogram.

F9

> Position the cursor within, or just after, the name of a keyword or predefined subprogram, and press F9. WinOOT displays the corresponding entry from the Reference Manual.

Tracing the Execution of a Program

WinOOT provides two ways of tracing the execution of a program. It can execute the program slowly, highlighting each statement as it executes the statement. It can also execute the program one statement at a time, which is useful for debugging.

To execute the program slowly, click the **Turn Trace On** button and then the **Run** button. You can adjust the speed of execution by adjusting the setting of the **Trace Speed** slider in the **Control Panel**.

During slow execution, the message on the **Turn Trace On** button changes to **Turn Trace Off**. To resume normal execution, click this button.

To execute the program one statement at a time, start the program by clicking the **Run** button and then click the **Pause** button. The program stops executing and enables the buttons **Step**, **Step Over**, and **Step Return** on the **Control Panel**.

Clicking the **Step** button advances the program by one statement. If the statement contains a call to a subprogram, the statements in the subprogram are not traced. The **Step Into** button is used to trace the statements of a subprogram. Click it when a statement that calls a subprogram is highlighted. Click the **Step Return** button to execute the rest of the subprogram quickly and return to the statement following the call.

Index

Object Oriented Turing
From Holt Software

Object Oriented Turing, with its multi-window, user friendly, integrated programming environment, brings the future of software engineering to the classroom and the home computer. Object Oriented Turing lets you make immediate use of the paradigms and methodologies of object oriented programming.

OOT is constantly upgraded on a wide range of hardware platforms:

  PC (DOS and Windows), SUN 3, SUN 4, DEC, MIPS, SGI and RS6000.

Additional Object Oriented Turing materials are also available directly from Holt Software. These include

- Turing Reference Manual
- OOT User's Manual.

For more information about upgrades to Object Oriented Turing, or about these additional materials, please contact:

Holt Software
203 College Street, Suite 305
Toronto, Ontario   M5T 1P9
CANADA
1-800-361-8324